The Self Awakened

The Self Awakened

Pragmatism Unbound

Roberto Mangabeira Unger

HARVARD UNIVERSITY PRESS

Cambridge, Massachusetts

London, England

2007

Library of Congress Cataloging-in-Publication Data

Unger, Roberto Mangabeira.
    The self awakened : pragmatism unbound / Roberto Mangabeira Unger.
        p.   cm.
    Includes index.
    ISBN-13: 978–0–674–02354–3 (cloth : alk. paper)
    ISBN-10: 0–674–02354–4 (cloth : alk. paper)
    1. Philosophy.   2. Pragmatism.   I. Title.
    B832.U55   2006
    144'.3—dc22   2006041136

Contents

The Self Awakened

The Philosophy of the Age

Its promise of freedom from many-sided dogma, its abandonment of the claim to see the world from the stars, its embrace of the awkward situation of the human agent, struggling against the institutional and conceptual structures that shackle him, its offer to help him loosen and reinvent these structures so that he may become greater and more vital as well as less deluded—none of this would have been enough to make pragmatism what it is today: the philosophy of the age.

Pragmatism has become the philosophy of the age by shrinking. In the hands of many of its votaries, it has been turned into another version of senility masquerading as wisdom. They think they have grown up. In fact, they have fallen down. As we have lost confidence in large projects, whether of theory or of politics, we have been taught how to live without them rather than how to recover and remake them in other, more promising forms. This doctrine of shrinkage, of retreat to more defensible lines, of standing and waiting, of singing in our chains, is the dominant philosophy of our time, expressed in the writings of professors as well as in the climate of educated public discussion. And many of its most influential formulations use the label "pragmatism."

This book is not about how to read James or Dewey, Heidegger or Wittgenstein. However, it starts from the premise that certain tendencies in the evolution of the most general ideas available to us— tendencies often described as pragmatism—have been emasculated, philosophically as well as politically, and in this way made more palatable and less useful. It is never too late to change course. I offer here both an argument for why to do so and a proposal for how to do so. The point is not to rescue pragmatism; it is to represent and raise up our humanity. Imagination and hope will be our twin guides.

1

Rejected Options

We awake in a particular world: not just the natural world we inhabit but the world of the institutions and practices, including the discursive practices, that hold sway around us. For better or worse, these practices stand between us and the absolute frame of reference, the view from above, from the vantage point of the stars.

However, we always experience ourselves, both as individuals and in concert with others, as sources of initiatives that may resist the established structures of organization and belief. What should be our attitude to such structures of established organization and common belief? Should we surrender to them and try to make the best of them, exploiting, however we can and by such light as they themselves provide, their hidden possibilities of transformation? Or should we seek to establish a position from which to pass judgment on them?

No question comes more naturally when we think free (if only a little bit) from the pursuit of immediate goals in an immediate context. No question comes more naturally because to think at some distance from the pressures of urgent action is already to act as if our relation to the structures we find around us were open to some form of resistance, as if we could distinguish between them and us and ask what to do about them. The answers that have been given to this question in the history of philosophy fall into a small number of alternatives. There have been four main options.

The first option has been belief in access to the truer, deeper order hidden far beyond the established structures of society and culture, beyond even common belief and perception. This higher order is both fact and value: at once the innermost core of reality and the source from which alone an imperative to live one's life in a particular way can result. All else is shadowy convention or illusion.

The access to this higher reality requires a break. This break must ordinarily be precipitated by some heartbreak, undermining our attachment to the world of shadows and opening the way for our ascent to the vision of the real situation.

Once we gain access to this higher reality through the appropriate itinerary of self-subversion and reorientation, we possess a standard by which to judge the established structures, bringing them into conformity with the pattern lying beyond. The characteristic product of this reformation is a parallel and reciprocal ordering of society and of the self: each force within society and within the self assumes its proper place.

In the history of Western philosophy, we associate this orientation most strongly with Plato. In fact, it has been the dominant form of philosophical ambition throughout much of world history. Many of those who have announced the end of the quest for the hidden, standard-setting reality have merely continued it under other names. No wonder they have habitually relied on the same structure of disappointment and conversion that has played so central a role in the views they profess to repudiate.

The characteristic claims made by this first tendency in the world history of philosophy come up short against a double objection. They demand that we devalue the reality and the authority of established practices and beliefs on the basis of someone's ideas: the speculative proposals of a particular philosophical teacher. They require that we change our lives and our societies out of a speculative conviction without having before us any detailed understanding of transformative constraint and transformative opportunity.

A second option has been to abandon the quest for the deeper, canonical reality in favor of a retreat into the human world: our central experiences of understanding the world, satisfying one another and hoping for happiness. Such experiences rest on certain presuppositions, without which we could not make sense of understanding, of obligation, or of hope for happiness. Having inferred these presuppositions of our humanity from our experience, we can then use them to judge and to reshape this experience. The system of the presuppositions remains invariant and provides the perspective from which to confront established institutions, practices, and beliefs and to reform them.

We identify this route of philosophical thinking with Kant. It has nevertheless had many other expressions in the history of Western and non-Western philosophy. Its preliminary decisive move—one it shares with pragmatism—is the abandonment of the perspective of the stars: man is the measure; we have no other. It has not, however, succeeded in its attempt to separate the unchanging presuppositions from the variable historical material they inform: the stuff of the real societies and cultures in which we live. Either these presuppositions have too much content to be changeless, or they have too little content to guide our individual and collective actions. We can no more separate our views of the sources of moral and social obligation from the content of our personal and social ideals than we can disentangle the modal categories of possibility and necessity from the substance of our cosmological beliefs.

The idea of the changeless and standard-setting framework turns out to be yet another version of the attempt to see with the eyes of God, even if it is ourselves we see with these eyes. Paradoxically, it denies precisely what is most godlike about our ability little by little to rethink and remake each feature of our situation, including those features we had been tempted to list among the unchanging assumptions. We are more historical beings than this doctrine is willing to allow.

From this realization arises the third of the major intellectual options presented to us by the history of our ideas and attitudes about the institutional and conceptual structures we find established around us. According to this approach, such structures represent incidents in a history: the history of our individual and collective self-construction. They exemplify types of consciousness or of social and economic organization. Law-like forces drive forward the success of these systems of organization or consciousness. The history of the succession, cul-minating in a final resolution of contradictions or a final fulfillment of humanity, provides the sole standard from which we can judge our institutions and our cultures. Only the imagination of the whole suc-cession and the presentiment of its final end provide us with the higher knowledge with which to see through our immediate circumstances by placing them in this larger and definitive context.

This is the option that we find realized in the philosophy of Hegel as well as in many of the ambitious social theories of the nineteenth and twentieth centuries. It is a paradoxical enterprise. We arouse the transformative imagination and will by placing history on their side. Then we put them back to sleep by suggesting that a predetermined history does their work for them. Theory claims privileged insight by looking back from the vantage point of the anticipated end and by distancing itself from the troubled, dangerous perspective of the agent.

A fourth option—a shrunken pragmatism—is simply to abandon the attempt to find above or beyond the societies and cultures with which we are engaged a place from which to judge their institutions, practices, and discourses. All we have is the world such as we experience it, with such enlargement of our experience as memory and imagination are able to provide. We decide which parts of our experience have the greatest value and which deserve to be sloughed off. And in the persis-tence of conflicting forces and contrasting tendencies we find oppor-tunities for transformation in the midst of constraint.

An implication of this point of view is to deny us guidance about what direction to take for our projects of challenge and change. All we can do is to follow the promptings of what we consider to be our better selves or the thrust of what we know to be our strongest desires. What is it that we think we see when we see beyond the arrangements estab-lished and the beliefs enacted around us? Are we deluded to believe that we can occasionally turn the tables on the worlds in which we find ourselves?

A further consequence of this position is to exclude the possibility that we might be able to transform the character of our relation to the social and cultural worlds we inhabit rather than just to change, little by little, the content of the arrangements and beliefs that comprise them. It is a mistaken view. Institutions and ideologies are not like natural objects, forcing themselves on our consciousness with insistent force and reminding us that we have been born into a world that is not our own. They are nothing but frozen will and interrupted conflict: the residue crystallized out of the suspension or containment of our struggles.

Consequently, the structures of society and culture never exist univocally, in just one way, with just one degree of force. They exist more or less, in degrees. They may be so arranged as to bar themselves as much as possible against challenge and change. We shall then experience a lengthening of the distance between the ordinary moves we make within the established framework and the exceptional moves by which we change it. The result will be to naturalize the social and cultural setting of our lives and to place the transformative will and imagination under a spell.

Alternatively, however, our societies and cultures may be so arranged as to facilitate and to organize their own piecemeal, experimental revision. We then shorten the distance between routine moves within a framework and exceptional moves about the framework; we experience the latter as a direct and frequent extension of the former. As a result, we denaturalize society and culture: we unfreeze them. It is as if, in the physical world, a rise of temperature were to begin to melt down the stark distinctions among things, returning them to the indistinct flow from which they came. To the extent we move in this direction, the facts of society and culture cease to present themselves to our consciousness as an inescapable fate.

This is no mere speculative contrast. Our most powerful interests turn out to be engaged in this denaturalization of society and culture, in this radicalization of experimentalism, in this turn from fate to invention: our material interest in practical economic and technological progress, our moral and political interest in the emancipation of individuals from stultified social hierarchies and divisions and stereotyped social roles, and our spiritual interest in being able to engage with a world—wholeheartedly though not single-mindedly—without having to surrender to it. The philosophy we need—a radicalized pragmatism—is the theory of this turn; it presents us with a way of approaching our situation, both in general and in particular, that informs this attack on fate and fatefulness. It is the operational ideology of this subversive and constructive practice. Yet this fourth option provides us with no way to understand the circumstances or the capabilities that can make sense of such a reorientation.

The four positions I have described are positions about society and culture. They regard the immediate human theater of action rather than the nonhuman setting of our lives: our place in nature. Their subject is the variety of grounds on which we may resist and transform this human world, or abandon resistance and relinquish transformation.

We are accustomed to imagine the immediate context of human life in society and culture as a little place within a big world—nature, the universe, being. What we think of that world, and what we think of our thinking about it, seem, according to this habit, to be what matters most in the definition of a philosophical position. Thinking about us and about our relation to the man-made constructs seems a mere sideshow.

It is not. We and our actions are the beginning; the rest is the rest. Our most constant and powerful yearnings and interests have to do with ourselves and with our relation to one another. Our perceptual and cognitive equipment is built on a scale suited to operate within the limited horizon of human action. It is only by force of disappointment with this nearby, human world that we contrive and pretend to view it from a godlike distance. And it is only by crazed ambition, perpetually arising from entrenched features of our situation, that we set our sights on distant objects.

If we are to become freer, including freer thus to scan reality as a whole, escaping the confines of our more immediate world, we can do so only by gaining greater freedom of insight and action in this world. This fact justifies a classification of philosophical positions that distinguishes them from one another by their implications for politics: that is to say, for the remaking of society and culture.

The view I develop here is one that begins in dissatisfaction with the four positions I have described. The future of our most general ideas lies in the intransigent radicalization of this discontent—to an extent and in a direction that the dominant orthodoxies of contemporary thought in the social sciences and the humanities as well as in philosophy are unwilling to tolerate.

2

The Perennial Philosophy
and Its Enemy

Consider the work of a radicalized pragmatism from a standpoint that is at once more simple and more general than the perspective of the preceding pages. The criterion of classification of philosophical positions here is no longer the attitude toward the basic arrangements of a society and a culture. It is the attitude toward the reality and the authority of difference: differences among things and among people.

In the world history of philosophy there has been a dominant view: in fact, so dominant that it alone deserves a label coined by Leibniz—the perennial philosophy. Yet this view has been rejected with ever increasing fervor by the major voices of philosophy in the West. For the most part, the philosophy of the West has been in dissent from a conception that has prevailed, outside the West, in many traditions of thought. This Western dissent has yet to find a secure basis because it has never pushed its rebellion against the dominant view far enough. One way to define the task of a radicalized pragmatism is to say that it is the radicalization of this dissent.

The dominant and the dissident views are defined by their metaphysical conceptions—in particular their understanding of the reality of change and distinction such as we encounter them in the phenomenal world. Each of them also implies a distinct approach to the problems of politics and morals. In this sense, the set of intellectual options explored in the following pages contains within itself, as a part of a larger whole, the alternative positions about social and cultural order discussed in the preceding pages.

A single doctrine about difference and being has prevailed in the world history of thought. According to this hegemonic view, the manifest world of distinction and change is an illusion, or if not simply an illusion, then a shallow and ephemeral expression of a more real unity of being. The manifold within which everything seems to be what it is and to be different from everything else is not the ultimate reality. The illusory character or the superficial nature of difference in the manifold applies as well to the differences of greatest and most urgent significance to us: the differences among persons. The perennial philosophy dismisses these differences as misleading.

Ultimate reality is a single force—energy, spirit, being—that appears to us under the disguise of division, difference, and distinction. However, such separations, culminating in the individuality of persons, are—if not illusory—epiphenomenal. They report how we ordinarily meet and perceive the world, not how the world really is. At best, they are transitory and superficial. They fail to cut down to the roots of being.

Insofar as we represent the world in the form of this differentiated manifold, we do not grasp it for what it ultimately is: a unity prior to all difference. And insofar as our cravings remain engaged in this realm of distinction and difference, we are condemned to disappointment and suffering. On the one hand, we find ourselves imprisoned in the body, in its pain and its slow ruin. On the other hand, we are forced to choose at every turn between frustration and boredom. When we momentarily escape the pressure of unmet desire, we find ourselves entrapped in situations that fail to do justice to our powers.

According to the perennial philosophy, insight into reality enables us to free our minds and wills from the tyranny of illusory or superficial distinction and change, and from the falsehoods, misdirections, and disappointments to which this tyranny subjects us. We participate in the attributes of divinity—impersonal and ultimate reality: unity, self-containment, and inaction. This reality lies beyond time as well as difference. It is an eternal present to which our causal judgments, predicated as they are on temporal sequence, fail to apply.

One version of this perennial philosophy differs from another in its account of the relation between fundamental being and apparent difference. Some versions represent the latter as insubstantial illusion.

Others attribute to it a lesser but shallow and short-lived reality. These in turn vary in their picture of the genesis of passing difference out of a single and permanent being.

The attempt to free both the imagination and the will from the stranglehold of manifest difference points toward a particular solution to the problems of existence. The solution is the imitation of impersonal divinity and the mastery of its attributes of inactivity and indifference, freed from all restlessness. If the goal is absorption in ultimate reality beyond superficial and ephemeral difference and therefore beyond the limits of the body and of its situation in social space and historical time, then the mark of success is serenity. We can become happy by making ourselves indifferent to the disappointments and sufferings that result from our entanglement in the world of shadowy difference and insubstantial change.

We achieve such happiness through enlightenment about the true character of the relation between ultimate and universal spirit and the apparent, differentiated manifold. By virtue of such enlightenment, we share in divinity and escape the prison houses of our physical and social embodiment. Art, because it represents the world to us free from the shackles of desire and repulsion, may provide us with a foretaste of such enlightenment and such happiness.

This perennial philosophy, and the ideal of happiness through invulnerability that it helps support, enjoy their appeal because they respond to some of the basic contradictions of human existence. We all have an experience of consciousness, which is also an experience of infinity. We understand particular events and states of affairs by grasping them as instances of repeatable types or general ideas; thus even our insight into the particular refers implicitly to a horizon stretching indefinitely beyond it.

Even in our most accomplished exercises of analysis, as in mathematics and logic, we can never reduce our insights to ideas that can be justified and generated by a closed set of axioms; our powers of insight outreach our capacities of proof. Our ability to master language is characterized by a recursive ability—a power to string words and phrases together in endless but significant combinations—a power to which linguists have given the name "discrete infinity." In the life of desire, we find at every turn that our most intense longings, attachments, and addictions constantly transcend their immediate objects. We ask of one another more than any person can give another: not just respect, admiration, or love, but some reliable sign that there is a place for us in the world. And we pursue particular material objects and satisfactions with a zeal that they cannot and, in the end, do not sustain. Having relentlessly pursued these objects, we turn away from them, in disappointment and discontent, as soon as they are within our grasp. Only the beyond ultimately concerns us.

The sense of a permanent power of transcendence over all limits— of openness to the infinite—is thus inseparable from the experience of consciousness. However, this sense is countered by two other circumstances that work together to shape our experience: the anticipation of death and the impenetrability of existence. If on the one hand we were immortal, though unable to decipher the meaning of our existence, or at least its place in the history of the universe, the mysteriousness of our lives would lose some of its terror. There would always be for each of us a tomorrow, another chance either to discover part of the truth of our situation or to console ourselves, through some diversion, for the inaccessibility of that truth. If, on the other hand, although doomed as we are, we understood why the world exists and why we have in it the place we do, we would enjoy access to a source of direction. However limited in scope and indeterminate in implication, that guidance would nevertheless be reliable in authority.

We cannot, however, count on either of these two varieties of relief. On the contrary, the inescapability of death and the mysteriousness of existence immeasurably increase each other's terrors, closing every exit to escape or solace. Together, they impart to our lives the character of a headlong rush, from one enigma to another, seemingly endless and open at the start, then startlingly brief when reviewed in memory toward the end. Everything in this combination of mortality and impenetrability underlines our imprisonment within the all too finite particulars of the decaying body and of our accidental place in society and in history.

This experience of imprisonment belies the impulse of transcendence intrinsic to consciousness and characteristic of all our activities of inquiry, speech, and desire. The perennial philosophy draws its inspiration from the urge to confront this intolerable contrast between the transcending impulse of consciousness and our entrapment in mortality and mystery. The nature of its response is to redefine our situation so as to reassert, in the presence of circumstances that seem to deny them, the prerogatives of context-transcending spirit.

The perennial philosophy does so, however, only by also denying the ultimate reality of the perceptions of distinction and change that determine our picture of the world and of life in society. This denial turns out to exact a cost more terrible than the sufferings from which it would deliver us.

The relation of this philosophy of impersonal and timeless being to the practical concerns of moral and political thought is loose but powerful. If the perennial philosophy is, in the world history of thought outside the West, the predominant metaphysic, a particular view of the parallelism of moral and political order has also been the leading formula of political and moral theory throughout that history. According to this view, the well-ordered society is one in which each group occupies its place and performs its role within a predetermined division of labor. Some rule and think; others fight; others buy and sell; others yet till and reap. The social hierarchy reflects, and must be reflected by, a moral hierarchy—an ordering of the faculties of the soul: reason or spirit over will; will over appetite.

Disorder in society and disorder in the soul feed on each other. They have the same character: transgression or confusion of the specialized moral and social roles on which right depends. The external order of society and the internal order of personality reinforce each other; each begins to fall apart if unsupported by the other. Disorder, beginning in one of the two halves, soon spreads to the other half.

The connection of the perennial philosophy with this doctrine of hierarchical order in soul and society is not immediately apparent. Moreover, although the two sets of views—the metaphysical and the practical—have sometimes been formulated by the same philosophers, they have much more often been put forward by different thinkers and different schools of thought. However, even when living separate lives, the two bodies of belief have regularly coexisted in a broad range of civilizations and historical periods. Everything happens as if, despite their seeming distance and even contradiction to each other, they were in fact allied. What is the meaning of this working partnership between partners with such widely differing motives, ambitions, and tenets?

The world may be strife and illusion, but its troubles, sufferings, and dangers do not dissipate simply because they have been denied solidity and value. Once devalued, the world—especially the social world— must still be managed. We must prevent the worst from happening. Those who can apprehend the truth of the situation, divining ultimate being under the shadows of mendacious difference, and permanence under the appearance of change, are a happy few. Their withdrawal from social responsibility in the name of an ethic of contemplative serenity, inaction, and absorption into the reality of the One fails to solve the practical problems of social order. On the contrary, such a retreat threatens to leave a disaster in its wake: the calamity of a vacuum of initiative and belief. Into this vacuum steps the doctrine of hierarchical specialization in soul and society.

Seen through the sharp and selective lens of the perennial philosophy, this doctrine may be no more than a holding operation, as inexorable in its claims on those who must govern society as it is groundless in its metaphysical justification. There is then no surprise in seeing it most often represented by traditions of thought different from those that have adhered to the perennial philosophy.

Some in the world history of thought, however, have claimed to discern a more intimate connection between the doctrine of order and the perennial philosophy. If ultimate reality is spirit residing in all the apparent particulars, and most especially in living beings, then identification with universal spirit creates as well a basis for universal solidarity or compassion. The same compassion can then reappear in a commanding place among the highest faculties of the soul. It can therefore also be most closely identified with rulers and priests. The bonds of reciprocity, of mutual allegiance and devotion, among superiors and subalterns as well as among equals, can be founded on the expression and the worship of universal spirit, manifest among us as compassion and solidarity.

It is a belief we find articulated in philosophical and religious teachings as different as those of Buddha and Confucius. It reappears in that uniquely relentless Western statement of the otherwise un-Western instance of the perennial philosophy—the teaching of Schopenhauer. This belief turns the doctrine of social and moral order into something more than an effort to contain calamity and savagery in this vale of tears and illusions: into a concerted effort to soften the terror of social life, shortening the distance between ultimate being and everyday experience.

The perennial philosophy suffers from both a cognitive and an existential defect. The former is manifest in its vision of the world, and the latter, in its quest for happiness through serenity, and for serenity through invulnerability and distance.

Its cognitive flaw is its failure to recognize how completely and irreparably we are in fact embodied and situated. Not only our sufferings and our joys but also our prospects of action and discovery are engaged in the reality and the transformation of difference: the differences among phenomena and among people. To understand a state of affairs, whether in nature or in science, is to grasp what it might become as it is subject to different directions and varieties of pressure. Our imagination of these next steps—of these metamorphoses of reality—is the indispensable sign of advance in insight. When we deny the reality—at least the ultimate reality—of differences, we sever the vital link between insight into the real and imagined or experienced transformation.

The existential failing of the perennial philosophy is the revenge of this denied and unchained reality against the hope that we would become freer and happier if only we could see through the illusions of change and distinction. The point of seeing through these illusions is supposed to be greater freedom on the basis of truer understanding.

However, the consequence of the required denial of the reality of particulars may be the inverse of the liberation it promises. Having declared independence in the mind and ceased war against the realities around us, we find ourselves confined within a narrowing space. In the name of freedom, we become more dependent and more enslaved.

We may cast on ourselves a spell temporarily to quiet our restless striving. However, in so doing we deny ourselves instruments with which to explore the real world. We forego the means by which to see how everything in it can become something else when placed under resistance. By the same token, we lose the tools with which to strengthen our practical powers. We become cranks, slaves, and fantasists under the pretext of becoming free men and women. It is true that there will always be moments when we can transport ourselves, through such self-incantation, into a realm in which the particulars of the world and of the body, to which we have denied ultimate reality, cease to burden us. However, we cannot live in such a world; our moments of supposed liberation cannot survive the routines and responsibilities of practical life.

The alliance of the perennial philosophy with the practical doctrine of hierarchical specialization in soul and society has been the predominant position in the world history of speculative thought. Its major opponent has been a direction of thinking that, though exceptional in the context of world history, has long been the chief view in Western philosophy. The expression of this view in philosophical texts, however, is secondary to its broader articulation in religion, literature, and art. It is not merely the artifact of a tradition of speculative theorizing; it is the mainstay of a civilization, though a mainstay that represents a radical and uncompromising deviation from what has elsewhere been the dominant conception. Today this deviation has become the common possession of humanity thanks to the global propagation of its ideas by both high and popular Western culture. Its assumptions nevertheless remain inexplicit and its relation to the representation of nature in science unclear. To render this Western deviation from the perennial philosophy both perspicuous and uncompromising is a major part of the work of a radicalized pragmatism.

The hallmark of the deviation is belief in the reality of time as well as in the reality of the differences around which our experience is organized: in the first instance, the reality of the individual person and of differences among persons; in the second, the discrete structure of the world we perceive and inhabit. It is the view of individual personality that is most central to this belief system; everything else follows as a consequence.

The individual, his character, and his fate are for real. Each individual is different from every other individual who has ever lived or who will ever live. A human life is a dramatic and irreversible movement from birth to death, surrounded by mystery and overshadowed by chance.

What individuals can do with their lives depends on the way society is organized and on their place within the social order, as well as on achievement and luck. What happens in biographical time turns in large part on what happens in historical time. For this reason alone, history is a scene of decisive action, and everything that takes place in it is, like individuality itself, for real, not an illusory or distracting epiphenomenon obscuring a timeless reality. History is not cyclical but rather resembles individual life in being unilinear and irreversible. The institutions and the beliefs we develop in historical time may expand or diminish the life chances of the individual, including his relative power to challenge and change them in the course of his activities.

The reality of difference and of transformation, rooted in the basic facts of individual experience, then becomes the model on which we see and confront the whole world. Nothing is more crucial to the definition of such an approach to the world than its way of representing the relation between its view of humanity and its view of nature. This representation is subject to three related misstatements that narrow the reach and weaken the force of the alternative it offers to the perennial philosophy. In the process of criticizing and rejecting these alternatives, we come to see more clearly just what is at stake in the advancement of this alternative conception. Many of the most influential positions in the history of Western philosophy—including the "rejected options" discussed in the previous section—represent variations on qualified and inadequate versions of the alternative.

I propose to call these misstatements of the Western rebellion against the perennial philosophy phenomenalism, naturalism, and democratic perfectionism. Phenomenalism and naturalism have appeared in other settings as variations on recurrent positions in the history of metaphysics, without regard to the contest between the perennial philosophy and its enemy. Democratic perfectionism is a modern heresy, making sense only against the background of the Western apostasy.

The simplest misdirection—and the one easiest to dispose of—is phenomenalism. By phenomenalism I mean the belief that the manifest distinctions in the world, such as we perceive them, are for real: they represent the reality on which we are most entitled to rely. Phenomenalism would be defensible only if we had godlike powers and could legitimately identify the differences we perceive with the distinctions that in fact exist.

Our perceptual apparatus is very limited; it is built on the scale of the actions an organism like ours, unaided by tools that magnify its powers and broaden the theater of its activities, might undertake. We can outreach this apparatus by building instruments and machines—the tools of science—and by placing our interpreted perceptions under the light of alternative theories. We can understand the differences that make up the world only by passing through the differences we perceive. These perceived differences, however, are not reality; they are only our first gateway to reality. Phenomenalism would award us by stipulation the insight we can achieve only by effort, tentatively, fallibly, and cumulatively. It is a hallucination by which we mistake our flawed and fallible perceptions for the deliverance of reality.

The most influential incomplete rebellion against the perennial philosophy might be labeled naturalism. In one form or another, it has been the ruling view in the history of European metaphysics. Its influence is so far-reaching, and so much taken for granted, that it has been felt with equal force in the rationalist and the empiricist traditions.

Naturalism continues to underlie the most ambitious metaphysical projects of analytical philosophy. It upholds the reality of difference in nature, in history, and in personality. It sees metaphysics as an extension into more perilous territory of the same impulses to understanding and control that animate our scientific and political endeavors. Its implications for how we should live our lives may be indeterminate, but if only for that reason—enshrined in the supposed distinction between fact and value—they offer no support for the ethic of serenity through indifference to change and distinction. In all these respects, naturalism breaks decisively with the perennial philosophy. It does so, however, under the influence of false ideas.

To understand the core idea of naturalism, imagine two domains of reality and then a vantage point of insight outside them. The first domain is the wide circle of nature, studied by natural science. Metaphysics explores the implications, presuppositions, and limitations of the scientific picture of nature. Nature is peopled by different kinds of beings. It is also governed by regularities or laws. As natural beings, with mortal lives and limited perceptual apparatus, we participate in this natural world. How we do so, and what if any aspects of our experience resist being understood as mere incidents of nature, represent standard topics of dispute in this intellectual tradition.

Within nature there is a second, smaller concentric circle of conscious existence. It is enveloped by nature and subject to its laws. However, it has special features. It develops in irreversible historical time, marked by singular events and personalities, for which general laws, whether of nature or society itself, cannot fully account. Moreover, it is organized around experiences of consciousness, of intentional action, and of agency that cannot be fully understood as mere extensions of nature. This is the domain explored by the social sciences and the humanities and pertaining most directly to our human concerns. The experience of personality and the knowledge of the personal may resist complete assimilation to nature and natural science. They may even, on some accounts, express our participation in a wholly different order of being—the realm of spirit. Viewed objectively, however, from the outside, they form no more than a small and fragile part of nature.

If, as scientists and philosophers, we are able thus to represent the relation between nature and society, it is because we occupy, in our projects of inquiry, a third place. The third place is the position of a godlike mind. From this position we can look down on the domains of nature and of society, and understand society as a small and exceptional part of nature. From this imaginary standpoint, the human world may appear less intelligible than the natural one because it is less evidently subject to the law-like regularities we claim to discern from the godlike position.

However, this picture is only an illusion by which we flatter ourselves into imagining that we possess a measure of independence we do not in fact enjoy—not at least without a long and halting struggle. We are not in a godlike place, equidistant from nature and society. We are square in the middle of the experience of the personal and of the social. It is of this world alone—the world we make and remake—that we can hope to have more intimate and reliable knowledge.

As we look out from this world into nature—or even into ourselves as natural beings—we are required to outreach, with the help of mechanical devices and speculative theories, our immediate or remembered experience. We look out from the only place on which we can really stand—a particular human place—into the greater darkness of a broader reality. Insight, now relatively detached from action and analogy, becomes distant and unsure.

The error of naturalism is not to suppose that we are wholly within nature. We are: even our most distinctive characteristics—including what I later call the totalizing, surprising, and transcending characteristics of the mind—are themselves natural and the outcomes of a natural history.

The mistake of naturalism lies in making a promise it cannot keep: that a mind embodied in a dying organism will see the world as if that mind were universal spirit; that it will grasp the world as the world really is, through progressive convergence to the truth; and that the reward of its disinterestedness will be its penetration into the inner nature of reality, not all at once, to be sure, but slowly and cumulatively. In this sense, modern naturalism is an attempt to reverse the outcome of Kant's philosophical revolution: his idea that our insight into nature always remains mediated by the presuppositions imposed on us by our natural constitution. According to the message of that revolution, we are never able definitively and completely to escape those presuppositions. From the standpoint of the naturalistic error, our inevitably controversial ideas about society and culture appear to be less reliable and less penetrating than our disinterested ideas in science about nature and the universe, driven by our theories, developed with our instruments, and vindicated by our experiments.

In clinging to the fantasy of the view from Alpha-Orion, from the vantage point of which society appears as a more or less exceptional corner of nature—more puzzling because more lawless rather than more understandable because more immediate—we blunt the force of the rebellion against the perennial philosophy. From the godlike place above both society and nature, we formulate a unified vision of the natural and social worlds. Naturalism attributes to that picture a purchase on reality greater than the one we can hope to achieve, without divine prerogative, from within our situation.

Naturalism and phenomenalism recognize the reality of the world of change and distinction, which the perennial philosophy would deny. However, they fail to take account of how mysterious our existence is and how impenetrable the world remains to the mind. In this way, they hedge on the rejection of the perennial philosophy by offering us a lesser form of the illusory consolation the perennial philosophy holds out; they suppose, falsely, that the world in whose differences and transformations we are inescapably entangled is a world we can in principle understand. Phenomenalism denies the fact and the implications of the impenetrability of the world naively, by identifying reality with our perceptions. Naturalism denies the fact and the implications of the impenetrability of the world more subtly, by surveying the human world from a distance, the distance of the godlike place from which human affairs appear to us as a little part of the great map of nature: more familiar, yet less rule-bound and therefore less intelligible.

There is a third way, alongside phenomenalism and naturalism, in which Western thought has insisted on the reality of distinction and change while dimming their terrors by mischaracterizing their force. Let me call this third unfinished rebellion against the perennial philosophy democratic perfectionism. By democratic perfectionism I do not mean the metaphysical and moral claim that there is a well defined ideal to which a person, and indeed every type of being, tends according to its nature—the doctrine to which the label "perfectionism" has been traditionally applied. What I mean is the belief that a democratic society has a unique, indispensable institutional form. Once that form is secured, it creates a setting within which every individual who is not unlucky can raise himself to freedom, virtue, and happiness. Not only can he achieve by his own efforts a modest prosperity and independence; through the same self-help, he can enhance his own physical, intellectual, and moral powers. He can crown himself a little king, thriving in this dark world of change and distinction from which the perennial philosophy had unjustifiably and unnecessarily promised release.

Democratic perfectionism has had its home in the country that has most ardently repudiated everything with which the perennial philosophy and its ethic of serenity are associated, the same country that took pragmatism to be its national philosophy—the United States. A first hallmark of democratic perfectionism is the belief that a free society has an institutional formula that, once discovered (as it supposedly was by the founders of the American Republic and the framers of the American constitution), needs to be adjusted only in rare moments of national and world crisis and, even then, only to adapt its enduring truths to changed circumstance. This institutional dogmatism, denying the truth that the promises of democracy can be kept only by the ceaseless experimental renewal of their institutional vehicles, amounts to a species of idolatry. It nails our interests, ideals, and collective self-understandings to the cross of contingent, time-bound institutions.

A second keynote of democratic perfectionism is the belief that, barring the extremes of misfortune and oppression, the individual can lift himself physically, intellectually, and spiritually. Once the predetermined institutional blueprint of a free democratic society is put in place, the instances of bad luck and injustice that block the path to effective self-help will, according to this view, be infrequent. Such extraordinary circumstances will justify extraordinary remedies.

Every individual will have it within his power to achieve an attribute of divinity: self-sufficiency. The accumulation of property, indeed the profusion of things consumed or accumulated, becomes an alternative to dependence on other people. The raising up of the individual by himself, fulfilled at last in a measure of self-sufficiency, is the next best thing to the victory over death he cannot hope to win.

Thus, the institutional dogma tainting democratic perfectionism sets the stage for the cult of self-reliance. It does so in two distinct ways.

For one thing, failure to push our democratic ideals by experimenting with their institutional expression encourages us to naturalize the social setting of individual existence. As a result, we lose the sense of how much our private experience, even in its most intimate recesses, remains hostage to the way society is organized. No part of our experience depends more directly on society and its organization than the equipment and opportunities at our disposal for the development of our own selves.

For another thing, the institutional formula of democratic perfectionism, with its attachment to nineteenth-century conceptions of property and contract, fits with an idea of self-reliance. This idea downgrades the claims of social interdependence. The denial of dependence and of interdependence substitutes for the denial of death, as if we could enjoy the self-sufficiency of the immortal until we died.

We live among particulars, but we always want and see something more than any particular can give or reveal—thus our restlessness, our boredom, and our suffering. We are certain to die, although we find in ourselves tokens of undying spirit—thus our sense of living under the pressure of an intolerable contradiction between our experience of selfhood and our recognition of the unyielding limits nature imposes on our existence. We can see only dimly beyond the boundaries of the social world that we ourselves make—thus our confusion, our inability to place our undeniable suffering and our apparent accomplishments within a context of all contexts that would keep them safe from doubt and denigration.

The perennial philosophy responds to these facts by denying the reality—at least the ultimate reality—of the world in which we encounter difference and transformation. It urges us to respond by distancing ourselves from the illusions and entanglements of this world. The end of distinction and change is supposed to spell the end of both suffering and illusion. However, the differentiated and changing world, though relatively impenetrable to the mind, is nevertheless the only world in which we have reason to believe. In trying to flee it, we are more likely to make ourselves smaller than to make ourselves freer.

Rejecting the perennial philosophy, phenomenalism, naturalism, and democratic perfectionism recognize the reality of this world. In so doing, however, they downplay some aspect of the background facts to our existence—facts to which the perennial philosophy, with its focus on an ultimate, unified being—beyond difference and transformation— provides a misguided response. Phenomenalism and naturalism suppose that the world is more manifest to the mind than it in fact is, or can be. Democratic perfectionism mistakenly sees in individual self-help a path to self-sufficiency in the face of mortality.

Our task, however, is to affirm the reality of difference and transformation while accepting the force to the background facts to which both the perennial philosophy and its major rivals in the history of thought respond: the disproportion between our universalizing longings and our particular circumstances; the comparative weakness of any insight we can hope to gain into the nonhuman world; the impossibility of finding a context of all contexts—an indisputable and invariant frame of reference—that would give meaning and direction to our experience; the certainty that we shall die as ephemeral natural beings despite the infinity-oriented character of our desires and thoughts.

The best and truest philosophy would be the one that did justice to these facts. Acknowledging the reality of distinction and change and the fateful importance of what happens in history, it would put its insights at the service of our empowerment.

3

Pragmatism Reclaimed

Pragmatism as a Starting Point

Some will object that the argument presented in this book has no unique relation to the philosophical tradition of pragmatism. It could start out from the agendas, the conceptions, and the vocabularies of several other traditions of thought, recent or long past. What matters, they will insist, is the content of the ideas.

They will be right. The ideas advanced here can be developed with the materials of other traditions of thought. These ideas have no exclusive relation to pragmatism or indeed to any other accredited school of philosophical doctrine. The point is indeed not to rescue and reinvent pragmatism. It is to pull ourselves together, now that we can no longer share the illusory ambitions of classical metaphysics or resign ourselves to the dogmas and practices of the specialized forms of inquiry that are available to us. It is to create a world of ideas about the mind and nature, the self and society, vindicating the great revolutionary attempt to marry science and democracy, experimentalism and emancipation, the humanization of society and the divinization of humanity.

The single idea that resounds on every page of this book is the idea of the infinity of the human spirit, in the individual as well as in humanity. It is a view of the wonderful and terrible disproportion of that spirit to everything that would contain and diminish it, of its awakening to its own nature through its confrontation with the reality of constraint and the prospect of death, of its terror before the indifference and vastness of nature around it, of its discovery that what it most shares with the whole of the universe is its ruination by time, of its subsequent recognition that time is the core of reality if anything is, of its enslavement to orders of society and culture that belittle it, of its need to create a world, a human world, in which it can be and become itself even if to do so it must nevertheless rebel against every dogma, every custom, and every empire, and of its power to realize this seemingly impossible and paradoxical program by identifying, in each intellectual and political situation, the next steps.

In an age of democracy and of peaceful or warlike communion among all parts of humanity, philosophy, like poetry and politics, must be prophetic. The content of its prophecy is a vision of how it is that we may respond, right now and with the instruments at hand, to the experience of being lost in a void that is made up of time, into the beginning and end of which we cannot see, and that is indifferent to our concerns. It is a prophecy of the path of our unchaining and of our ascent in a world of time, in which we remain always bound to death and forever denied insight into the ultimate nature of reality.

No philosopher or philosophical tradition in the last two centuries has had a monopoly on this prophecy. It is everywhere.

In retaking and developing this vision, there is no one place to begin; there are many places. Faithful to the doctrine of this book, I care less about the point of departure than that there be one; that we achieve clarity about the direction; and knowing the starting point and the direction, that we be able to identify next steps.

That pragmatism has been the national philosophy of what is now the dominant power in the world renders the label suspect. For what could be more suspect as a source of philosophical insight than apparent flattery of the powerful? Nevertheless, there are pragmatic reasons to use the label "pragmatism" and to pillage the pragmatist tradition for some of the ideas we most need now.

The first reason is that the tradition of pragmatism contains in distorted or truncated form many of the conceptions that we most require if we are to advance and to reconcile the two projects that enjoy—and deserve to enjoy—greatest authority in our world: the empowerment of the individual—that is to say, his raising up to godlike power and freedom—and the deepening of democracy—that is to say, the creation of forms of social life that recognize and nourish the godlike powers of ordinary humanity, however bound by decaying bodies and social chains.

The major source of the attraction of these ideas lies in their focus on a picture of the human agent. According to this picture, the human agent is irreducible to any set of causal influences that may weigh upon him. He is incapable of being fully contained and governed by the social and cultural orders he develops and joins. For such a view, prophecy speaks louder than memory, and one lives for the future the better to live more freely and fully in the present. Orientation to the future is just another way of describing the structures, of organization and of consciousness, that can define a present that provides us with the instruments of its overcoming.

These themes, further explored in the following pages, do not suffice to justify commandeering the label "pragmatism." For they can be found as well in other intellectual traditions—Christian, romantic, or historicist. Hegel or Bergson could, on these grounds, stand in the place of James and Dewey: my line of argument here is no further from the German and the Frenchman than it is from the two Americans. (In fact, the philosopher with whose teachings the ideas of this book have in certain respects the closest kinship was neither a pragmatist nor my close contemporary. He is Nicholas of Cusa, who lived from 1401 to 1464.)

The seizing of the label "pragmatism" relies, however, on two additional reasons. One additional reason is that pragmatism, though diminished and domesticated, represents the philosophy most alive today. It lives not among professors but in the world. Moreover, it remains the most characteristic philosophy of what is today in every dimension the dominant power. The use of the label "pragmatism" is therefore attended by the danger of power worship: the peril of becoming a genuflection to the national philosophy of an imperial democracy. What can alone save it from such abasement is the radical nature of the change of direction it proposes: a change of direction not

only in the doctrines and methods associated with the American pragmatists but also in the broader forms of consciousness that are spreading
throughout the world under the sponsorship of the leading power.

The world needs the full, intransigent development of what I characterized in the preceding section as the major alternative to the perennial philosophy. It needs to develop this alternative in aid of its commitments to the radicalization of democracy and the divinization of the
person. The teachings of the American pragmatists are a version of this
alternative. However, they are an inadequate, truncated version, which
sacrifices the central themes to a range of costly and unnecessary concessions, especially concessions to the view earlier called naturalism.
On the other hand, the forms of consciousness most closely associated
with the American national culture, and now propagated throughout
the world, have global significance. They amount to lopsided, misdirected versions of beliefs that should be dear to experimentalist democracies that are friendly to the empowerment and transcendence of
the individual.

It matters that the label "pragmatism" describes the characteristic
national philosophy of the dominant, globalization-shaping power. It
matters because the struggle over the direction of this philosophy, and
of the forms of belief and sensibility it represents, then becomes a contest over everyone's future as well as over the content of an alternative
to the perennial philosophy.

Another additional reason to use the name "pragmatism" is that a
fight over the meaning and value of pragmatism today soon becomes a
struggle about how we should relate the future of philosophy to the
future of society. Philosophy matters on two accounts. On one account,
it matters because it is like politics: it is not about anything in particular;
it is about everything. On another account, it matters because it is like
us: it does not fit; it is the residue in thought of what cannot be contained in particular disciplines or be brought under the control of particular methods.

As in logic and mathematics, our capacities for inference and invention outreach what any closed system of axioms can justify without
contradiction; as in natural science, our powers of discovery and the-

orizing go beyond what any antecedent understanding of our scientific beliefs can accommodate, and end up requiring retrospective revision of how we understand the practice as well as the content of science; as in cosmology, more clearly, but in all its sister sciences generally, our thinking about the structure and history of the universe reshapes our understanding of the supposedly invariant modal categories of possibility, necessity, and contingency, rather than taking these categories as immutable givens, so in philosophy we take up a form of thinking that has as its subject the limits of all other subjects. In this way, we confirm the power to act and to think beyond regulative limits, and then, after the fact, to reposition these limits, as a defining characteristic of our humanity and our intellects.

Philosophy is a concentrated deployment of the transgressing faculties of the mind. This fact is at the root of the special relation between the doctrinal claims or arguments of a philosophical system and its thematic orientation or intention. It also reveals a hidden and vital level of our thinking: conceptions laying roots in an experience of the world that, once translated into distinct ideas, can be assessed, challenged, and revised.

It is precisely in this spirit that I here approach pragmatism and justify my use of its name. Let us treat the key doctrinal claims of American pragmatism as an unsatisfactory representation of themes more deserving of attention than the technical concepts and arguments by which we know them. Let us approach these themes as an expression in the realm of thought of a major strand in the national consciousness and culture of the American people. Let us view this strand as an incomplete and distorted version of a political and intellectual program that holds immense interest for all humanity. Let us recognize this program as a response to the range of human interests at stake in an effort to develop an alternative to the perennial philosophy.

To use the name of pragmatism is to assert that an argument over the future course of the ideas and attitudes historically associated with the pragmatist tradition are useful right now in advancing these goals. I proceed in three steps: first, distancing the argument of this book from some of the conceptions that were central to the ideas of the American pragmatists; then exploring how my argument is nevertheless intimately connected with themes—attitudes, gestures, and hopes—on which American pragmatism, like many other modern philosophical traditions, laid great store but to which its most distinctive philosophical claims were unable to do justice; and finally discussing how these themes were misdirected in a national culture that now enjoys worldwide influence.

Ideas of the Pragmatists

Consider three of the most characteristic ideas of the American pragmatists: Charles Peirce's approach to the meaning of concepts, William James's theory of truth, and John Dewey's doctrine of experience. None of these ideas is immune to decisive objections. All are inadequate and misleading expressions of the larger, not fully developed themes that make pragmatism a subject of continuing interest. What is most valuable in each of them comes down, in the end, to something negative: the way each helps dispel an enslaving superstition of the mind.

That the meaning of a concept lies in the difference the concept makes—that it is to say, in its use within our practices and in its effect on them—is a salutary rebuff to every attempt to separate meaning-making from its practical context. Our moves within every such context are guided by guesses about the future that are also, unavoidably, proposals for the future. It is a conclusion in which many of the greatest philosophers of the last century have agreed.

What this approach to the meaning of concepts fails to address, however, is the distinction as well as the relation between the difference a concept makes to an understanding of part of reality and the difference it makes to our efforts to master and to change our situation: between our theoretical or contemplative and our political or reconstructive practices.

A central thesis of this book is that the connection between thought and practice is most intimately and fully realized only when our minds are addressed to our own affairs—the concerns of humanity. When we direct our thoughts to nature, even if to see ourselves as fixtures of nature, we loosen the connection between thought and practice. When we loosen it, we are tempted to assume the posture I earlier called naturalism. We survey both the human and the nonhuman worlds from a supposedly godlike distance. We treat the achievement of such distance as the realization of our longing for transcendence.

Thinking in this way, we see natural science, conducted from the viewpoint of the stars, as the pinnacle of human understanding: the point at which the mind most completely overcomes its enslavement to immediate and ephemeral circumstances. Consequently, we treat the reciprocal entanglement of insight and resistance as an intellectual embarrassment.

If these beliefs—hallmarks of naturalism—provide the background for the thesis that use of a concept determines its meaning, the thesis belongs to the arsenal of the forces a radicalized pragmatism must oppose. The association of such a view of how concepts gain meaning with an understanding, like Peirce's, of objectivity in thought as convergence of belief by ideal observers (or ideal observers under ideal conditions) reinforces the naturalistic bias.

If, however, we rid ourselves of the naturalistic bias, we change the way we understand the thesis that concepts gain their meaning from the difference they make. In our thinking about ourselves our concepts are weapons, either helping lend a false semblance of naturalness and necessity to the organized settings of action and thought, or helping us to become masters of the context. In our thinking about nature—or about ourselves as purely natural entities—our concepts are extrapolations and metaphors, by which we try to see and comprehend a world external to our wills and imaginations: a world we did not make. In the first situation, the use from which the concepts gain meaning is the making, unmaking, and remaking of society and culture. In the second situation, it is our effort to acquire a proxy for forbidden knowledge—the knowledge we might have if we were not embodied spirits and mortal organisms, validating our claims to insight only by our powers of prediction and control. We are accustomed to bring these two situations under the same rubric of knowledge. We should rather recognize that they are as different as looking into a mirror and peering into the dark.

A second characteristic idea of American pragmatism is William James's theory of truth. This theory asserts that the representation of reality and the experience of desire are internally related. An element of what we want to be the case properly and even inevitably enters into our judgments of what is the case.

James's defense of this idea against the charge that it amounted to a philosophy of wishful thinking took the form of a series of generic qualifications. Instead of qualifying it, however, we should reinterpret and radicalize it. The agent—according to James's qualifications—may prefer a belief that satisfies a "vital good" to one that does not if the choice is momentous and urgent, the evidence is inconclusive, and the appeal of the good is overwhelming. In this way a doctrine corrosive of naturalism was deprived of its force, having been made plausible only by being first made safe. The result was to squander an opportunity to develop part of the intellectual apparatus useful to the advancement of a cause, at once philosophical and political, to which James had every reason to be sympathetic.

The problem of the relation between what we want and what we judge to be the case arises with unique urgency in a particular context. This context is the relation between insight into social reality and proposals for social reconstruction. The relation is reciprocal. Programmatic imagination depends on insight into transformative opportunity. Without such insight, and bereft of any credible view of how structural change happens, we find ourselves reduced to the idea that realism means simply remaining close to what already exists.

Conversely, to grasp a state of affairs, whether in nature or in society, is to see what, under different conditions, it might become. In nature we are reduced to limited interventions in a world we hardly control or understand. In society and culture everything that seems fixed is simply frozen politics or interrupted struggle. The inventions, the conflicts, and the compromises, in thought and in practice, are all there is; there is nothing else. The penumbra of next steps, interacting with our more general ideas about self and society, represents the practical residue of the idea of the possible in our social experience.

Every social world must be normalized to become stable; its arrangements, even if originating in violence and accident, must be seen to embody a set of possible and desirable images of human association—pictures of what relations among people can and should be like in different domains of social life. Against the background of the two-way relation between understanding and transforming, the imperative to normalize and to moralize turns all of our most powerful social ideas into self-fulfilling prophecies. In acting on such ideas, people reshape the social world in the image of these ideas. However, they do not do so freely; they come up against the "stubborn facts": the constraints of scarcity, of contradiction between means as well as between ends, and of sheer ignorance and confusion.

Any social theory that would escape the illusions of false necessity without surrendering to the fantasies of an unchastened utopianism must make sense of this clash between the self-fulfilling prophecies and the recalcitrant facts. Instead of qualifying James's theory of truth to death, as James himself, misled by naturalism, ended up doing, we should see it as the summary formula of an insight into the character of social experience. Its most pertinent setting is therefore our understanding of our own individual and collective selves, our societies and cultures. Turned into a view of everything—into an account of the margin of maneuver the mind enjoys in its transactions with the non-human world—it loses both clarity and direction. It will then be eviscerated to be saved. What then remains of it may not be worth saving.

Dewey's conception of experience—a third characteristic teaching of American pragmatism—provides yet another example of the betrayal of a radical vision by a naturalistic compromise. Two ideas struggle for supremacy in this conception; they cannot live in peace.

One idea is the picture of the human agent thrown into a constrained but nevertheless open world—a world in which everything can become something else and nothing is permanent. The most important feature of such a world is that it allows for novelty: for things that are really new in the sense that they do not merely make real a possibility that had been backstage to the actual world, awaiting the events that would serve as its cue to step onto the stage of actuality.

The second idea is the view of the individual as a mindful organism, cast in an evolutionary narrative of which he is not the master. Ideas and arrangements are tools, allowing him to cope with his situation; their most important feature is their instrumental character. If we are to take seriously the view of man as a situated organism, the toolmaker is himself a tool: a tool of natural evolution. Even in the most keenly felt experiences of his life, he will be the unwitting plaything of impersonal forces that are indifferent to his concerns and destructive of them. In this spirit, Schopenhauer presents our sexual and romantic experience as the cruel means by which nature, before grinding us down, forces us to serve her goals. No naturalistic view of humanity and its predicament is coherent or complete unless we are willing to push it to the bitter limit of this disturbing result.

These two ideas cannot both be right. Suppose that ultimate predominance falls to the second idea: the toolmaker who is himself a tool, the mind made to serve instrumentally the stratagems of the dying organism, held within a natural world that has no use for its concerns. Then, the first idea—the self as resistant agent, making its way through a sea of contingencies—must come to little. The naturalization of man will be his dehumanization. The motives that led us to seek solace or escape in the perennial philosophy will gain new strength.

Dewey's conception of experience, like the whole line of historical pragmatism and of its counterparts in other naturalistic strands of modern philosophy, leaves this ambiguity unresolved. By so doing, it greatly weakens its most fertile proposal: the view of the agent struggling with constraint and contingency, and using contingency to loosen constraint.

A radicalized pragmatism, more faithful to its own intentions, must resolve this ambiguity decisively in favor of the agent and his ambitions. But how? The naturalistic picture of the confined and dying organism contains a powerful truth. A philosophy that takes sides with the agent must not deny this truth. It must, however, reveal how we can redirect thought and reorganize society so that the vision of the agent able to use contingency against constraint becomes more real, and the picture of the toolmaker made into a tool of natural processes indifferent to his concerns becomes less real.

The issue is not which of the two ideas holds more of the truth today.

Rather, the issue is how the first idea can be made to hold more of the truth than the second idea tomorrow; how we can make a tomorrow in which the first idea holds more truth than the second. It is the contest over the future that is at stake in the controversy over this view of experience.

Peirce's doctrine of how to give meaning to concepts, James's theory of truth, and Dewey's conception of experience all have several elements in common. They draw their enduring interest from underlying motivations that they fail to make explicit and even betray. In each instance, an insight into humanity and self-consciousness is compromised by being represented—unadvisedly—as a claim about knowledge and nature in general. Each of these ideas fails to recognize that far from being a model for our knowledge of humanity our knowledge of the nonhuman world can be only its dim extension. Each imposes on pragmatism an overlay of naturalism. Philosophers for whom human agency was supposed to be everything took up once again the ancient and universal quest for a place above both human and the nonhuman reality. They should instead have agreed to see the nonhuman world from the only place we really have—a place within the human world.

Thus, the misadventures of these three characteristic ideas are telltale signs of a fundamental equivocation. The effect of this equivocation is to deprive us of means with which better to serve the cause of democratic experimentalism and better to advance the rebellion against the perennial philosophy.

Central Themes: Agency, Contingency, Futurity, Experimentalism

These ideas nevertheless draw their misused power—their residue of distorted insight—from their relation to four great themes to which they—and many of the other doctrines with which they were associated—fail to do justice. These themes are: agency, contingency, futurity, and experimentalism.

The first theme is *agency*. The human agent, shaped and manacled by context and tradition, by established arrangements and enacted dogma, fastened to a decaying body, surrounded in birth and death by enigmas he cannot dispel, desperately wanting he knows not what, confusing the unlimited for which he longs with an endless series of paltry tokens, demanding assurance from other people, yet hiding within himself and using things as shields against the others, somnambulant most of the time yet sometimes charged and always inexhaustible, recognizing his fate and struggling with it even as he appears to accept it, trying to reconcile his contradictory ambitions but acknowledging in the end or, deep down, all the time that no such reconciliation is possible or if possible not lasting: this is the one topic from which there is no escape.

The knowledge we can have of him and of his constraints and constructions is the intimate, piercing knowledge that most closely resembles the knowledge God can have of His creation. Such knowledge as we can gain of nature outside ourselves, or even of ourselves as natural entities outside the realm of consciousness—that is to say, of theorized life—will be less full and less reliable. It will be open to contradiction not, as are our human endeavors, in the content of its claims and undertakings, but in its most basic procedures and concepts. The reasons for this frailty of our knowledge of nature are both natural and preternatural.

The natural reason for the frailty is that we are not built as gods but as ephemeral natural beings, with a finite scope of perception and experience. The further we move away from the range in which thought shadows action and action embodies thought, the more must we infer unseen reality from ambiguous signs. The test of success then becomes practical even when it seems to be theoretical: that when we act upon a piece of nature on the basis of our inferences, what happens is not incompatible with what we had conjectured. However, in arguing the merits of rival theories, although we may fancy ourselves philosophers enjoying the view from the stars, we are in fact lawyers contending with irreducible ambiguity and foreclosing alternative solutions out of practical need: sometimes the need to achieve some effect in nature; always and immediately the need to put our scientific concepts and instruments to use and to describe what a part of the natural world would be like if those instruments and concepts were adequate to describe it.

The preternatural reason for the frailty is that the most important trait of the agent—his power to spill over, to not completely fit, to contain within himself irrepressible resources of transgression and transcendence—produces very different results when applied to the human and the nonhuman worlds. In the human world, it makes reconstruction possible, for better or for worse. The impulses and interests not countenanced by the present order become seeds of another order. And this other order may differ in quality as well as in content from the order it replaced: it may have a different relation to the constructive freedom of the individual or collective agents who conceived it.

Everything in the context—our context—can be changed, even if the change is piecemeal. And the change, in the form of an endless series of next steps, can take a direction, revealed, even guided by ideas. We can develop practices and institutions that multiply occasions for our exercise of our powers of resistance and reconstruction. If spirit is a name for the resistant and transcending faculties of the agent, we can spiritualize society. We can diminish the distance between who we are and what we find outside of ourselves.

However, we cannot spiritualize nature. We can choose only between doing something to it and leaving it alone. We remain restricted to this choice even in our greatest scientific accomplishments. Here, in our relation to the nonhuman world, the significance of our not fitting remains focused on a single intense but narrow target: our ability to conjecture and to experiment beyond the limits of what the prevailing theories and the accepted methods allow, and then retrospectively to revise our assumptions in the light of our discoveries. In the end, however, we can have no hope of turning nature into us.

The second theme is *contingency*. When applied to the natural world, the modal categories of necessity, possibility, and contingency have no meaning that is independent of our ideas about how nature works. One branch of natural science in particular—cosmology—bears directly on the sense in which the necessary is necessary; the possible, possible; and the contingent, contingent. A particular conception of necessity, possibility, or contingency is simply a shorthand allusion to a particular theory or family of theories.

In any body of ideas about nature, some states of affairs will be represented as more "necessary" than others in the sense that their givenness depends on fewer conditions. However, even the most necessary of necessary events and relations will be infected by an element of factitiousness: of being a certain way just because it is. Not even a "steady-state" cosmology can explain why the universe, any universe, must be so designed as to have the quality of self-propagation or self-subsistence. That the universe has turned out to be one rather than another is the irreducible element of contingency in the cosmology most supportive of the necessity of constant relations in the universe. The precise sense in which these relations are or are not necessary cannot be inferred from any explanation-independent lexicon of modal categories. This sense depends on the substance and implications of our ideas about the universe and its history—or its way of not having a history, of being timeless, if time is an illusion.

In our human experience of humanity, however, contingency takes on a special meaning. This special meaning is of central importance to a philosophy that would free our understanding from the shackles of naturalism. This contingency is no mere idle speculation; it is a weight that bears heavily down upon us. We struggle in vain to deny or downplay it. This weight is the compacted combination of distinct elements.

One component is the irreducible sense—preserved under even the most necessitarian cosmology—in which the universe and its history—the broader setting of our lives—are simply and unexplainably there.

A second constituent is our inability in the study of any part of nature to determine, conclusively and definitively, which theory is the right one. Not only is our knowledge limited, but our efforts to establish unchanging premises and methods are tainted by insoluble contradictions.

A third part is the fateful character of our historical struggle over the shape of society and culture. Even the most intimate and basic aspects of our experience are colored by the dogmas of culture and the institutions of society. We cannot rigidly divide our experience into the personal and the collective, the transient and the permanent. Historical time seeps into biographical time.

A fourth element is the role of luck and grace in human life: having or not having lucky breaks, receiving or not acts of recognition and love from other people. The blind fortune that presides over our birth— out of the consequences of the accidental coupling of our parents— pursues us in the big things as well as in the little ones.

The experience of contingency resulting from the combination of these four facts threatens to overwhelm us. It offends and frightens us because of its apparent irreconcilability with our equally powerful sense of being context-transcending, embodied spirit. Among the devices we have deployed to fight against it the most persistent in the history of ideas has been the perennial philosophy. We should give up this fight against the experience of contingency: we can conduct it only at de-structive cost to our powers of self-construction as well as to our clarity of insight.

The third theme is *futurity*. Whether or not time is for real in the vast world of nature, of which our knowledge always remains at once remote and contradictory, is a subject that will always continue to arouse con-troversy. That time is for real in human existence is not, however, a speculative thesis; it is a pressure we face with mounting force, so long as we remain conscious and not deluded, in our passage from birth to death. The temporal character of our existence is the consequence of our embodiment, the stigma of our finitude, and the condition that gives transcendence its point.

We are not exhausted by the social and cultural worlds we inhabit and build. They are finite. We, in comparison to them, are not. We can see, think, feel, build, and connect in more ways than they can allow. That is why we are required to rebel against them: to advance our interests and ideals as we now understand them, but also to become ourselves, affirming the polarity that constitutes the law-breaking law of our being.

To seek what goes beyond the established structure and represents, for that very reason, the possible beginning of another structure, even of a structure that organizes its own remaking, is to live for the future. Living for the future is a way of living in the present as a being not wholly determined by the present conditions of its existence. We never completely surrender. We go about our business of passive submission, of voiceless despair, as if we knew that the established order were not for keeps, and had no final claim to our allegiance. Orientation to the future—futurity—is a defining condition of personality.

So fundamental is this feature of our existence that it also shapes the experience of thinking, even when our thoughts are directed away from ourselves to nature. Ceaselessly reorganizing our experience of particulars under general headings, constantly breaking up and remaking the headings to master the experience, intuiting in one set of known relations the existence of another, next to it or hidden under it, finding out one thing when we had set out to find out another, and discovering indeed what our assumptions and methods may have ruled out as paradoxical, contradictory, or impossible, we come to see the next steps of thought—its possibilities, its future—as the point of the whole past of thought.

Futurity should cease to be a predicament and should become a program: we should radicalize it to empower ourselves. That is the reason to take an interest in ways of organizing thought and society that diminish the influence of what happened before on what can happen next. Such intellectual and institutional innovations make change in thought less dependent on the pressure of unmastered anomalies and change in society less dependent on the blows of unexpected trauma. In any given historical situation, the effort to live for the future has consequences for how we order our ideas and for how we order our societies. There is a structure to the organized revision of structures. Its constituents, however, are not timeless. We paste them together with the time-soaked materials at hand.

The fourth theme is *experimentalism*. It is less a separate idea than it is the combination of the other three. What it adds to them is a conception of the new and of its creation. Consider the problem in the context of production and of its relation to science. To understand a state of affairs is to grasp its possible transformations: what it could become under different conditions or as the result of different events. These transformations of the established situation—the penumbra of the next steps—are what we mean, or should mean, by the possible.

We can turn some of these imagined variations into things. Then, science becomes not the basis of production but production itself.

A way to accelerate the production of the new is to turn the way people work together into a social embodiment of the imagination: their dealings with one another mimic the moves of experimental thought. To this end, the first requirement is that we save energy and time for whatever cannot yet be repeated. Whatever we can repeat we express in a formula and then embody in a machine. Thus, we shift the focus of energy and attention away from the already repeatable, toward the not yet repeatable.

Other features of work as permanent innovation build on this basic achievement. We rethink and redesign our productive tasks in the course of executing them. Consequently, we do not allow rigid contrasts between supervisory and executing roles to be established. The divisions among those who perform different specialized tasks become fluid—the plan on the march. Rather than allocating competition and cooperation to different compartments of human life, we join them together in the same practices. And just as we revise our tasks in the course of carrying them out, so too, in the course of the experiences engendered by this productive activity, we begin to revise our understanding of our interests and even of our identities. In this way, the form of practical cooperation comes to reflect the combination of analysis, synthesis, and what Peirce called abduction: the leap of speculative but informed conjecture. The organization of work becomes practical reason on horseback.

Politics, especially democratic politics, carries experimentalism to another level. It does more than organize a distinct domain of social life, alongside the domain of production. It sets the terms on which we can change all the other domains. The overriding criterion by which to measure our success in approaching an experimentalist ideal in politics is success in making change less dependent on crisis. A calamity—often in the form of economic collapse or armed conflict—can break any order. Even in the partly democratized societies of the contemporary world, those who would reform the established social order will ordinarily need to count on crisis as their ally. To render politics experimental is to dispense with the need for this ally. It is so to organize the contest over the mastery and uses of governmental power—and indeed over all the institutionalized terms by which we can make claims on one another—that the present arrangements and practices multiply opportunities for their own revision. Change becomes internal.

Our stake in making change endogenous has many sides. By its direct effect, it serves our interest in being masters of the partial, contingent context within which we operate: in not having this context imposed on us as a natural fact or an irresistible fate. By its indirect effects, it advances two other families of interests. The first is our interest in the subversion of entrenched social divisions and hierarchies, which always rest on institutions and beliefs that are relatively insulated from constant attack. The second is our interest in accelerating practical progress by enhancing our power to recombine people, machines, and ideas.

Thus, experimentalism in politics is deeper in reach and more general in scope than experimentalism in production. However, this political experimentalism is itself a species of a yet more general idea and more ambitious practice: the idea of never being confined to the present context, the practice of using the smaller variations that are at hand to produce the bigger variations that do not yet exist. Experimentalism is existential bootstrapping; it is about changing the context of established arrangement and assumed belief, little by little and step by step, as we go about our business.

Viewed in this light, experimentalism is the solution to a metaphysical problem. The problem is that we must organize experience and society in order to do anything at all but that no single organization of experience and society does justice to our powers of insight, invention, and connection. The solution to this problem has two parts. The first part is to develop a way of moving within the established context that allows us to anticipate within the context the opportunities that it does not yet realize and may not even allow. The second part is to arrange society and thought so that the difference between reproducing the present and experimenting with the future diminishes and fades.

The result is to embody the experimental impulse in a form of life and thought enabling us more fully to reconcile engagement and transcendence. We then become both more human and more godlike.

Two Misreadings of Pragmatism

As a philosophy, pragmatism failed to do justice to the themes of agency, contingency, futurity, and experimentalism, which inspired it; the pragmatist philosophy sacrificed them to naturalism. (As an expression of American national culture, it failed to do justice to the possibilities of life under democracy; it sacrificed them to democratic perfectionism.) The equivocations of Peirce's view of how to determine the meaning of concepts, of James's theory of truth, and of Dewey's doctrine of experience illustrate characteristic forms of this sacrifice of the vision to the prejudice.

The vision took sides with the human agent, unresigned to belittling circumstance. The prejudice insisted on the misguided attempt to find a basis for thought and judgment higher than the perspective of humanity. The consequence was to prevent pragmatism from living up to its vision and from embodying a more intransigent and powerful alternative to the perennial philosophy.

We should rescue the vision from the naturalistic concessions that have compromised it in the history of American pragmatism. Whether we choose to apply the label pragmatism to the product of this rescue is an open question. I propose that we answer it affirmatively on a combination of pragmatic grounds.

Such a redirection of pragmatism amounts to the unchaining of a shackled vision. To unchain it, we must oppose two ways of understanding the pragmatist tradition that have recently been in the ascendant: a deflationary and a nostalgic-heroic reading. The former is anachronistic; the latter is archaic. Both are inimical to what we should value most in this tradition.

The deflationary reading sees pragmatism as a precursor of "postmodernism." Its characteristic conceit is that every historical setting is its own law. To pass judgment on it on any terms other than its own would be to lay claim to a foundational context-overriding insight that no one can hope to achieve.

This idea represents a confusion of a good negative idea—that there are no fixed points in the history of knowledge and experience—with a bad negative idea—that we cannot see, think, or create more than the established structure of society will allow. The bad negative idea represents a straightforward denial of the theme of futurity or transcendence. It also amounts to the key claim made by the fourth of the four rejected options explored earlier in this book.

One way to tell that the bad idea is bad is that it makes no practical sense on its own terms. It offers an empty gesture. The deflationary thesis implies that discourses about discourses—higher-order proposals about criteria, methods, and foundations—are a waste of time. The only justifiable meta-discourse is the one that proclaims the useless and illusory character of all meta-discourses. What matters is to have first-order proposals about the reconstruction of our arrangements and our ideas.

The energy, the authority, and the fecundity with which we devise first-order proposals depend, however, on our ability to see beyond the limits of the present context. Every important innovation in thought or in society is likely to require a minor rebellion: an anticipatory realization within the present context of possibilities—of insight, experience, connection, and organization—that could be more fully realized only through a change in the context: which is to say, in the institutional arrangements and enacted ideals that define it.

Thus, the first-order initiatives that matter most come pregnant with alternative futures; they are prophecies as well as reforms, and their agents and votaries have no choice but to make war on whatever in their situation belies their prophecies. Such a practice amounts to a living refutation of the idea that we are prisoners—lucky or hapless as the case may be—of the social and cultural world in which we find ourselves.

The ideas that inform such innovations inevitably combine in themselves elements of first-order and of higher-order proposals. If, for example, they are new theories in a science, they may imply changes in the practice and self-conception of that science as well as in its assumptions about necessity, possibility, and contingency. If they are social reforms, they may leave a mark on people's understanding of their interests as well as on the institutional organization of society. In each instance, a first-order initiative will come adorned by a higher-order reform of ideas or arrangements.

What we should repudiate therefore is not the prophetic ambition of a higher-order discourse that demonstrates its power by the power of the proposals it informs. What we should reject is the high-flown emptiness of a meta-discourse that reveals its sterility by its failure to make any such proposals.

The deflationary reading of pragmatism is, by an apparent paradox, just such a sterile evasion. It denounces ambition in the name of modesty, and it rejects reach for the sake of effect. However, its champions are distinguished from their own philosophical heroes by their programmatic silence. Having conceived a higher-order discourse that has as its only message the uselessness of all meta-discourses and the exclusive value of first-order proposals, they then abandon the field, disarmed of any such proposals, to the dominant forces in society and in thought. Failing to recognize the openness of the boundary between first-order and higher-order projects, they remain deficient in the very types of ideas to which they assign the highest value.

The nostalgic-heroic reading of pragmatism seeks to defend the pragmatist tradition against the trivializing historicism (or "postmodernism") of the deflationary reading. Under the pretext of venerating the classic American pragmatists, it represents them as professors of philosophy concerned with familiar debates about realism, relativism, and objectivity. The result, however, is to produce a fossil that accentuates their time-bound flaws of vision rather than liberating for our use today the most disquieting, perplexing, and energizing elements in their doctrine.

On such a view, the central thesis of pragmatism was something about the last sustainable line of defense during the long retreat of Western thought from overweening confidence in our power to see the world with the eyes of God. There is indeed much in the writings of the classic American pragmatists that lends itself to such an interpretation. However, it is precisely the part most vitiated by the illusions of naturalism.

The mistake committed by this strand in pragmatism is the confusion of two impulses: one, to be rejected; the other, to be preserved. The impulse to be nurtured is the impulse to discard the dualisms that continue to haunt speculative thought: between subject and object, between freedom and necessity, between spirit and nature. Our experience of action and connection dissolves these dualisms.

It matters, however, what direction we take as we dissolve them: what we do with our lives and societies from day to day. The dualisms are indeed hallucinations. They arise from attempts to step outside the realm of action and to look at ourselves from the outside, contemplatively, rather than from the inside, actively. Almost everything that is most valuable in the philosophy of the last two hundred years has contributed, directly or indirectly, to the campaign against them.

The impulse to be rejected is the impulse to tell a story about the dissolution of these dualisms that is detached from any particular reconstructive intention or project. Such a story will look like a superscience. It will explain just how the dualisms are dissolved in nature and how experience—our experience—forms an inseparable part of the natural world. In so doing, it will repeat, in one form or another, the confusion exemplified by Dewey's doctrine of experience: the confusion between knowing that we are natural beings—as we are—and attempting to provide a full account of our human experience in naturalistic language—which we cannot. It is as if we could dispel the darkness surrounding our scientific knowledge by suddenly turning on the lights, only without having to do the work of natural science and without being limited by the specialized, tool-bound, and therefore also ephemeral character of all scientific conjecture.

The classic pragmatist philosophers, just like Hegel, Bergson, or any number of their other peers, mistakenly pushed the dissolution of the dualisms into a way of understanding and practicing philosophy as a naturalistic superscience. The nostalgic-heroic reading of pragmatism turns its campaign against the relativism and the historicism of the deflationary reading into a commemoration of that mistake.

By virtue of this mistake, we risk a double loss. One loss is loss of clarity about our situation. It does not follow from our envelopment within nature that we can map out this envelopment and describe our situation from the outside as if we were not who we in fact are. We can extend, through theorizing and toolmaking, the range of an apparatus for perception and reasoning that is built to the scale of an ephemeral, situated organism. However, we can do so only by localized but cumulative steps.

As our views leave the ground of the phenomena that are manifest to us, they turn into an allegory, remote from our intuitive understanding. We can justify them, at their periphery of inference and application, by the practical results—the experiments and the intentions—that we are able to produce by taking them for real.

On this loss of clarity about our situation there follows a loss of direction in our deeds. We cannot see the world with the eyes of God. We can nevertheless change our situation—not just the elements of our circumstance but the relation we have to it. To produce a form of thinking that can support and guide transformative action while dispensing with the illusions of a naturalistic superscience is one of the ambitions of a radicalized pragmatism. It is also the needed sequel to the dualisms against which philosophy has rebelled.

Pragmatist Insights and American Mistakes

Pragmatism, however, is not merely a doctrine expounded in books. It is the most characteristic philosophy of the country that has become the dominant power in the world. It is not enough to take it at its word as a series of conceptual proposals, diverted by the prejudices of naturalism from the reconstructive impulses animating it. It is also useful to understand it against the background of the national experience and the national project to which it has given a philosophical voice.

Viewed in this light—as it has been in the larger world outside professorial philosophy—pragmatism has provided less a group of theories of meaning, truth, and experience than a set of attitudes to the practical problems of life and society. In this context, the difficulty with pragmatism has not been the temptation to confuse sympathy for science with surrender to naturalism. It has been the temptation to allow the content of its method to be compromised by the flaws of the national culture for which pragmatism has spoken. The error has not been naturalism; it has been the view I earlier labeled democratic perfectionism—together with phenomenalism and naturalism, one of the major ways in which modern thought has been distracted and deflected in its effort to offer a full-fledged alternative to the perennial philosophy.

Every culture must draw the line between the alterable features of social life and the enduring character of human existence. When we understate the extent to which the whole order of society and culture represents a frozen politics—the containment and interruption of fighting—we become the slaves of our own unrecognized creations, to which we bow down as if they were natural and even sacred. To replace a political vocabulary by a theological one, we then commit a sin of idolatry, confining infinite spirit within the perimeter of its finite constructions.

If, on the other hand, we deny our own ignorance and finitude, and imagine ourselves able to escape them by acts of self-help or self-incantation, we risk losing not only our clarity but ourselves. We trade real reconstructive power for a pretense that begins to imprison us. The perennial philosophy—and, to a lesser extent, phenomenalism, naturalism, and democratic perfectionism as incomplete escapes from it—are themselves such forms of false transcendence and illusory liberation.

A major element in American culture understates the mutable nature of social life while exaggerating the extent to which the individual can escape the consequences of his mortality, his fragility, and his cluelessness about the ultimate setting of human life.

The source of the denial of the alterability of social life is a species of institutional fetishism: the belief that the genius of the founders and the favor of providence enabled the American Republic to hit, at the time of its foundation, on the definitive formula of a free society. The cult of the Constitution is merely the limiting case of this comprehensive idealization of an abstract conception of the market, of democracy, and of free civil society, unjustifiably identified with a particular, contingent set of institutional arrangements. This structure supposedly requires adjustment only at extraordinary moments of national crisis.

However, it is part of the project of human empowerment and

freedom to diminish the dependence of change on calamity. The greater this dependence, the smaller our chance of combining engagement in a particular world with critical distance from its assumptions. And the greater the chance that institutions and habits will hold our opportunities of practical cooperation and passionate attachment hostage to a scheme of social division and hierarchy. In both these ways, institutional fetishism will make us less free, less godlike, less human. We shall be able to engage only by allowing ourselves to be marginalized. We shall succeed in connecting with others only by becoming masters or underlings, and in affirming our freedom only by betraying our attachments.

Failure adequately to acknowledge the mutable character of social life coexists, in this vision, with a misunderstanding of our ability to deal with death and weakness. The individual imagines that he can lift himself up, all by himself, through repeated acts of self-reliance and self-construction. He accumulates things to depend less on people. He toys and tinkers with practices that he hopes will steel him against fate and quiet his terrors. Anxious to achieve a modest prosperity and independence, he dreams himself in his little realm—his business, his property, his family—a small-time king, self-crowned and self-anointed. In all these ways, he contrives to lift himself above both the dangers of life and the fear of death. The historical world of institutions and practices becomes a backdrop to the cycles of individual existence. It is a view that radically and dangerously underestimates the extent to which our efforts at self-construction are at the mercy of blind luck, of the social order, and of what others may give or deny us, by way of intangible grace as well as tangible help.

It is true that in American experience this idea of self-making exists alongside a great wealth of forms of association, of voluntary cooperative action, extending, by a series of concentric circles, around the perimeter of the individual and his concerns. However, voluntary association is likened to a bubbling over of the energy and the magnanimity of individuals who stand solidly on the ground of their own existence. It is a form of consciousness that comes and goes, becoming stronger or weaker. It takes for granted, as its setting, the structure of established social life, naturalized as an intrinsic part of a scheme of ordered liberty. It is a spirit, filling, or failing to fill, an institutional vessel that it need not and cannot reshape, and that is in turn powerless to preserve it.

Married once to naturalism as a philosophical doctrine, pragmatism has been remarried to this democratic perfectionism as the philosophical expression of a set of national attitudes. The price of the first marriage has been to blunt the force of the underlying themes of agency, transcendence, futurity, and experimentalism by combining them with ideas antagonistic to them. The price of the second marriage has been to corrupt the expression and the radicalization of those same themes at the hands of what is in fact a Western heresy. It is a heresy in the sense that it diverts and corrupts, through its error in drawing the line between the mutable and the immutable features of our existence, a way of thinking about humanity and history that for the last two hundred years has been taking the world by storm.

Wrapped in the language of the attractive liberal experimentalism that the pragmatist philosophy provides, this form of consciousness confines the promises of democracy and economic progress to a dogmatic institutional formula—a particular institutional version of representative democracy, of the market economy, and of a free civil society. And it equates the project of individual emancipation and self-fulfillment with a moral program that denies or misrepresents the relation between self-help and solidarity.

This heresy is now armed, and identified with the power of the United States. It is in the interest of humanity to resist it and to deny to its sponsors the prerogatives of Constantine.

If pragmatism is to push forward its own animating themes of agency, contingency, futurity, and experimentalism, it must purge itself of its partnership with this sectarian democratic perfectionism as well as of its association with naturalism. The result may not resemble the pragmatist philosophy that history has delivered to us. It nevertheless deserves the name of pragmatism if anything does because it speaks to what, from the beginning, mattered most, and had most promise, in that tradition of thought.

4

The Core Conception
Constraint, Incompleteness, Resistance, Reinvention

A Conception of Humanity

The future of philosophy lies in the development of an unsettling conception of humanity—of human action, thought, and potential. It is unsettling both because it contradicts many of our received ways of thinking and because it implies a radical criticism of society and culture as they are now established. In another sense, however, this conception is also orthodox: it results from the generalization and the deepening of some of the most characteristic tendencies of thought in the last two hundred years. If the pragmatist tradition has any special claim to speak for these tendencies, this authority lies in the vehemence with which it has attacked some of the intellectual obstacles to their advancement. What is at stake in a discussion of the radicalization of pragmatism is therefore the future of these impulses in thought and of their significance for society.

We cannot grasp the character of this view of humanity without appreciating the reversal of intellectual priorities on which it rests. The philosophy of the ancients assumed the superiority of the impersonal over the personal. Impersonal reality was assumed to be both the subject matter of our most reliable knowledge and the source of our strongest values. The divine itself was pictured on this model of impersonal but fundamental reality, and the anthropomorphic representation of God was dismissed as a concession to the vulgar.

At times the superior authority and reality of the impersonal found expression in views that affirmed the reality of the phenomenal world and at other times in ideas that represented the phenomena as diluted expressions of more hidden and more real models. Placing as they did ultimate reality and value far from the immediate concerns of the troubled and striving agent, such beliefs devalued transformation and self-transformation through struggle. They sought for the mind and the self the disengagement, the serenity, and the invulnerability that they associated with the divine.

The religious, moral, and aesthetic movements that have shaped our civilization and through it set the world on fire have wholly reversed this priority. They have affirmed the precedence—in fact, in knowledge, and in value—of the personal over the impersonal. It is our own world—the world we create through action—that we can understand more intimately and confidently; the rest of reality we master only by an overreaching that we cannot avoid and cannot trust. Having made our own world, we can remake it. We can, as Marx said, "make the circumstances dance by singing to them their own melody."

These same tendencies in our civilization have repudiated the ethic of invulnerability that forms the most constant and universal element in the moral reflection of high cultures throughout world history. In its place, they have put the idea, so persistently explored in some of the most characteristic literature of the modern West (such as the nineteenth-century novel) that the individual develops strong and independent personality, he raises himself up and makes himself more divine, through conflict with society and within himself. The road to self-possession and self-construction passes through a selective lowering of defenses, the creation of zones of heightened reciprocal vulnerability.

Not the least service that democracy renders to humanity is to create a climate more favorable to such exploration. It does so both by its assault on the extreme and entrenched forms of inequality and by its espousal of the idea of the capacity of ordinary men and women for transformation and self-transformation.

Within what understanding of the world, of the self, of society, and of thought, can we best develop this revolutionary impulse in our civilization, testing its credentials and working out its consequences? The pragmatism that is worth saving and radicalizing is just another name for the philosophy that takes this question as its own.

The most troublesome element in this philosophical enterprise is its very first move: the assertion of the primacy of the personal over the impersonal, the determination to begin from where we are, in our human world. Debates about pragmatism have emphasized traditional disputes about the objectivity of knowledge and the authority of natural science. They approach the problems raised by the pragmatist philosophy as if they were mere variations on familiar controversies over skepticism.

It is less in these variations, however, than in the implications of the claim of the priority of the personal over the impersonal that we can find both what is most puzzling and what is most promising about pragmatism, and to its meaning and grounds I soon return. If only we could take this claim to the hilt, the relation of pragmatism to skepticism would appear in another light. Skepticism can be managed by a set of time-tested countermoves. Once radicalized, pragmatism however, can be contained only by reversion to the pagan ascendancy of the impersonal over the personal, an ascendancy that the West—and the whole world in its wake—have long since struggled to overthrow.

Elements of a Conception

Three ideas about the self and about humanity in its relation to the institutional and discursive settings of human action are central to such a philosophical program. We misunderstand these ideas if we fail to see them in relation to one another. I state each of them both as conceptions of the individual self and as views of our humanity.

The first idea is that we have our being in the particular: particular bodies as well as particular societies and cultures, shaped by distinctive arrangements and beliefs. There is no natural and definitive form of our individual and social being, no extraneous space to which, by an act of intellectual and moral transcendence we could travel, the better to pass judgment on the particular. In a sense, there are only the particulars.

Our equipment for cognition and action is soaked in particularity; it is best suited to the temporal and spatial scale on which a mortal, embodied being must act. It is a natural fact about us that we see unaided only what is around us and feel most readily what threatens or delights us here and now. Most of our thoughts hang on our actions, preceding them as scouts or following them as historians and judges.

The second idea is that the habitual settings of action and thought, especially as organized by the institutions of society and the conventions of culture, are incapable of containing us. Although they shape us, they never shape us completely. Even when they do not invite us to defy and to change them, we can defy and change them nevertheless. There always remains in us a residue or a surfeit of untamed and unexhausted capability.

This transcendence of the self over its formative circumstances occurs in every department of human experience. At one pole of a spectrum of possible experience, it happens in our most general and abstract ideas—in mathematics, for example, where our powers of discovery and invention outreach our ability to bring our concepts under the control of a closed and complete set of axioms. At another pole of that spectrum, it takes place in our social and cultural life, when, for example, under the aegis of the rules of a particular regime of contract and property we devise forms of cooperation that suggest, foreshadow, or even require a different set of contract and property rules.

The uncontainable character of the individual mind and self is repeated in the experience of humanity as a whole. No possible list of social and cultural orders exhausts the collective powers of the species. The historical succession of such orders never culminates in a full and definitive reconciliation between spirit and circumstance.

This perpetual misfit between us and our situation is prefigured in the most basic facts of our natural constitution, beginning with the plasticity of the brain and with the relative openness and indirection of our most elementary drives. It is echoed throughout every level of our experience, including our most ambitious projects in thought, politics, and art. Its supreme expression in the realm of ideas is the notion of the infinite. That a flawed and finite being, living an ephemeral life in the midst of impenetrable ignorance about the meaning of this existence and the outer reaches of reality, should take the idea of the infinite into itself as something that would raise it up, that it should transact with this idea on tense but intimate terms, that it should experience its relation with other selves as capable of being transfigured by infinite longing, longing that nothing and no one can quench—all this testifies to just how much this stigma of our humanity brands us.

The fine texture of our experience recalls to us the same truth of our misfit and shows how this misfit may become a source of power. We must give much of our lives over to routine and repetition. We repeat because time and capacity are scarce. We embody in machines whatever we can repeat and bring under a formula. Repetition frees energy and time for what we do not yet know how to repeat. It enables us to move outward to the penumbra of the new. Our interest is to accelerate this oscillation, using the repetitious to serve the unrepeatable.

We do not quicken the tempo of this procedure merely for the sake of its particular material and moral benefits. We quicken it for its own sake, which is to say for the sake of the experience of mastery over the terms of our existence and of intimacy with the infinite that it makes possible. The philosophical instrument of this acceleration is a radicalized pragmatism.

The third idea is that we can do more than innovate in the content of our social and cultural contexts. We can innovate as well in the character of our relation to them; we can change the extent to which they imprison us. Not only can we do so, but we must do so if we are to realize our most powerful interests in material progress, in the liberation of individuals from entrenched social division and hierarchy, and in the creation of a world that is able to acknowledge and to support us as the world-transcending agents we know ourselves to be.

Our activities fall into two classes. Some activities are moves within a framework of organization and belief that we take for granted. At the limit, the framework remains unchallenged and even invisible. We naturalize or sanctify it, treating as natural fact or sacred imperative the collective product of our own hands. Other activities are moves about the framework. Such activities change the framework the only way it ordinarily can be changed: piece by piece and step by step.

Society and thought can be organized to lengthen the distance between the ordinary moves we take within the established limits and the exceptional moves by which we redefine these limits. When we lengthen this distance, transformation depends on trauma; ruin becomes the condition of change. Alternatively, society and thought can be arranged to shorten this distance. We shorten the distance by arranging our social and discursive practices so that the transformation of the structures becomes a constant extension of the way we go about our ordinary business. Transformation will become less dependent on calamity. It will be rendered banal and be sucked into our everyday experience.

We split the difference between being inside a particular framework that decides for us what we must do and being outside such a framework, forced to decide everything for ourselves. It is the next best thing to the divinity we are denied. Given that we cannot inhabit the context of all contexts, the natural and definitive space of reason and society, we can at least create a framework that helps propel us outward beyond itself.

The shortening of the distance between context-preserving and context-transforming activities is the price of practical progress, including economic growth and technological innovation. It creates a setting in which experimentalist cooperation can flourish. It enlarges our freedom to recombine people, machines, and practices in the light of emergent opportunity. It is a requirement for the liberation of the individual from a strongly rooted hierarchy and division: any scheme of rigid social ranks and roles depends, for its perpetuation, on the naturalization or the sanctification of the arrangements that reproduce it. And it gives a chance for a fundamental experience of freedom and empowerment: the experience of not having to choose between fidelity to our context-transcending selves and engagement with a particular world.

A radicalized pragmatism is the operational ideology of the shortening of the distance between context-preserving and context-transforming activities. It is thus a program of permanent revolution— however, a program so conceived that the word "revolution" is robbed of all romantic otherwordliness and reconciled to the everydayness of life as it is.

Our acts of going beyond the established institutional or discursive context of our habitual actions and thoughts leave us in a condition that can be described with equal justification as being at a loss and knowing more clearly just what to do. The naturalization of formative arrangements and beliefs lends to ordinary existence and thought a quality of narcoleptic compulsion. We forget the purposes of our activities and deliver ourselves to them as if they were self-directing. The rules of engagement and success become embodied in the framework. When we think the thoughts or do the deeds that the framework does not permit, demonstrating that there is always more in us than there can be in the organized setting of our action, we deprive those rules of some of their force.

Where, at this moment of the stretch or the transgression, can we find guidance? The answer is that we find it by a double move. We can no longer understand our interests and ideals as we had understood them when we were acting safely within the framework. We explore what they mean now that we have changed some of the institutional or conceptual presuppositions on the basis of which we had been acting. We try to make the purpose outlast its familiar setting. However, we cannot renew its life without reforming its content. At the same time, we should ask ourselves what would best strengthen our revisionary power in thought and society.

The ideas at the center of an unchained pragmatism amount to a way of thinking about our relation to all the habitual contexts of our action. When we judge the value of any initiative, we should take into account its effect on this relation. We should ask whether it develops or undermines our attributes of agency, transcendence, futurity, and experimentalism.

Let me give an example drawn from the institutional organization of democratic politics rather than from the methodological organization of natural science. It is an appropriate example to offer, given the priority of the personal and the social over the impersonal and the natural in the definition of a radicalized pragmatism.

Consider a series of connected proposals for the institutional reorganization of democratic politics. I return to these proposals in greater detail later, as part of a program of social reconstruction. Here I present them more briefly as instances of a revisionary practice that can change every aspect of our circumstance, piece by piece. They do not form an indivisible system. They nevertheless reinforce one another. They arise from similar concerns. They can be implemented piece by piece and step by step through a process of combined and uneven development.

First, we uphold the liberal objective of fragmenting power while repudiating the conservative objective of slowing down the political transformation of society. If we are faced with an American-style presidential regime, for instance, we provide for mechanisms enabling the two deadlocked political branches of government to break the deadlock by calling anticipated elections for both branches of government. Either branch would have the unilateral right to call the elections. To exercise this right, it would have to run the electoral risk. By this simple expedient, we transform the presidential regime into a device for the quickening of democratic politics.

Second, we introduce a series of reforms that have as their combined effect a heightening of the level of organized popular mobilization in politics: public financing of political campaigns, free access of the political parties and social movements to the means of mass communication, electoral regimes designed to strengthen the parties. We raise the temperature of politics without abandoning the commitment to institutional organization. We do so convinced that there is a relation between the structural fecundity of a form of political life and its energy level, yet also aware that energy without organization remains both ephemeral and dangerous.

Third, we extend the understanding and practice of federalism as a form of experimentation. For example, we encourage the development in particular territorial units or sectors of the economy and the society of countermodels to the main policy and institutional solutions adopted in national politics. Under certain conditions designed to prevent abuse and oppression, localities or groups can opt out of the general legal regime and produce another one. It is as if society, in advancing along a certain path, were to hedge its bets.

Fourth, we deepen the conception and strengthen the tools of basic human rights. To thrive in the midst of accelerated innovation, the individual must be and feel secure in a haven of protected vital interests and capabilities. He must enjoy a social inheritance of basic resources on which he can draw at turning points in his life. People sometimes find themselves caught in localized forms of disadvantage and exclusion from which they are unable to escape by the normal devices of self-reliant individual action. The state, acting through a distinct branch of government, specially organized and equipped for this purpose, must be able to intervene in the particular practice or organization, restoring its victims to a condition of effective agency.

Even the partial implementation of a project defined by its commitment to these four sets of reforms would alter our preexisting conceptions of political freedom and political equality in the process of drawing on them. Yet it would also achieve some of its authority and its direction from the service it would render to a conception of our humanity—the very conception defined by the three ideas I have just discussed. This conception is itself not constant. It has a life and a history but no permanent essence. It draws meaning and force from the ways in which we realize it in life and in thought.

The philosophy of the future is a philosophy of how we create futures, different futures. The reorganization of democratic politics is an example of the revision of a practice: an example of unparalleled interest because it deals with the terms of a practice that sets the terms on which we innovate in many other practices. We make ourselves more godlike without pretending to escape the defining circumstances of finitude and mortality.

Philosophical Attitudes Associated with These Ideas

These ideas about humanity imply three philosophical attitudes. Together with the ideas, the attitudes form the core of the program for thought explored in this book.

The first attitude is commitment to the marriage of theory and action. Our views of the self and society—the views standing at the center of a radicalized pragmatism—are never more than a deepening of the ideas of an ordinary agent in ordinary life. We loosen the bonds tying ideas to action to give them greater generality, but we do not untie these bonds. There is no fundamental difference between the quality of our self-reflection in the grip of activity and the character of our speculation as we take a step back. The philosopher is master of no secrets forbidden to the agent.

The continuity of reflection in context with theory against context does not exempt speculative activity from a unique pressure. It is the perennial temptation of specialized thinking to identify the routines of a society and the conventions of a culture with the way things rightly or necessarily are. Unexpected crisis brings us up short, revealing the particular and the contingent for what they are, depriving them of the specious patina of authority and necessity. We should not, however, need to wait to be shaken up to free ourselves of our superstitions. Instead of waiting, we can imagine. Imagination does the work of crisis without crisis.

The second attitude is the rejection of the spectral idea of possibility. We think that before something became actual it was possible. As a yet unrealized possibility, it was waiting around as a ghost for the cue that would allow it to walk on to the stage of actuality.

Together with this spectral view of possibility goes the notion that we can at least in principle be able to demarcate the outer horizon of the possible states of affairs or of the possible worlds. Whatever happens in fact in our world amounts to a subset of this larger reality.

From the vantage point of reflective action, however, the possible is not the antecedent of the actual but its consequence. Something new has emerged in the world, something we may have ourselves created. It may have arisen in violation of the rules of possibility and propriety codified in the preexisting regimes of society or of thought. We then rearrange our view of the constraints on the transformation of certain pieces of the world. This rearrangement is our image of the possible. Correctly understood, it is an afterglow that we now mistake for an antecedent light.

So it is that we cannot know looking from any point in historical or biographical experience what the outer limits of the forms of social organization and personal experience may be. If there are limits, they are likely to be movable ones. To make sense of the reality of constraint, we need to credit the power of sequence and grasp the limitations imposed by our natural constitution as well as by our historical situation. However, we need not resort to the idea of a fixed horizon of possibility.

Our most general ideas about self and society arise from the extension of our most vivid local experience, corrected by a studied recollection of past events and the imagination of a future direction. Such an imagination shows us how we can turn what we have into something else and what we can turn it into: memory into prophecy.

The spectral idea of possibility results from antipathy to the new. The new, according to that idea, is not completely new because it was already stalking the world as the possible. It is only when we divorce thought from action that a view so foreign to the experience of engagement and action begins to force itself upon us as if it provided an antidote to the unavoidable delusions of an embodied self.

The third philosophical attitude is denaturalization of the most important objects—the materials from which we make our human world of society and culture. The institutional and ideological structures forming this world are not there as natural objects with a single, invariant mode of being. They exist more or less. Their thingness—their presentation to us as natural facts or even as inescapable fate—is a consequence of their relative insulation against challenge and change.

Unlike natural facts, these human facts can exist more or less. The greater the distance between our context-preserving activities and our context-transforming ones, the stronger the sense of their existence. They exist more strongly because we act and think more weakly. The force that is sucked out of us is drawn into them. The shorter the distance between out context-preserving and our context-transforming activities, the less clearly do these structural facts exist. We are strengthened because they are weakened.

The naturalization of the social world is therefore a hallucination that constantly turns into an imprisonment. We cannot escape this prison simply by thinking differently. We have to reorganize society and culture to become more free. Nevertheless, thinking differently dispels some of the illusions that keep us enslaved.

The three philosophical attitudes I have invoked and defended have their home in the human world. We cannot carry them into our thinking about the nonhuman world around us. Our inability to do so is the source of the antinomies of the impersonal, considered in the next part of this book.

In the nonhuman world, we must divorce divorce theory from practice, with results that plunge our thinking into insoluble antinomies. Through experiment guided by theory we can relieve the consequences of this divorce. We thus produce in natural science a pale but powerful proxy for the intimate bond between reflection and action.

In this natural world we find ourselves in a realm in which we cannot either embrace or discard the spectral idea of possibility without poisoning our ideas with confusion and contradiction. We may try to make sense of the world as a reality that is ultimately timeless and therefore governed by history-less laws. We thereby force ourselves into the desperate effort to mark out the frontiers of the possible. Abashed by the paradoxes into which this effort drives us, we try to dispense with the idea of the possible as the shadowy forerunner of the actual, only to discover that in so doing we fatally weaken the conception of a lawlike universe. Turning our thoughts to nature, we find ourselves unable to dissolve things into the actions from which they arose and therefore unable to distinguish among degrees of being.

The structures of society and culture are fighting turned to stone; they are what comes into existence so long and insofar as we interrupt our practical and ideological struggles over the organization of life in society. When the fighting escalates again, the structures dissolve into the collective action and imagination from which they arose. When we fashion structures designed to invite their own reconstruction, we make them into both superior instruments of our power and more faithful reflections of our humanity.

We can find in nature parallels to this birth of structure out of structure-destroying and structure-creating action. As our power over nature increases, we can ourselves unleash these forces. However, when things in nature melt down, even by virtue of our intervention, it is not into us that they melt. They remain as strange and alien to us when formless as they were when formed.

5

Time and Experience
Antinomies of the Impersonal

The Source of the Antinomies

The only world we can know with confident immediacy is our own. In relation to it, we stand, collectively though not individually, in the position of God the Creator. Its frozen structures are simply the residues of what can once again become at any moment our unfrozen relations with one another. From this molten mass of intersubjectivity, of reciprocal testing across the barriers of distinct bodies and separated consciousness, arise the institutions of society and the dogmas of culture.

Our cognitive equipment is designed on the scale of this world and of its immediate natural setting. However, because it is marked by the preeminent attribute of plasticity, of relative functional indefinition, of permanent disquiet at the tension between limited context and insatiable longing, unstoppable striving, capability exhaustible only by death, we reach out beyond our immediate settings.

This reaching out—transcendence in a theological vocabulary—is implicit even in our most banal experiences of understanding and desire. We relate particulars to prototypes and try to capture as much of their particularity as we can by accumulating or combining these prototypes. With these prototypes—our concepts about kinds of things or events—we scoop out as much of the particularity of the particulars as we can. However, something of the particularity remains uncaptured; we cannot tell how much. That is why we call particulars ineffable. This receding horizon of the particulars as they are scanned by the understanding recalls the general structure of our situation. Our relation to our own organized contexts of action and thought is analogous to this relation of the particulars to the understanding. In us, as in the particulars that the understaning seeks to grasp, there is an inexhaustible residue. A similar situation arises in our relations with other people. We treat acceptance and recognition by the other person as a token of definitive assurance about our place in the world, an assurance that the other is never able to provide. We demand the unlimited from the limited.

As we move further away from this human theater and turn our minds to distant nature, our ideas fall into contradictions. These contradictions are the antinomies of experience. We cannot solve them. Neither, however, are we entirely powerless to deal with them. We can diminish the restraints under which they place our insight and our power, and reestablish in our dealings with nature a paler version of the more intimate and complete knowledge we can gain of our own world. This rescue operation makes natural science possible.

Natural science therefore provides us with a knowledge that is less perfect than the knowledge we can have of our own social and cultural constructs, or of one another, or of ourselves as reflected in the mirror of the other person. However, we can diminish its imperfection and increase its power by certain temporizing expedients. As a result, we blunt the force of the antinomies, although we cannot overcome them.

All the antinomies of the impersonal can be reduced to two: the antinomy of time and the antinomy of objectivity.

The Impersonal and the Personal

The understanding of the antinomies of time and objectivity rests on a certain view of the relation between our experience of ourselves and our insight into nature. The philosophical tendency I earlier labeled naturalism shares with the perennial philosophy the view that the impersonal has higher value—and allows for more secure knowledge—than the personal. In certain important respects the argument of this book, faithful to much of what is most distinctive and most disconcerting in the culture of the modern West, qualifies and even reverses this hierarchy of value and insight. Now is the time to define more clearly and precisely the content and basis for this qualification or reversal.

Nothing in this line of reasoning denies that we are part of nature. Nothing in it appeals to the existence of an evanescent spiritual substance exempt from nature and its laws. The issue is how best to approach the relation between nature within us, as we meet it within a world of human initiative and connection, and nature outside us, as we deal with it beyond the frontiers of our engagements with others and with ourselves. In exploring this relation, we do not contrast the human to the natural; we contrast the natural experience of humanity to the human experience of nature.

Two facts—natural facts—play a commanding part in shaping the natural experience of humanity. By virtue of the first of these two facts, our action-oriented knowledge has an advantage over knowledge dissociated from action. By virtue of the second natural fact, the part of action-oriented knowledge that addresses our own world—the human world—is capable of attaining a penetration that no other part of our knowledge can rival. Together, these two natural facts suggest reasons to reject the idea that the most reliable knowledge is the knowledge of the impersonal. In so doing, they also contribute to the background of beliefs supporting the preeminent value of the personal.

The first such natural fact has to do with the character of the mind as a problem-solving device, built on the scale of a dying organism. Our ideas shadow our actions, and our actions are ordinarily undertaken to seize opportunities and avoid dangers. On this human scale, thought comes incessantly up against the resistance imposed by nature surrounding us and embodied in us.

We do not encounter this world immediately, because we are not disembodied and universal spirit. We encounter it only within the glittering realm of our perceptions. And so philosophy debates whether the deliverances of perception are reliable tokens of the real nature of the world or only a hallucination, exercising authority by the weight of its own consistency.

However, we go on, relying on a principle of efficacy. We are like blind people carrying canes to feel the obstacles before us. Our successful conjectures are rewarded by not hitting and falling and by moving forward to our desired destination. Whether or not the message of the senses reveals reality, we find guidance and correction in the resistance that nature imposes to our wills—but only in the small theater in which we are able to act.

The mind would not be capable of solving problems in the fashion distinguishing it if it failed to possess the attributes that make its problem-solving activity so different from that of a machine or a zombie. To solve problems in the way it does, the mind must be able to represent a situation as a whole; it must be totalizing. This totalizing impulse is what makes consciousness what it is. And because every such totalizing representation is incomplete and contestable—good for some things and not for others—mind as consciousness must forever contend with a clash of representations: with ambiguity, doubt, and darkness.

To solve problems in the way it does, the mind must also be able to make moves it never made before, according to rules it can formulate, if at all, only after making them. It must, in other words, be capable of not repeating itself. This impulse of surprise, invention, and transcendence, when combined with the totalizing impulse, turns consciousness into what we call imagination. It counts for much in the power of the mind to address the problems of action-oriented experience.

The second natural fact has to do with one species of our action-oriented knowledge: knowledge of our own world, of society and culture. Of this world, we can hope for a knowledge that is unlike any other because it is the knowledge that the creator has of his creation. This knowledge conforms to a principle of construction: we can come to know, with a transparency unrivalled in any other part of our experience, what we have made. Here and only here can we hope to dispense with the rod of the sightless and to see with eyes wide open.

The godlike perspective that both the perennial philosophy and modern naturalism attribute, in their different ways, to our disinterested knowledge of the natural order applies, with far greater propriety, to our human knowledge of the human world. However, it does not do so automatically or evenly; its increasing applicability is the outcome of a successful transformation of social and cultural life in a particular direction.

The arrangements of society and culture are fighting petrified; they survive on the interruption or containment of practical and visionary strife. The more society and culture are organized to increase the distance between our context-preserving and our context-transforming activities, the more these arrangements take on the appearance of natural facts. They appear to us as givens, as our collective fate. Indeed, that is what, in a sense, they then become.

It is only by a long struggle, occupying much of the entire history of mankind, that we reform society and culture to diminish the distance between the ordinary moves we make within an institutional and ideological setting we take for granted and the extraordinary moves by which we reshape that setting, piece by piece and step by step. A sign of our success is that change becomes less dependent on calamity and better able to come from within, as an extension of our ordinary activities.

To some extent, the imagination can anticipate movement in this direction and do the work of crisis without crisis. To that extent, it can denaturalize the false necessities of society and culture, presenting them as the constructions that they are. In this effort, however, it dare not expect to be entirely successful. The transmutation of our institutional and ideological assumptions into false facts of nature is not merely a piece of false consciousness, capable of being dispelled by an act of enlightenment. It is an actual fact, produced by institutions and practices that remain entrenched against challenge and change, except when forced by external trauma or by ordinary conflict, aggravated until it gets out of hand. The naturalized arrangements of society and culture are always partly opaque—not only because they wear the mendacious semblance of nature, and represent the accidental course of conflict as rational or necessary, but also because they exhibit and facilitate the empire of the dead over the living.

In reforming society and culture to place them more wholly within the reach of the transforming will, we also place them more completely

within the grasp of the transformative imagination. Insofar as we succeed—and we only ever succeed haltingly and relatively—the principle
of construction—the knowledge the maker can have of his artifact—
applies with stronger force. We become greater and freer, and enjoy
deeper insight into a world of our own making.

The counterpart to the principle of construction in our moral consciousness is the impulse of iconoclasm: refusing unconditional reality
and value to the contingent and flawed worlds we build and affirming
that there is always more in us, individually and collectively, than there
can ever be in them. The most complete expression of this iconoclastic
commitment is the development of forms of life and consciousness that
provide us with the means and occasions to resist and reform them. In
this way, they save us from having to choose between engaging wholeheartedly in them and keeping the last word, of resistance and transcendence, to ourselves.

The creation of such societies and cultures is an achievement rec-
ommending itself by its power to promote our most fundamental interests: not only our interest in mastery over context, of which it is the
most direct manifestation, but also our interest in the experimental
recombination of people and resources for the sake of economic growth
and our interest in the permanent subversion of all entrenched schemes
of social division and hierarchy for the benefit of our ability to give
ourselves to one another as the radical originals we all believe ourselves
ultimately to be rather than as placeholders in any such scheme.

The penetration that results less fully from the principle of problem-
solving and more fully from the principle of construction has a cost.
The cost is that the knowledge promised by problem-solving and construction is, for better and worse, interested. Just as the penetration
increases as we move from the first principle to the second—from the
blind man's use of his stick to the insight a human creator can have
into his social and cultural creation—so too the significance of the
interestedness increases with this same move: the pragmatic residue in
our thought grows. What we know comes to be contaminated by what
we will.

Our problem-solving conjectures, on the scale in which thought is able to accompany action, have only the pragmatic residue of the blind man's rod: we judge them by their use in enabling us to walk ahead without being knocked down. The resistances we encounter can support alternative conjectures, and the superiority of some such conjectures over others may change as we redirect our efforts.

Our conceptions of humanity and society contain a pragmatic residue in a much more radical sense. Not only do we use them as weapons in a contest of interests entangled in visions, but we are also unable to expunge from them the quality of self-fulfilling prophecies. To take them as guides is to give them some degree of transformative power. This power will not be unlimited—the unacknowledged constraints within and around us will not dissolve under the pressure of wishful thinking—but it will be real. It results from many sources: that the idea of society—even the idea of a free society, based on cooperation among individuals assured of equal opportunity and respect—has no unique and uncontroversial translation into a particular organization of human life; that our understanding of interests and ideals is relative to the practices and institutions in which we imagine them capable of being realized, so that there is an internal relation between our thinking about those ideals and interests and our thinking about these institutions and practices; that consciousness is always individual and embodied in an individual organism, whereas society and culture are collective constructions, not immediately under the control of the individual will and imagination; and, above all, that none of our forms of life in society and culture exhaust our resources of insight and experience, which always transcend them.

For all these reasons, our thinking about the world we make remains forever plunged in the shadows of ambiguity, projection, deception and self-deception, will masquerading as insight, idea hoping to become reality. However, all of these taints are less the exception to the special penetration we enjoy in the realm to which the principle of construction applies than they are the price we must pay for the exercise of this power.

Suppose we leave the realm of our knowledge of our made world, in which the principle of construction, with its promise of insight from within, holds good insofar as we succeed in creating societies and cultures that give us the means with which to challenge and change them. Suppose that having left this refuge of the imagination turned in on its own collective creations, we then continue traveling away from the setting of our inner experience until we cross the frontiers of our knowledge of that part of the natural world in which our thoughts continue to shadow our actions. At last, we turn outward to the microscopic or macroscopic realities lying beyond our immediate reach. Here is the place of science.

We must now reproduce the conditions that allow us to form reliable conjectures in the world that we can reach. We do so by extending the blind man's cane through the tools or instruments of the scientist. We do so as well by staging experiments that simulate the blind man's experience of hitting with his stick against barriers or of finding his way open by forming hypotheses according to his experience of resistance or advance.

Before it can become a tenet of natural philosophy or a working assumption of natural science, our idea that all reality is governed by a web of causal connections represents an act of faith. It is an act of faith in our ability to make sense of the whole of reality in a fashion that remains in communion with those elementary experiences of finding our way, with the stick of the senses, in our proximate world. As the blind man is rewarded by reaching his destination if he draws the best inference from his use of the stick, the scientist is rewarded by predicating experimental results if he knows how to make the most of what his tools allow him to hypothesize.

The further away we move from the activity of the will and the imagination directed to the human world we build, and then away even from the parts of nature we can touch directly, relying on tools to extend the range of our senses and on experiments to broaden the scope of our collisions with nature, the greater the likelihood that such knowledge as we are able to achieve will be contaminated by an ineradicable metaphorical overlay. The most fundamental of these metaphors will be the idea of universal causation itself, followed by other familiar and general ideas like force, matter, and energy. And just as the pragmatic residue compromising the convergence or objectivity of thought is greatest precisely where can we hope to gain the most incisive knowledge—insight into the social and cultural worlds we collectively build—so the metaphorical overlay is heaviest when our thinking about nature is most universal and ambitious because most detached from ourselves.

This contamination of knowledge by metaphor will, however, be compensated by a disinterestedness that is the reverse side of the interestedness underlying the existence of the pragmatic residue in our ideas about ourselves. Evidence and experiment may still support alternative representations, conjectures, and theories. However, our choice among them will be less distracted by our stake in making the world—our world—one way rather than another. We may well have such a stake because of our methodological, metaphysical, or theological preconceptions, but it will be weaker and less evident. The criteria of success will be simplified. Convergence of a kind we cannot expect in our beliefs about society and humanity will be feasible. (Only when, in rebellion against the fragmentary character of scientific knowledge, we insist on searching for an explanation of everything, and on discovering what such an explanation means for our place in the world, will the problem of the pragmatic residue emerge with a vengeance within science itself. As they become more comprehensive and less bound by evidence and experiment, our ideas about nature cease to be separable from our projects for ourselves.)

We may be tempted to misinterpret our limited and distinctive success in scientific prediction and technological control as a sign that we see the world as it really is. We may try to forget that we see it imprisoned in the view from the dying organism and claim to see it with the eyes of God. We may then begin to treat our knowledge of the human world as a dimmer, more controversial form of our more reliable, convergent, and progressive knowledge of nature and the universe.

The perennial philosophy made this mistake in one form. Modern naturalism makes it in another. It amounts to a delirious misunderstanding of our situation. Our disinterestedness is the other side of our remoteness; we see a distant reality through a glass darkly, embodied as dying organisms, using and abusing the totalizing and transcending powers of consciousness, extending our senses through tools and our experiences through experiments. We can hope to describe and explain that reality only by resorting to ideas that require many layers of translation into a language we can use to describe what we find in the world close by: the world in which thought remains wedded to action.

Against this hallucination we must save ourselves by a humility that serves as the counterpart in our ideas about nature and the universe to the iconoclasm that should inspire our beliefs about society and culture.

The Antinomy of Time

The antinomy of time reveals the conflict between the reality of time—the historical character of the universe—and the causal picture of the world. Suppose that time is an illusion, an epiphenomenal feature of human subjectivity rather than an objective attribute of nature. Then we cannot make causal judgments or provide causal explanations of events without deluding ourselves. For all relations will be simultaneous. The true structure of the world will be a grid of simultaneous reciprocal constraints. If we call this grid causality, we shall be playing with words. The world truly seen will be an eternal manifold that only a divine mind, free from the toils of mortality and finitude, could register. For it is not only causality that would be left groundless; life itself as we experience it—our terrified, dazzled passage from birth to death—would be a hallucination.

Suppose, on the contrary, that time is for real, going all the way down to the ultimate organization of nature. Then we can make causal judgments in only a very limited and revised sense. The universe will have no permanent laws to inform such judgments. The law-like regularities on which we base our causal accounts will be but approximate and provisional accounts of certain states of universe. These states will be limited in time, even if a very long time. There was a time when these laws did not apply, even approximately, and there will be another time when they no longer hold.

If we claim that higher-order laws govern the succession of states of the world and of their transient laws, we invoke the existence of another reality up above the present universe. We imagine that this higher reality is not itself engulfed in time.

When we accept the notion that time goes all the way down, that there is nothing it does not invade and ravage, we do not foreclose the right to provide causal explanations in a drastically revised sense. We generalize analogically from particular states of the universe, located in time. We say that so long as certain defining features of these states remain stable, certain law-like regularities apply. However, we realize that even as we invoke such regularities to establish a basis for our causal explanations, they may be in the process of being undone.

A social and an economic order, once stabilized through the interruption of conflict over its institutional and ideological foundations, exhibits regular relations. If we allow this order to be naturalized and if we lose sight of our power to challenge and change it, we may be tempted to mistake its routines for the universal and eternal laws of social and economic organization. When we repudiate such a mystification, we can think of the transformation or the succession of the orders only by inference from the record of past experience and by the prophetic intimation of unrealized transformative opportunity. Such also is the character our thinking about nature must assume—although with less intimacy and confidence than our thinking about humanity—if time does indeed go all the way down.

Our conventional view of causation therefore makes no sense. For either causality is, like time itself, an illusion or, because of the reality of time, it lacks a ground beyond time. To think causally must then be at best to think by a series of concentric circles, of widening ripples, around our immediate experience. The middle ground on which time exists but not too much—in which it is more than illusion but less than a master—is only a wish. It is a wish to escape the tyranny of time over thought, given that we cannot escape its tyranny over life.

In the human world, we can and do resolve the antinomy of time by seizing on its second side. The history of social theory demonstrates that even in our thinking about society and the self we do not come easily to this acceptance of the historical character of our being. We come to it nevertheless.

We cannot solve the antinomy of time as it infects our understanding of nature. However, we can attenuate its force by developing in a natural science a diluted counterpart to our historical understanding of humanity. It is an accident of the historical development of modern science rather than a revelation of any deep and persistent feature of science that Galileian quantification and Newtonian mechanics preceded Darwinian natural history. Then cosmology began to accustom us to the idea that the universe itself has a history. Failure fully to accept this idea of the natural history of the universe allows us to cling to the prejudice that an unhistorical physics can lay the foundations of scientific knowledge.

If the universe had a beginning, at what point did the laws that we now associate with its operation come into force? To save timelessness from time by resorting to the conception of higher-order laws is to compound prejudice with special pleading. For how can we infer the supposed laws of all possible worlds except by extension from the world that in fact exists?

To carry the idea of natural history to the hilt, expanding its scope from the history of life to the history of the universe, is to weaken the barriers between our thinking about nature and our thinking about ourselves. It is to draw the former closer to the latter, and to see it for the more compromised and shadowy form of knowledge that it is.

The Antinomy of Objectivity

The second antinomy to which our experience of the impersonal falls victim is the antinomy of objectivity. The force of this antinomy is to undermine our confidence in the reliability of our perception of the world as a representation of reality. It is to the definition and the possible resolution of this antinomy that much of Western philosophy since Hume and Kant has been devoted. I restate it here for the purpose of exploring further the implications of the view that our knowledge of nature becomes more reliable only insofar as it comes to share some of the attributes of our knowledge of humanity.

If we think through the implications of our causal ideas about the world, we find ourselves driven to the conclusion that the world as we see it and experience it is only the world conveyed to us by our neurological and perceptual apparatus. It is an internal phantasm delivered to us by the brain and by the senses. We have no way of grasping the relation of this phantasm to the world on its own—the world as God would see and know it. Not only do we see from a point outward into reaches of increasing darkness but we also find ourselves imprisoned in frail and mortal bodies and supplied with perceptual equipment built to the scale of the setting of our action. We can extend the reach of this equipment by machinery (the tools of scientific investigation), but we cannot jump out of ourselves.

Yet in acting and living, we do embrace this phantasm as a manifestation of the reality of the world. We credit the resistance we encounter to our actions as a continual reality check. The anxieties aroused in our minds by the suspicion of the phantasm then seem to us to be themselves phantasms, brought upon us by a misguided effort to reach beyond ourselves and to equate access to objective reality with freedom from the condition of embodied being. We can neither give up this overreaching nor abide its implications.

Fear of the phantasm is forced on us by our causal thinking about the way in which reality gets translated into the experience of a limited, embodied being—each of us. We describe the shadow cast by reality on the subjectivity of an organism. We can compare only shadows to shadows. So the same causal thinking may itself be part of the phantasm we are unable to trust as a revelation of reality.

In acting and living, we must rely on the message of the senses, managed and corrected by our interpreted experiments. Yet the suspicion of the phantasm is an event that takes place within this acting and living. It is a consequence of consciousness, not a metaphysical delirium. For our consciousness includes the recognition of our own embodied state, a realization that we are not God. The idea of objectivity or reality—the objectivity available to a finite and embodied being, not the objectivity available to God—remains divided against itself.

In the human world, we resolve the antinomy of objectivity in favor of action and life. The world outside us is not the world viewed from the vantage point of the stars but the world seen from the perspective of other people. This external but nonetheless human reality takes two forms: intersubjectivity—the dealings among minds—and institutional or ideological structure—the shared arrangements and assumptions on the basis of which such dealings take place. One is the liquid, and the other is the solid form of social life.

These twin forms of the human world may be estranged from us, or we from them. Nevertheless, each comes from us and returns to us: from and to the collective us, if not the individual us. In confronting them, we do not confront a purely external reality to which the antinomy of objectivity might apply.

We live reflected in one another's consciousness and recognition, discovering and developing ourselves through encounter with others. Our self-consciousness remains empty until it is filled up by the memory of such encounters. Intersubjectivity is internal to subjectivity.

The institutional and ideological structures of society are simply the temporarily petrified remains of our adventures in association and the monuments of our temporarily interrupted struggles. They then become as well the templates within which our routine practical and discursive activities develop. We can know them more intimately and confidently than we can ever know things and events in nature; they are the ejected residues of our collective selves.

These structures may wear the specious semblance of naturalness. However, we can denaturalize them. We can do so in one way by intensifying and broadening the conflicts on the interruption of which they are built. We can do so in another way by reorganizing them to ease their own revision, thus enhancing our power over them and through them, and bringing them closer to us.

Our relations to these organized institutional and ideological settings of normal life and thought ordinarily pass through three stages. In the first stage there is an explosion of conflict and invention. Such are the foundational moments in history, the times of re-imagination and reconstruction. They set for us a direction, an agenda, a view of a future worth having and of the best way to reach it.

These are not moments of revolution in the dreamy nineteenth-century sense—the violent, sudden, and wholesale substitution of an entire organized form of thinking and living by another one. They are episodes of revolutionary reform. Part of the established framework of arrangements and ideas gets changed. The change, however, is enough to require a realignment of all the unchanged parts.

In the second stage the foundational conflicts subside, and the resulting institutional and ideological structures cool down. In this period of diminishing light and heat, the task of general ideas is not only to work out systematically the implications of the foundational agenda but to prolong its life and its force in the absence of the engagements and the contests from which that agenda arose. So it is, for example, that a theory of justice couched in seemingly abstract and unhistorical terms may in fact lend a patina of justification to the homely realities of the revolutionary reforms that ushered in the social-democratic settlement of the mid-twentieth century, with its commitment to compensatory redistribution through tax-and-transfer and its abandonment of more radical attempts to reorganize both politics and production. Such theories attempt to make the light last without the heat.

In the third stage the foundational moment recedes too far away from present experience to address it with clarity and authority. It can no longer speak effectively even through the vehicle of doctrines that would bring the dead to life. So people bicker, without guidance, or they wait around for another collective crisis that can rescue them from littleness and confusion.

No set of social and cultural innovations is more important than the one that allows us to hasten the succession of these stages, compacting them into another. Mastery over context makes us more godlike and creates a setting favorable to the advancement of both our material interest in practical novelty and our moral interest in individual emancipation.

This account of the genealogy of structures suggests by comparison the sense and the extent to which we can contain the burden placed by the antinomy of objectivity on our knowledge of the natural world. As the doctrines of the ideologists revive, in the cooling down stage, the radiance of a darkening agenda of social and cultural life, so do the experimental practices, tools, and ideas of natural science allow us to carry into our knowledge of nature traces of the immediacy and the intimacy of our knowledge of humanity.

For the distinguishing trait of experimental science is to combine tools and ideas in ways that allow us to broaden the theater of understanding and of action in which we face the world. An experiment is an intervention into the transmutations of nature to discover how things work by discovering what they turn into under various conditions of pressure. But it is we who intervene. An experimental idea is the speculative extension of such practical intervention. By marrying experiment to speculation, we put ourselves in a dimmer version of the circumstance of the Creator. We remake nature or we imagine it remade. By this expedient we free ourselves, if only partly and tentatively, from suspicion of our beliefs, and we live once again, unafraid, in the light of the actual.

6

The Reality of Time

The Transformation of Transformation

Time Is Real

There is no truth more important to acknowledge if we are to understand ourselves and our place in the world.

The reality of time is not a meaningless platitude; it is a revolutionary proposition, incompatible with much of traditional science and philosophy. In particular, it is anathema to the perennial philosophy, which takes as a core tenet the unreality of time. For divine and ultimate being, and for the mind insofar as the mind participates in such being, all events in the world are, according to that philosophy, simultaneous. There is only an eternal now.

However, it is not the perennial philosophy alone that resists recognizing the reality of time. The logical or mathematical relations among propositions, even when they refer to events that seem to take place in time, seem themselves timeless. Thus, after ridding ourselves of the influence of the perennial philosophy, we may continue to find a conspiracy against recognition of the reality of time established in the inner citadel of our mental life.

The implications of this division of our experience are not limited to our logical and mathematical reasoning; they extend as well to our practices of causal explanation. From this fact arises what I earlier called the antinomy of time. If time goes all the way down, there are no timeless laws of nature. Each law has a history; each changes. Then, however, our causal judgments are rendered unstable and insecure because there are no permanent laws underwriting them.

In some sense yet to be explained, the laws and the phenomena may change together. Yet they do not change miraculously; they change for cause. On the other hand, if the reality of time is superficial, if it fails to go all the way down, then causal explanation must be limited in its reach to the same degree and in the same sense. Where time fails, causality fails, and simultaneity takes over.

If time were unreal, however, nothing in our situation would be what it seems to be. For every facet of our lives is soaked in time. Agency, contingency, futurity, and experimentalism would make no sense as major aspects of our experience. Our lives would be tunnels of illusion from which we could escape, as the perennial philosophy recommends, only by identifying with a timeless, hidden reality.

If, however, resistance to full recognition of the reality of time has a foothold in the nature of our thinking, at least of our logical and mathematical reasoning, rather than just in a philosophical tradition that we are at liberty to repudiate, we find our experience divided against itself. How are we to understand this division and to master it? To affirm the reality of time and grasp what this affirmation implies is to find another starting point for the development of an alternative to the perennial philosophy. Such an alternative would make good on the picture of a real self, struggling about the future in a real world, a world of time, that it does not control and barely understands. I develop, in the form of five theses, a view of the reality of time and of the consequences of this reality for us.

The Thesis That Time Is the Transformation of Transformation

Time is the contrast between what changes and what does not change. More precisely, it is the contrast between what changes in a particular way and what either does not change or changes in some other way. Time is a real feature of the world because this contrast between what changes and what does not change is an important part of the way the world is.

Time is therefore the product of a relation. Time is the relativity of change: of some change relative to other change, or to absence of change. According to another thesis of this chapter, everything changes sooner or later, but not at the same time or in the same direction or in the same way. On a definition equivalent to the one that defines time as the contrast between what changes and what does not change, time is therefore the unevenness or heterogeneity of change—of its rates as well as of its scope and direction. In speaking of a contrast of relative rates of change, however, this alternative definition falls into circularity; it depends on a conception of time to define the nature of time.

If time is the contrast between what changes and what does not change, how can we measure it by clocks? Clocks are just devices by which we mark intervals in a process of change, relative to some absence of change or to some change of a different sort.

If time is the contrast between what changes and what does not change, it is also the transformation of transformation. If change were uniform—in pace, in scope, in direction, and in foreseeable outcome— it would not be change. We could not time one series of changes in relation to another. Time would not exist, or it would exist in a vastly diminished sense.

Suppose the progress of events in the world were governed by a single, unchanging set of laws. Suppose that variety in the pace, scope, direction, and outcome of change were itself always law-governed. Suppose further that the laws of nature minutely determined everything that happened, or would ever happen, until the end of time. There would be no underdetermination of the events and of the phenomena by the laws: the laws would thoroughly shape all particulars. Chance and catastrophe—including the production of vast reversals out of relatively small disturbances—would be ruled out.

In a universe of this kind, time would be much less real than it is in a universe in which the laws of nature have a history, changing change. Under such a Laplacean regime we could in principle foretell the end of all things in the beginning of all things, not just as beings who can become more godlike but as beings who can attain God's insight. For such a mind in such a world, the difference between the causal sequence of events and the mathematical or logical relations among concepts would shrink: the relation of consequences to their causes in our understanding of nature would closely resemble the relation of conclusions to their premises in logical and mathematical thinking. Under certain interpretations of these circumstances, time might still be said to exist, but only barely. However, that world is not the real world, and that mind is not our mind.

Does the reality of time presuppose the reality of space or of any particular ontology? It presupposes only three propositions about what exists: that there not be nothing—the postulate of reality; that there not be only one thing—the postulate of plurality; and that the things constituting the manifold of reality be in some relation to one another—the postulate of connection. The postulates of plurality and of connection require further elucidation.

It may seem at first that if there were only one thing, that one thing might change without prejudice to its oneness. There would then be time. However, the change could not occur without occurring in particular parts of the one and without changing the relation among all its parts. Thus, plurality would emerge within the one; the one would no longer be, if it had ever been, just one.

Of the three postulates of the reality of time, the most suspect is the postulate of connection. Yet there can be no transformation of transformation if things are not somehow connected. The crucial term here is not "connected;" it is "somehow." If time goes all the way down, the nature of the connections that there are may themselves change; indeed, if experience and science serve, they will change. We cannot prospectively demarcate the outer horizon of these changes. What seems to be disconnection in natural reality, as in social and mental experience, may simply be prelude to connection in new form. There never has been a human vision of the world that dispensed with the postulate of connection, nor—given the totalizing quality of consciousness, its impulse to represent worlds—does it seem there could ever be one. Even under a simplified and radicalized interpretation of Leibniz's monadology, for example, the monads connect, if not by direct action and reaction, then by their joint and organized participation in the divine intelligence.

If space is the organization of plurality, which is the meaning of the postulate of connection, then time presupposes space but continuously remakes it. The physics of the twentieth century represented the spatialization of time. It might have come closer to the truth about the world if it had explored the temporalization of space. It would therefore be misleading to describe space and time as being fundamental in the same sense or to the same degree.

The idea that time is fundamental—that it goes all the way down—would be misleading if we understood it to mean that time is a demiurge creating something out of nothing. However, time is not a demiurge; in fact, it is not a thing or even a being. The manifold defined by the postulates of reality, plurality, and connection is at once the condition of space and the condition of time. It is time-space.

Once we guard against the misunderstanding of time as a thing more powerful or more basic than space, we can define more precisely the meaning of the idea that time goes all the way down. It is simply this: that there is nothing that does not change, including the organization of connection, which is space, and including change itself and whatever laws may govern it. This idea may at first seem unexceptionable. To take it seriously, however, turns out to require rebellion against some of our most entrenched assumptions about science and ourselves.

Change might abolish itself. The world would then stop for a while—time suspended—but only until it changed again into a changing world. In such a world there would be no life and therefore no mind. Its changelessness, in addition to being temporary, would be unknown.

The three postulates—of reality, plurality, and connection—may at first seem to constitute a proto-ontology, as if they amounted to a minimalist version of a teaching like Aristotle's metaphysics of being. In fact, however, they are the prelude to an ontology only when misread against the background of the history of classical Western metaphysics. All they say is: something happens.

The thesis of the reality of time requires rejection of the whole project of ontology. The legitimate successor to ontology is a history of nature, historicizing the laws of nature as well as the kinds of things and of relations that arise in the course of this history. The effort to develop a theory of the types of being that there are in general, not just at a particular moment, betrays resistance to recognition of the reality of time.

To reject the project of such a timeless ontology is to deny that there is something—basic types or natural kinds of being—that escapes time. No, nothing escapes time, as the next thesis holds; nothing is changeless and therefore timeless. That is the sense in which time goes all the way down.

However, to affirm that time goes all the way down is not to disregard the brute facticity of the world. Time itself could not have produced any of the three facts—of reality, plurality, and connection—that are presupposed by the thesis that time is the transformation of transformation. A world ruled by time, understood in the sense of this thesis, is a world of reality, plurality, and connection, full of particulars that have a particular history because they are one way rather than another and that are the way they are because of the history from which they have resulted. It is therefore also a world to which the spectral idea of possibility fails to do justice.

In this world it is true that we understand phenomena or states of affairs only by imagining the conditions under which they can become something other than what they are now. However, it is also true that an immense distance separates the real, adjacent possible—what a part of the world, or the world as a whole, can become next—from two fictions, closely related to each other, that debase or discount the reality of the world.

One of these fictions is the spectral idea of possibility, with its view of possible worlds and of possible states of affairs. According to this view, such worlds and states of affairs enjoy every attribute of real being except actual existence. The other fiction is the ontology of possible worlds, with its claim that the real world—the universe or the universes that exist, or have existed, or will exist—is just like those phantasmagorical entities—the ghostly, nonactualized possibles—except that it happens to wear for a while the garment of actuality.

These reflections show that affirmation of the reality of time makes common cause with affirmation of the reality of the world. The reality of time and the reality of the world—and of its attributes of plurality and connection—are two sides of the same truth.

In thinking about time, we inevitably confuse time as an experience of progression toward death in our finite lives with time as an objective feature of reality. The view of time as the transformation of transformation may seem misguided because it may appear unconnected with what time means for us. However, we can make sense of our time-soaked experience, and vindicate the view of the self and of its place in the world outlined in the preceding pages, only if we treat inquiry into time as inquiry about the world as well as about us. If humanity did not exist, time would exist nevertheless.

The salutary insistence on understanding time as a feature of reality rather than merely as an attribute of our experience sets the stage for complication and confusion. We must grasp the connection between time as part of external reality and time as part of internal experience.

The Thesis That Time Holds Sway over Everything

Everything changes sooner or later. This proposition means that the laws of nature also change.

A few remarks about the history of modern science help explain the content and reach of this thesis. Twentieth-century physics overthrew the distinction between the phenomena of the natural world and a changeless background of space and time against which these phenomena occur. The background became part of the phenomena.

In undermining this distinction, however, the physics of the last century nevertheless upheld the contrast between an invariant background of natural laws and a changing physical world. For the thesis that everything changes sooner or later to hold, what thought did to the background of space and time it must now do to the background of timeless laws. It must be the case that the laws themselves change and that they somehow change together with the phenomena they govern.

This idea is puzzling, but it is not nonsensical. That it is not nonsensical is shown by our having already learned to think this way about history (in social theory) and even about life (in biology). Consider one of the basic moves made by the classic social theories of the nineteenth century: the attempt to reinterpret as laws of a particular type of social and economic organization what were falsely viewed as universal laws of society and economy. Thus, Marx attacked the English political economists for having represented as universal and timeless laws of the economy that are in fact laws of capitalism.

Now, it is true that in Marx's social theory there are higher-order laws supposedly governing the succession of economic and social systems and therefore as well the succession of the special laws applying to each of these systems. However, that idea of higher-order laws is the first part of Marx's social theory to have been abandoned by his latter-day successors. The chastened Marxist who has relinquished belief in the higher-order laws but clings to the idea that different social and economic orders have their distinctive laws of operation and transformation is precisely in the intellectual circumstance that we may be tempted to regard as senseless, when in fact it is merely baffling.

The history of modern biological thinking has accustomed us as well to the view that the phenomena and the laws governing them have developed at the same time. The phenomena of life and the laws governing life are coeval. Before there was life there was nothing to which the laws could apply.

The point is worth generalizing. The history of modern science developed in such a way as to inspire a powerful prejudice. Newtonian mechanics and Galileian quantification came first and provided the model for the most ambitious and rigorous thought. Biology and natural history came to be seen as weak physics, and social science as weak biology. This contingent history of ideas helps account for the ease with which we embrace as preeminent and even universal a view of the reign of timeless laws that has in fact been merely a tenet of one style of scientific thinking.

Let us not replace one dogma by another: the view of biology as weak physics and of history as weak biology by the opposing view of physics as crude biology and of biology as crude history. Our attitude toward the relation between phenomena and their laws of reproduction or transformation, and of both to time, should remain, insofar as possible, uninfluenced by the accidental history of thought. Free from the shadow of this history, we are then able to consider without prejudice the idea that the laws of nature have a history.

To say that the laws have a history is to say that they develop together with the phenomena they govern. We cannot place them beyond time; they are down below, in the middle of the events. The laws underwrite causal connections. The character of these connections as well as their specific content change together with the change in the laws. A change that is far-reaching and persistent enough will not just replace one cause by another; it will alter the way and the sense in which a cause brings about its effect.

Because everything in the world changes sooner or later, including the laws governing change, the nature of contingency and necessity is also susceptible to revision. We are familiar with the idea that what we mean by the necessity of the most necessary relations varies according to our views of how nature works. Among these views, our beliefs about the history of the universe have special importance. However, it is not only our understanding of the necessity of the most necessary relations that changes in accordance with our ideas about the workings of nature. It is also the nature of this necessity of the most necessary relations that changes according to changes in the way the world actually works.

The movement from one set of laws and phenomena to another is not uncaused and miraculous simply because no higher and eternal set of laws stands over it, commanding, once and for all, its direction. However, if time goes all the way down, nature gives laws to itself as it goes along. The character of every causal connection, played out in time, changes accordingly.

If change of the laws does not take place by chance, if it is not miraculous, is it not caused? And if it is caused, must it not be caused by what happened before? A mind sufficiently penetrating and encompassing would anticipate, together with the transformation of the phenomena, the transformation of the laws. We would have rescued something of the idea of timeless laws. Time, if not defeated, would at least be contained.

This picture would present too impoverished a view of nature, however. Nature may develop in such a way that a structure arises, initially by chance, within the limits set by the preexisting reality, which then makes possible forms of self-transformation that cannot be reduced to the simple opposites of necessity and chance. Such an event in the history of the world was the appearance of life. If it happened in this form, which is close to us and to our concerns, who is say that it has not happened, and will not happen again, in forms we would now be unable to anticipate or even to describe?

These ideas about the inclusiveness of time are consistent. Their appearance of paradox vanishes once we cast aside the prejudices suggested to us by the way in which modern science happens to have developed. But are these ideas true? They are at least as compatible with our present insight into nature as the beliefs that would limit the reach of time and establish a place for timeless laws. We have a reason to prefer them and, in preferring them, to act on them: they describe a world that is less alien to us than the world would otherwise be—a world that is as time-drenched as we, the death-bound, are. Moreover, although we cannot put these ideas directly to empirical test, they can inform agendas of scientific thinking that can be subject to such probing. For the same reason, they can help inspire particular conjectures in particular sciences.

For example, a puzzling feature of the universe is the existence of certain constants or parameters with precise but seemingly arbitrary values. Among these arbitrary parameters in contemporary physics are the masses (and the ratio of the masses) of the elementary particles, the strength of the different forces or interactions, the cosmological constant (the energy density of space), the speed of light, Planck's constant, and Newton's gravitational constant. These values, under present views, are arbitrary in the sense that they have defied all attempts to account for them on the basis of the laws of nature we are now able to discern. Might we not suppose that they are the vestiges of earlier states of the world in which other laws held sway? They would then be like the monuments of a dead civilization, written in the hieroglyphs of a language we have not yet learned to decipher.

Three of these unexplained parameters—Newton's gravitational constant, Planck's constant, and the speed of light—are intrinsically dimensional: to the extent they fail to vary, we can take them to define the units by which we measure everything else—including time, mass, and energy. Their function as part of the equipment by which we measure the world may give them some exemption from the nagging question about why each of them has one value rather than another.

However, the enigma of brute, irreducible facticity then attaches all the more strongly to the remaining unexplained parameters. These residual parameters are unitless or dimensionless ratios. The mystery of their having one value rather than another stares us in the face. (If the dimensional parameters do vary, then the ratios of their values at different times are also dimensionless numbers, with the result that the mystery applies to them as well.)

The riddle of the unexplained parameters exemplifies a more general recurrent problem in the history of modern science: phenomena that are underdetermined by the laws of nature such as we can understand these laws. We witness this underdetermination of the phenomena by the laws in many aspects of the science of our own time: for example, in the proliferation of "string theories" in particle physics. A vast number of such theories are compatible with known phenomena and feasible experiments.

To such problems of underdetermination, there are, in general, three classes of apparent solutions: the dialectic of chance and necessity, the subsuming of the actual world under a range of possible worlds, and the recognition that the laws of nature change, in the course of time, together with the phenomena they govern. The third class of solutions is merely undeveloped; the first two are radically inadequate. Their shared flaw is their inability to come to terms with the reality and inclusiveness of time.

What seems to be underdetermined may be ascribed to probability: the roll of cosmic dice. It is a solution that becomes increasingly less satisfactory as we expand the scope of the explanatory work we expect it to carry out. This solution may have undeniable power in helping explain particular physical and biological events. Expanded, however, into a cosmological thesis, capable of elucidating the unexplained value of the seemingly arbitrary parameters, it is so incomplete as to be unavailing. It is the half rather than the whole of an answer, and it makes little sense without the missing half.

To justify the metaphor of the dice, we must be able to say how such dice are put together, and how they are rolled, and within what setting of changeless or changing reality the cosmic gambling goes on. No wager sets its own terms; a probabilistic explanation can work when operating within a framework determined in another way, not when it is used to account for the most general framework of natural events. On this vast scale, to make use of probabilistic thinking is to replace one mystery by another.

The appeal to possible worlds presents our actual world, governed by the laws we manage to discover, as simply one of an indefinitely large number of possible worlds. Such worlds are supposedly forever coming into, or going out of, existence, successively or simultaneously. From this view there arise two distinct approaches to the understanding of the unexplained or underdetermined factual residue.

One approach is to push the laws of nature many levels up, assigning them the role of governing what is common to the indefinitely many possible worlds rather than what is peculiar to the actual world in which we find ourselves. Their relation to the unexplained phenomena would then be like the relation of basic biochemical constraints and regularities to the accidental details of natural history.

The alternative approach is to push the idea of possible worlds many levels down, into the multiplication of many different ways in which the constituents of matter can interact. The way in which they do interact in our world will then be explained as one of such possibilities: the possibility that is consistent with our own emergence. We shall then read the seemingly arbitrary constants in our own world as part of the indispensable background to our emergence—thus converting, to our satisfaction, arbitrariness into providence.

In either of these two modes, the invocation of possible worlds amounts to an evasion rather than to an explanation of the enigmatic factual residue, including the mysterious parameters. It redescribes, instead of solving, the problem presented by that leftover and by these constants. It provides no account of why some possible worlds rather than others—in the large or in the small—become actual: the "anthropic principle," which presents the values of the parameters backward as part of the condition for our rise, stands in for a missing explanation. The intellectual sin of this latitudinarian perspective is the transmutation of a scientific enigma into an ontological fantasy: the vision of the possible worlds. Under the weight of this transmutation, science sinks into allegory; the actual world takes on some of the non-reality of the possible worlds so that the possible worlds can borrow some of the reality of the actual one.

The result is to rob the world of what, for science as well as for art, must be its most important attribute: that in all its present, past, and future particularity it is what is, or has been, or will be, given its all-decisive history. The real world is what it is, not something else. The more clearly we acknowledge this attribute, the deeper becomes, in our ideas about the world, the abyss separating being and nonbeing. The possible worlds of the rejected allegory would provide the *tertius* between nonbeing and being, and make the contrast between them less absolute.

The failure of these two ways of dealing with the factual residue—the dialectic of necessity and chance and the subsuming of the actual world under an array of possible worlds—drives us to a third position. According to this third thesis, there is facticity because there is history, because time goes all the way down and holds sway over everything. The phenomena change, and so do the laws. The parameters we observe in the world—some of them unexplained by the known laws of the observed world—may, according to a conjecture suggested by such a view, be explained by the laws of a previous state of the world.

On the analogy to customary law in human history, some natural change is law-governed, and some is law-changing. On the analogy to a way of thinking well established in certain traditions of social theory, though less familiar in natural science, discontinuous change may result, at the breaking points of such change, in changed laws.

That the laws of nature should be mutable, rather than a timeless backdrop to phenomena immersed in time, is a fact that complicates our understanding of causation. Views that equivocate with the reality of time, exempting part of nature, if only the laws governing it, from the reach of time, make the idea of causation incoherent, as my earlier discussion of the antinomy of time has shown. By contrast, a doctrine recognizing that the laws of nature remain within time rather than outside it results in complication, but not in incoherence, for our notion of causality. On the contrary, it gives us hope that we can make sense of this notion and improve it.

An aim of the argument of this book is to suggest a basis on which to reckon with the reality of time, in all our thinking and action, including our scientific practice. We have a stake in the generalization of such view: one of the results of such a generalization is to mitigate the foreignness of nature to our human concerns and experience. Like us, the world is open because, like us, it has no feature that time does not change.

The Thesis That There Is No Closed Horizon of Possible Worlds

There is no closed horizon of possible worlds, of possible states of affairs, within which we can confidently place the actual world or the present state of affairs. The possible states of affairs are not a timeless antecedent to the actual state of affairs; they are simply a penumbra around the actual.

They are a penumbra in two different senses: one anthropocentric, having to do with us; the other, impersonal, having to do with nature without us. The anthropocentric sense of the possible is to be what we can get to, individually or collectively, from where we are, with the instruments at our disposal. The possible is then the foreshadowing of a big or little revolution to be brought about by us. It is only in this anthropocentric sense that the possible has a clear meaning; a meaning within the narrow, illuminated space of what we can see because it pertains to us.

The impersonal sense of the possible is that which can happen next, given the laws that now govern nature but given also the way in which the transformations ruled by these laws may result in changes in the laws themselves, either directly causing them to take place or allowing them to occur. This impersonal sense of the possible is much less clear than the anthropocentric sense. It is less clear because we are powerless to peer beyond the veil of time, to a beginning and to an end, and to trace the limits or the logic of this self-transformation of the laws that takes place together with the transformation of the phenomena.

According to this view, the metamorphoses of reality do not happen within a closed configuration space, a horizon circumscribing possible states of affairs. That is part of what it means for time to be real and for it to go all the way down. It is another way of denying the spectral idea of possibility: the idea of the possible as a ghost stalking the world and waiting for a cue to come on to the stage of actuality. It is another means to affirm that something can be really new, that the new is not just the materialization of the ghost-like possible.

The idea of a closed configuration space is so well entrenched in our minds that it may seem a presupposition of any attempt to make sense of nature in causal terms. That it deserves no such honor is shown by the far more limited and contested role that it has in natural history or evolutionary biology in contrast to modern physics (insofar as physics has yet failed to take fully to heart the idea that the universe and its laws have a history). It is shown as well by the failure of every attempt to base social and historical analysis on the idea of an organized space of human possibility. The most notable of these attempts was the appeal to the idea of a deep structure, supporting a master narrative of historical evolution. Its characteristic claims were belief in a closed list of alternative types of social and economic organization, in the indivisible unity of each of these types, and in law-like forces driving their succession in history.

The absence of a closed horizon of possible states of affairs, in combination with a characteristic feature of our thinking, produces a conundrum about counterfactual explanation. This conundrum shows once again how confused and misguided are our familiar ideas about causation.

If there were a closed horizon of possible worlds, changes would take place according to a simple model of rule-following that distinguished clearly between the rules and acts under the rules. The rules would be the unchanging laws of nature, and the acts under the rules would be the phenomena the laws govern.

Because there is no such closed horizon, change occurs according to a more subtle model: like customary rather than statutory law. Under this model of customary law, no clear-cut distinction exists between the rules and the behavior to which they apply. Every new act goes into the stuff defining what the rules are at the same time that it either conforms to them or defies what, in their preexisting state, they were understood to be. Change changes change, and it does so either continuously or discontinuously, that is to say, in ways that are themselves susceptible to change.

To understand something, we must imagine it not only absent but also transformed. A view of how a phenomenon would behave, or of what it would become, under various conditions is what understanding it means. Counterfactual causal conjecture is thus indispensable to the deepening of insight into the world. It is, however, tainted by a flaw. We cannot expunge this flaw; it is built into the conditions of our understanding. We can only reveal it and, by revealing it, contain its dangers.

To understand something is to imagine it changed, by seeing how and when it might change and into what. However, every such change may result in a change in the ways in which things influence one another: it may change the laws. The common fallacy of the counterfactual analysis built into causal explanation is to suppose that when we change—or imagine changed—part of the world, everything in the changed world continues operating by the same rules as before. It is as if we suspended and replaced part of reality but upheld the whole regime under which that reality works. In fact, the regime cannot be upheld.

To know for sure how the regime changed, there would have to be higher-order rules governing regime change, and so on forever, in infinite regress. If time is radically real, however, there are no such higher-order rules, or at some point they cease to hold. The system fails to close at the top or on the outside; it is therefore, strictly speaking, no system at all. The course of inquiry does not then stop; it continues, albeit on darker and shakier ground.

Here we confront for the second time the paradoxical character of the causal thinking on which we must rely to form a picture of the world. The common, spectral idea of possibility to which we regularly appeal in the course of our thinking equivocates with time. If time were illusory, all phenomena or events would be simultaneous. Causation and causal explanation would therefore amount to fictions or delusions.

The idea of a closed horizon of possible states of affairs, and the spectral idea of possibility (states of affairs as ghosts stalking the world, waiting for the call to become actual), with which it is closely related, are attempts to admit that time is real, but only barely. The world would witness transformation, but not—not at least at the bottommost level—the transformation of transformation. Time would fail to go all the way down.

However, this metaphysical principle, although it may save the day for our equivocal idea of causality, seems ever less compatible with what we discover, despite our causal confusions, about nature. As we shall soon see, it contradicts the most striking and salient features of our temporal experience. It even threatens to help disarm us in our efforts to make a world for ourselves in the face of indifferent nature.

To take time, however, as fully real, rejecting the spectral notion of possibility and the idea of the closed horizon of possible states of affairs, is to recognize that no timeless laws support our causal explanations. It is to acknowledge that the counterfactual conjectures with which such explanations must work deny us any ground that will not shake. It is to assert that the project of a unified causal theory of everything is misguided in principle. It is to conclude that, although we may control the confusions of our ordinary view of causality and of our familiar practices of causal explanation, we cannot definitively dispel those confusions.

We should credit these confusions to an inescapable tension between the reality of time—more real than we are willing to admit—and the view of connection and inference to which we are led by a born enemy of time: our mathematical and logical thinking.

The Thesis That Mathematics Resists the Recognition of Time

Mathematics—and all the aspects of our thinking that participate in its nature—perpetually suggest to us the conception of a world without time. The relations among our mathematical notions are timeless even when we use such notions to represent events in time.

The development of the ideas summarized in the theses of the reality of time, of the inclusiveness of time, and of the absence of a timeless and closed horizon of possibility around the actual world encounters a source of resistance in the most intimate and most powerful expression of the mind: our mathematical reasoning. To understand how and why we face this resistance from within the mind to the recognition of the reality of time is to discover what is at stake in the affirmation of that reality.

Seen as the product of its natural history, the mind is a machine for solving problems. To solve problems, however, it must be more than a machine. Its formulaic and modular aspect must coexist with its plastic, surprising, and transcending aspect. These two aspects meet in the need to survey a situation as a whole and to relate its parts to one another. A capacity to grasp structures and relations is the crucial precondition of our problem-solving capacity. To enjoy this capacity, we cannot simply think according to established formulas, as if we were machines. We have to be able to think more than any preexisting formula will countenance, and then we have to establish the formulas that make sense of our insights after we have first made our formula-breaking discoveries. We must be able to construct new ways of understanding, of explaining, of seeing what stands before us, in the scene of imminent or imagined action, as an ordered whole or as a set of relations.

This power of the mind may be inseparable from the precise constitution of the brain. Its historical roots may therefore lie in the natural history of that brain and of its development, under selective pressure, as a problem-solving device. Nevertheless, once established, this faculty of representing the scene of action as structured wholes and bundles of relations outreaches the natural occasions for its emergence. It becomes a revolutionary principle for seeing the world as a whole. It ties our interest in understanding the manifest world to our stake in devaluing the actual, or at least any given way of representing the actual, by insisting on other possibilities of transformation and of vision.

The supreme expression of this power is mathematics. Viewed superficially, the character of our mathematical reasoning may seem to be fully accounted for by the combination of three attributes: explication, recursion, and equivalence.

The first and most general of these attributes is explication: to make explicit what is implied in a conception of a structured whole or of a bundle of relations. Such a conception amounts to a foreshadowing; its content is hidden. By representing the conception in mathematics, we are then able to work the content out: to show what was implied in the foreshadowing. To treat the worked-out conclusion as synonymous with the concentrated foreshadowing, and therefore to reduce mathematics to tautology, is to mischaracterize the procedure and to sleight both its difficulty and its value.

The second attribute is the pervasiveness in mathematics of recursive reasoning. Reasoning is recursive when it deploys a procedure to which it then applies. By using recursive reasoning, we are able to pass from enumerations to generalizations; we jump off from the particular to the general by suggesting the general rule implicit in what, up till then, had seemed to be a mere enumeration of particulars. The significance of recursive reasoning, and the respect in which it most strikingly differs from mere induction, is this: that it allows us to economize on strong premises and to reach strong and rich conclusions on the basis of weak and parsimonious assumptions. It does so by allowing us to discover structured wholes and bundles of relations not in our conjectures about any particular piece of the natural world but rather in our own efforts to think about notions we deploy in our efforts to represent all structured wholes and bundles of relations. It is as if finding ourselves surrounded by mud huts, we were to tear them apart and with nothing but their pieces build palaces.

The third attribute of mathematics is its fertility in the production of equivalent propositions. A large part of mathematical reasoning consists in showing how one analysis can be restated in the terms of another. To say that such equivalences are merely definitional, to reduce them to tautologies, is to miss the point of mathematical construction. The point is not to organize our conventions of mathematical notation, by clarifying which combinations of symbols are and are not synonymous, as if we already understood the truth and had only to organize better the language in which to represent it. The point is to empower ourselves in the ability to represent ordered wholes and sets of relations by distinguishing, at every turn, our ideas from their conventional expressions. We insist on our capacity to free ourselves from the stranglehold of any particular conventions in our understanding of relations and wholes.

If mathematics were characterized solely by these three attributes, it would not be what it is: the peerless expression of our vocation for surprise and transcendence in thought, of our infinity with respect to our own ideas. It would be merely a monument to our cleverness and versatility. It has, however, a fourth attribute that transforms the significance of the other three and reveals their underlying unity. This fourth characteristic is its effort to purify itself of any natural content— that is to say of any content that would limit its procedures of explication, recursion, and equivalence to the exploration of the nature, and of the laws and history of nature.

Here is the visionary element in mathematics, the driving and intoxicating force. It is the element that in the language of patristic theology we might call *kenosis*, an emptying out. What is emptied out, progressively and through great struggle, is the residue of restriction in patterns of connection and organization suggested to us by our natural experience and by our ideas about this experience, within science and outside it.

We may have developed the capacity to think about structured wholes and bundles of relations the better to solve problems under the shadow of a need to act in particular situations of danger or opportunity. Even, however, if this original task remained paramount, we might serve it best by generalizing the faculty to which it gave rise beyond any particular circumstance, beyond any given repertory of such circumstances. To achieve content by doing away with content: that is the paradoxical ambition sustaining this fourth, decisive feature of mathematics.

The frequency with which a branch of mathematics has been inspired by the effort to solve problems in natural science for which existing mathematical tools are inadequate does not belie the importance to mathematics of this evisceration of natural content. For such breakthroughs represent efforts to use the mathematical representation of nature as an incitement to see more, by way of order and connection, than we can discern in the natural world, as if we were to jump toward nature in the hope of jumping beyond it.

Thus, for the mathematician, mathematics is not the handmaiden of natural science; natural science is an instigator of mathematical progress, taking its place alongside the instigation that is internal to the self-obsessed history of mathematical analysis.

There is, however, a price for the greater freedom and power that comes with this denial of content. The price is the disappearance of time. The relations among our mathematical ideas are outside time. They are incapable of grasping time. In this respect, relations among mathematical concepts differ from causal connections, which always have time-bound events as their subject matter.

To be sure, mathematical ideas are commonly deployed in the description of time-bound events. Causal explanations may be represented in mathematical language; the mathematical physics of the modern age is the most famous child of the marriage of mathematics to natural science. Whole branches of mathematics, like the calculus, were first devised in the course of attempts to represent change, occurring in time. However, in those branches of mathematics that are directly concerned with the representation of relative change, the conceptual relations of explication, recursion, and equivalence are not themselves time-bound. They are timeless. They are not timeless merely in the weak sense in which the laws of nature are timeless when we imagine them not to have a history. They are also timeless in the strong sense of being incapable of mixture with the realm of time-bound events.

What is true of the propositions of mathematics holds more generally for the conceptual connections forming the subject matter of logic. No deductive inference and no logical contradiction take place in time. Only our thoughts about them are time-bound events.

The strangeness of mathematics, as the Trojan horse in the mind against time, can now be made clear. Mathematics is a science that does not have as its object the natural, time-drenched world, or the free development of arbitrary conventions, or a separate realm of mathematical objects that are like other natural objects except that like angels they remain invisible to our eyes. Mathematics is not the shadow of natural science, nor is it a game of mental tricks, nor is it the study of objects that would be like others if only they were material. Mathematics is the visionary exploration of a simulacrum of the world. It is the study of the world—of the only world that exists—except with time sucked out of it.

It is as if we were to take from nature its lifeblood—time—and by preserving it from corruption, make it eternal because it is timeless. It is paradoxically through the study of this simulacrum that we best arm ourselves to struggle against our enslavement to the limited ideas about order and relation that are suggested to us by experience and science. By distancing ourselves from the world that changes under the shadow of time, we equip ourselves better to deal with that world. We multiply the schemes of connection that we bring to our understanding of natural events. We affirm the second—surprising and transcending—aspect of the mind by expressing and developing the power of the imagination to outreach the impressions of nature.

It would therefore be a mistake to suppose that the two hundred years in which mathematics struggled to tame the idea of the infinite, and to subject the infinite to finitistic methods, can now be followed by another two hundred years in which it comes to do justice to the reality and the inclusiveness of time. Nothing need prevent us from enriching the mathematical instruments at our disposal for the analysis of discontinuous and differential change in the laws as well as in the phenomena.

However, this task presents difficulties of an entirely different order from those that surrounded the attempt to make sense of the infinite by cutting it down to size. Because mathematics is by its very character alien to time, it will not be able to show us how to think mathematically of a world in which the laws and the phenomena change together. The mathematics of time will never have its Cantor. We must first learn, by intuition, experiment, and theory, how to think of such a world—a world in time—physically. Mathematics may rationalize such an understanding, but it will not prophesy it.

Our mathematical and logical reasoning perpetually suggests to us the reality of a timeless world. We are tempted to mistake this embalmed world for the real thing. However, nothing is more real than time. In a sense it is the only real thing.

The Thesis That Human Experience Has an Inescapable Temporal Structure

Our experience has a particular temporal structure. We cannot understand ourselves without understanding this structure. It is a mistake to suppose that it is merely a source of distraction and illusion, something to suppress the better to achieve impersonal and objective insight into the world. We must indeed correct it. Nevertheless if we seek aggressively to suppress it, we do not come closer to a knowledge that is free from the shackles of the body. We merely enable the antitemporal element in our consciousness—the element represented in mathematics and logic—to take over.

We do not encounter time as disembodied and context-less beings. We encounter it within a particular situation. There is a human phenomenology of time: an experience of time and of ourselves as temporal beings. No element of our condition is deeper or more pervasive. This phenomenology of time has a definite and surprising constitution. Like everything in life and in reality, it too changes. Indeed, it develops historically, informed by ideas and influenced by arrangements, by practices, even by machines. In other words, the phenomenology of time is itself temporal. However, its continuities and discontinuities are some of the most fundamental continuities and discontinuities of our natures. There is nothing incoherent or fantastical about trying to change, individually and collectively, our experience of time. It is not futile or senseless; it is merely hard.

Being time-bound is what we most share with all reality. In a sense we are made of time. The analysis of the phenomenology of time therefore holds special interest. Through it we can understand both what distinguishes us from the world around us and what connects us to that world. Let us see it at first simplified, and then let us complicate the picture.

Two facts lie at the center of the phenomenology of time. The first fact is that we are living and dying organisms. The second fact is that we pursue projects and form attachments, and seek to sustain such projects and attachments against the ravages of time.

The foreknowledge of death is central to the first fact. The certainty and the intimation of death give our experience its quality of dramatic concentration. They account for the unilinear and irreversible character of our experience; there is not enough time to do everything over again differently, to have enough second chances. They define our experience of how human life is made meaningful and how its meaningfulness may be destroyed; we are unable to solve the problem of meaning by indefinite postponement, as if meaninglessness now could always be remedied by meaning later or by a power to gaze into the beginnings of time.

Our position as organisms living and dying in time lies at the root of the most daunting aspect of our experience: the incalculable and irremediable disproportion between the scale of a human life and the reality of the universe around us. This disproportion denies us the right to believe that we are in a partnership with the natural setting of our existence. We share its temporality, but we cannot share its scale.

The difference of scale is so absolute and definitive that it introduces into our experience of the world an element of pure terror. We face the permanent temptation to reduce the higher work of the mind—our religion, philosophy, and art—to supplying us with consolations against this terror. However, we do not need sugarcoating and lullabies. What we need is to see the situation for what it is, and to find a way to affirm our interests and our selves on that basis.

The certainty of death is a scandal and an affront because it imposes finitude and finality in the face of our experience of inexhaustibility. The fecundity of our experience in every dimension, from the making of things to the forming of attachments and the having of ideas, defies all formula and limitation. Death, however, is supreme limitation, and its certainty a formula that cannot be disobeyed.

Our experience of time, however, has a second aspect: through time and against time, we pursue projects and we form attachments. This second aspect changes the significance of the first and turns the temporal setting of our existence into an occasion for conflict of visions and for production of novelty.

In the temporal fate of our projects and our attachments, we see ourselves more clearly than we could see ourselves directly. Our relation to them is a large part of our experience of time. For one thing, they are the true clocks by which we measure time. They take time to form and to work out; and the steps and intervals in their making are the counting of our lives. For another thing, they are hostage to uncertainty and defeat because they are played out in time. Their susceptibility to destruction is our susceptibility to destruction. Their inability to tame the unforeseeable is our inability to tame the unforeseeable.

We form projects and undertake them; we form attachments and live them out. The projects and attachments are the sole response that we have open to us to the intense concentration and irreversible course of time in our existence. If there is a direction in our lives, it is their direction. If there is a meaning to our lives, it is their meaning. They define the boundaries of a world built on our scale rather than on the awful, humanity-destroying scale of the world around us. However, they can be overwhelmed, and in the end they will be overwhelmed by time. We may experience them as immortal, but they are immortal only so long as they last.

The relation between our situation as dying organisms and our pursuit of projects and attachments gains its significance against the background of another opposition: the contrast between the formulaic and the surprising aspects of our experience. Routine and repetition occupy a large part of our practical and mental lives. They are not mere dross; they represent both a principle of economy and a principle of integration.

As a principle of economy, they save our time for those activities that we do not yet know how to repeat under a formula and to embody in a machine. They thus allow us to shift the horizon of our attention away from the repetitious and toward the not yet repeatable. Habit deadens the experience of time; the shift from the habitual to the not yet habitual recovers it.

As a principle of integration, they enable us to organize our experience and our identity. Our habits are an essential basis of our sense of the self, of its continuity, and of its integrity. They are not a mere burden; they shape and empower. The continuity of the self, ensured through habit, is yet another precondition of our experience of time.

The dialectic between routine and invention is a fundamental feature of our humanity. It is not limited to behavior; it is the distinctive trait of the imagination. Our understanding of the world advances through a two-stage displacement. Call the first displacement distance and the second, transformation.

Kant described displacement through distancing when he defined imagination as the power to represent what is absent. The routine aspect of the life of perception and understanding is the marriage of our familiar experience of perception to a categorical scheme we leave unchallenged. The experience and the scheme seem inseparable: the latter, the straightforward expression of the former. Perception would then degenerate into staring. What we call understanding would cease to exist.

For there to be the human experience of understanding, we must let go of immediate perception—because it is not before us, or because we are able to treat it as if it were not—and to remember it as image. We must then be able to bring the particulars under categories, types, or kinds. Like lawyers, we must classify effortlessly much of the time, and we must confront doubt and ambiguity some of the time.

The distancing of immediate experience, recovered in memory and organized by understanding, brings trouble to the marriage of habitual perception with our categorical schemes and allows us to see forever anew. However, it is not enough; it does not suffice to characterize the work done by the imagination.

A second displacement must complete the effort of distancing: the displacement of transformation. Neither the imagination nor the imagined world would be what they are if we could distance ourselves from the immediate only to change the scene in which habitual perception weds familiar categories. The contestability of our categorical classifications is rooted in the transformation of the phenomenal events to which they apply.

The mind does not endlessly return to a fixed list of natural kinds of things; there is no such fixed list. In the world that exists—both the world as it is manifest in experience and the world as it is explored and haltingly revealed by experimental science—every thing of a kind can become some other kind of thing through some set of intermediate transformations under certain conditions. Such transformations may be numerous and complicated. They may take a long time. They may—indeed they will—result sooner or later in a change not just in the kinds of things that there are but also in what it is for one kind of thing to differ from one another kind, that is to say in the nature of natural kinds.

Consider the example of speciation in biological evolution. The emergence of the biosphere on earth did not just add new natural kinds to a previous list; it changed the machinery for the production of natural kinds—if we think of species as such kinds—and altered the meaning of the distinction among them. An igneous rock and a sedimentary rock do not differ in the same way or in the same sense in which one biological species differs from another. Moreover, the change in the nature of natural kinds did not happen only once, with the beginning of life. It kept happening. With sexual selection, for example, came a narrowing of the funnel of alternative body types but also a basis for the development of regulatory genetic mechanisms that would in time allow for what we have: our negative capability—our power to defy formula and to transcend constraint.

We are accustomed to regard the biological reinvention of difference as an astonishingly improbable exception to the universal organization of matter. We should rather think of it as an instance of a pervasive feature of the world: that the list of natural kinds changes in its character as well as in its composition. This feature is an aspect of the transformation of transformation, which is to say that it is an aspect of time and a consequence of its reality.

We imagine something by representing it not only as absent but also as changed. Change of phenomena or events merges into change of the natural kinds the phenomena or the events instantiate—how they differ as well as what they are. We cannot see to the outer horizon of possibility: the spectral idea of possibility is a delusion. Given enough time, there is no ultimate, closed space of feasible configurations. However, we can always see next steps of transformation by one means or another and to some extent or another. To do so is part of what it means to imagine, in time, a temporal world.

The chief expression of the standardized aspect of life in personality is a character—the rigidified form of a self—surrounded by a protective carapace of individual and social routine. Our relation to a character has the same nature as our relation to all the other ordered settings of our activity: we need it, and we need not to surrender to it. It is us, but we are more than it. The development of the personality requires both the embrace of habit and the shattering of habit, both the formation of character and the shaking up of character. Without such shattering and such shaking up, we make ourselves merely finite; we deny and suppress the surprising and transcending side of our nature.

One sign of the evil such a surrender does to us is the experience of boredom: an intimation of unused capacity, a rebellion of the infinite within us against the finite, a complaint of denied plasticity against imposed rigidity. Like all the most intimate aspects of our experience, it is not invariant; it is susceptible to criticism and transformation. As we organize the institutions of society and the practices of culture to lay themselves more fully open to challenge and revision, we become more susceptible to boredom. We form the idea of it; the idea helps create the thing itself.

Another sign of the same evil is the deadening of the sense of the passage by time: in losing the transformation of transformation within our own experience, we lose as well the means with which keenly to measure and therefore to experience the passage of time. Projects and attachments are displaced by routines and subtly bring us into a world in which the reality of time dims.

From this sleepwalking, inimical to life and destructive of our hopes for the divinization of humanity, we are saved by two opposing experiences. One of these time-revealing and self-awakening experiences is discontinuity from without—fortune and misfortune, reversal and misdirection: a manifestation of the truth that all our projects and attachments are hostage to time. As they are corroded from below by habit and by the silent despair accompanying it, they are threatened from without by the powers of a world over which we never hold sufficient sway. The result of this violent discontinuity, similar to the cracking open of a rigidified social order by war, is to reaffirm in our minds the reality of time. It is a reaffirmation that will have particular force if it represents for us more than change: change in how change takes place.

The contrary experience is the one we attain when we are able to deliver ourselves single-mindedly and wholeheartedly to our attachments and projects. Then it may seem that time stops—the time measured by outward events—and only internal time—the time measured by the working out of the attachment or the project—remains to be experienced and counted. We know that this release is ephemeral and that it will be slowly deprived of its life by habit and eventually undone through the ruination of time. We nevertheless achieve at such moments the only experience of timelessness that need not require illusion and indifference and that does not result in the destruction of vitality.

How could we have both of these experiences at once—the experience of being awakened by time-quickening disturbance from the great world outside us and the experience of giving ourselves without reservation to the time-suspended flow of our projects and attachments? We cannot: such a combination is ruled out by the finitude of our lives and by the partiality of our vantage point. It represents the idea of a type of happiness that must forever elude us, and its denial to us amounts to yet another expression of the difference between what it might mean to be God and what it does mean to become more godlike.

We cannot synthesize these two experiences; all we can hope for is to have more of both of them and to use the powers produced by the second the better to sustain the vicissitudes of the first, recognizing, with opened eyes, the unforgiving reality of time.

If we are asked, then, what time is, we should not answer only by saying that it is the difference between what changes and what does not change and that it is also the transformation of transformation. We should go on to describe the structure of the human phenomenology of time, acknowledging that it is universal in our existence and yet susceptible at the margin to cumulative reinterpretation and revision, in the light of our ideas and under the force of our arrangements.

We should not understand this structure of temporal experience only to reject it more completely as a delirium imposed on us by our nature—our nature as beings who, although they may be context-transcending spirits, are also dying organisms. It is rather the peculiarly human form in which we share in the universal reality of time. If we try to cast it off as phantastical, we shall not be left with a view from above or from outside ourselves; we shall simply render ourselves defenseless to the Trojan horse within us—the part of our thinking, especially logical and mathematical, that is recalcitrant to time. Surveying the world from that timeless perspective, we shall not see it without illusion; we shall see it less fully.

We have just one way: to embrace the reality of time and then to extend our powers of observation and understanding, through our mechanical and conceptual inventions, beyond the reach of our immediate sensible experience. In that operation, we shall at every turn have to trade our immediacy to the manifest world for a more remote and more general insight. The more immediate the experience, the more shaped it will be by the contingent facts of our embodied nature and of its evolution.

The more remote and general, although tested at the outer edges of causal conjecture, as in natural science, our thinking becomes, the more tainted by metaphor, although restated as scientific theory, it will also be. We can no more have a knowledge that is both intimate and general than we can combine in the same experience the sense of being awakened to the reality of time by disturbance from outside with the sense of being freed from the passage of time by engagement with our projects and attachments.

The unifying thread between the views from within and from without is recognition of the reality of time. Time goes all the way down, as change changes, and is the only thing that is always left.

7

Self-Consciousness
Humanity Imagined

The Imagination Disarmed: Rationalization, Humanization, and Escapism

The conception of the self and of the mind that is needed to provide an adequate replacement for the perennial philosophy must be realized in the practices of the social sciences and humanities to be realized at all. If a view of humanity informed by the themes of agency, contingency, futurity, and experimentalism is the core of a radicalized pragmatism, the realization of this view in the way we go about understanding who we are and what we can become is that philosophy itself. We have not succeeded in our intellectual program until we have transformed the practices by which we account for our experience and argue about our prospects.

Today, however, the social sciences and humanities are dominated by tendencies antagonistic to such a program. Three ways of thinking— rationalization, humanization, and escapism—are in the ascendant. Each has its headquarters in a distinct group of disciplines. The votaries of each oppose the champions of the others. Nevertheless, they work unknowingly together to disarm the transcending imagination and to inhibit the transforming will.

These tendencies normalize our view of society even when they seem to undermine this view. So long as the range of practical and ideological conflict over the terms of social life remains set, such normalization goes unquestioned. Its fundamental effect is to make the present arrangements and the habitual way of thinking appear natural and even necessary. In the past, social thought often produced such an appearance of naturalness and necessity by claiming that the structure of society was a product of constraints at once deep-seated and determinate. It sometimes added to this claim the further thesis that the transformation of the structure was driven forward by law-like forces. The workings of such forces produced a foreordained evolutionary succession of forms of social, economic, and political organization or a narrowing funnel of institutional possibilities.

The beliefs that have come increasingly to dominate the social sciences and the humanities yield a similar result more obliquely. They do so less by claiming that inflexible constraints or law-like forces underlie the present institutions, practices, and forms of consciousness than by disregarding or denying the imagination of transformative opportunity: the next steps by which, in thought and practice, we can get from a here to a there.

Only when there is a crisis—that is to say, a problem for which the established structure offers no ready-made solution—do we hit against the limits of our present ideas and methods. Only then does the search for alternative ways of thinking begin. However, in thought as in social life, a mark of experimentalism is that we not need to wait for crisis. The imagination does the work of crisis without crisis, making it possible for us to experience change without undergoing ruin. The imagination cannot do this work unless it is suitably equipped. We acquire the equipment we need by rebuilding the equipment at hand. Criticism of the ruling forms of social knowledge at any given time produces something of lasting value as well as of immediate usefulness: insight into what it takes to use theory against fate.

Rationalization is the tendency prevailing in the positive social sciences, and especially in the most influential of these—economics. The rationalizing tendency proclaims the practices and institutions of contemporary societies to have been vindicated by survival in competition with failed alternatives. A cumulative winnowing out shows what works. Success confirms superiority.

To understand the type of rationalizing now prevalent in the social sciences, we must grasp its prehistory: two entirely distinct strands of thought are entangled in our present practices of rationalization.

One strand comes from classical social theory. It is most fully exemplified in the teaching of Karl Marx. Its leading idea is that what we are tempted to identify as the universal laws of social, political, and economic experience are in fact the distinctive regularities of a particular institutionalized ordering of social life and of the enacted beliefs that inform it. We mistake the particular for the universal and the transitory for the permanent. The specific deep structure shapes the surface routines and conflicts of society.

In this classical social theory, the idea of the deep structure usually comes associated with other assumptions. One of these assumptions is the thesis of closure: there is a closed, predetermined list of structural options in world history like Marx's "modes of production": feudalism, capitalism, and socialism. The scope of the list may become manifest only in retrospect, but its composition is not up for grabs. The practical result is a radical constraint on the sense in which history is open.

A second assumption is the thesis of indivisibility. Each of these structures—for example, the feudal or the capitalist modes of production in Marxist theory—is an indivisible system. Its different parts stand or fall together. A practical consequence is that politics must consist either in temporizing reforms, moving within the limits of one of these indivisible systems or in revolutionary transformation, replacing one such system by another.

A third assumption is the thesis of law-like progression: an irresistible logic of transformation, arising from the internal tensions and contradictions of each institutionalized form of social life, drives forward a preordained sequence of institutional systems. Conflict and vision are powerless to create real novelty; they can reveal only the future that lay in store for us. As struggle intensifies, the logic of group or class interests becomes more perspicuous. The punishment of illusion about its content is political failure. A corollary of this thesis is that programmatic thinking has no place; history supplies the project, though not without heartbreak.

These three assumptions are false, and an understanding of politics shaped by them squanders reconstructive opportunity. There is no short list of institutional orders on offer to humanity; variation and invention in the character as well as in the content of institutional arrangements are therefore all the more decisive in importance. The successive forms of social, economic, and political organization are not indivisible systems, standing or falling together; their piecemeal reconstruction—revolutionary reform—is the exemplary mode of transformative politics. No set of irresistible forces determines the pace and direction of change; it is we who determine them. For the moment we continue to determine them under the awful discipline of calamity. Better if we could have change without catastrophe.

The way of thinking formed by these assumptions has long stopped being an obstacle to insight because it has long ceased to be believable. In the course of its slow descent, however, it has brought down with it the kernel of indispensable truth it contained: that in every historical circumstance we are the prisoners of a structure of arrangements and assumptions that we readily mistake for the nature of society and of humanity itself. We gain freedom and power by achieving some measure of intellectual and practical mastery over such a context, and we progress by reforming it.

We must rescue this insight from the decaying corpse of the necessitarian theories within which it remains encased. As we rescue it, we must also add to it an idea that was always alien to it: the idea that our interests require us, and our powers enable us, to change the character as well as the content of our accustomed settings of life and thought. We can forge frameworks, of society and culture, that allow and even encourage their own remaking, without crisis, in the course of our ordinary activities.

The main line of the evolution of positive social science has, however, been built on the rejection of any such intellectual program. This mainstream has rejected the contrast between the surface routines and the deep structure of social life, downplaying the element of fateful discontinuity and divergence in history. It has portrayed the unchallenged arrangements and assumptions shaping a society and culture as no more than the crystallized residue of ordinary conflicts and compromises.

Through this denial of the potential for radical discontinuity and divergence, it has led back to the very naturalization of established order against which classical social theory rebelled.

Nowhere do we see the nature and implications of this superstitious mixture of apology and explanation more clearly than in the most influential social science, economics. There, the denial of alternatives takes three characteristic forms.

The first form of the evasion of structure in economics is the retreat, in the most rigorous styles of economic analysis, from all controversial causal claims and prescriptive commitments into a haven of analytic neutrality. The price of such purity, however, is tautology and triviality. The pure science of tradeoffs and constraints, emptied of all controversial content, becomes the handmaiden of whatever empirical and normative ideas are supplied to it from outside. Like Pontius Pilate, it washes its hands. And like him, it asks, without waiting for the answer: What is truth?

The second form of the evasion of structure in economics is the identification, in the most ideologically committed forms of economics of the abstract idea of the market, and of market-based allocational efficiency, with a particular regime of property and contract. The same identification contaminates all the less overtly programmatic forms of practical economic analysis that nevertheless rely on the unwarranted and almost unreflective equation of abstract economic principles with particular institutional arrangements.

Such arrangements cannot in fact be inferred from the principles that supposedly underlie them; the effects attributed to them depend on local circumstance as well as on their relation to other arrangements in place. Like all the abstract institutional conceptions central to contemporary discourse, the concept of the market is institutionally and legally indeterminate; it lacks a single natural and necessary institutional translation. This theoretical thesis has now gained practical importance. We cannot now achieve our democratic and experimentalist goals merely by regulating the market or by compensating for its inequalities through retrospective redistribution. We can achieve them only by reorganizing the institutions that define what a market economy is.

The third form of the evasion of structure in economics takes place in many applications of economic analysis to policy debate. It is the avoidance of clarity about the relation between the regularities of economic life and the institutional and ideological background on which such regularities depend. This very issue led to the attempt by Marx and others to develop a practice of economic thought that would treat the constants of an established form of economic life as products of their specific institutional context rather than according them a false universality.

The method of the equivocation is to acknowledge in principle the dependence of the supposed constant relations—for example, among levels of saving, investment, and employment—on a detailed and contingent institutional background but then to disregard this qualification as irrelevant to the practice of argument about policy. What makes it plausible to disregard it is the narrowness, in the absence of war or depression, of the contest and controversy about structural reform. Failure to challenge the established arrangements, either in practice or in thought, is enough to lend the regularities of the moment a specious semblance of law-like necessity.

These two traditions of thought about society—the tradition of classical European social theory and the tradition of the positive social sciences—thus conspire to disarm the imagination. They do so by depriving us of a way of thinking about the institutional and ideological presuppositions of an organized form of social life—of how such presuppositions get established and of how they get changed.

In the absence of a credible conception of structural change, we fall back on a surrogate, fake criterion of political realism: the proximity to what already exists. This reliance on the standard of proximity then results in a dilemma that inhibits, discredits, and confuses the practice of programmatic argument. Of a proposal that seems close to what exists today, we say that it is feasible but trivial, and of a proposal that appears remote from what happens now that it is interesting but utopian. Thus, every proposal is made to seem either trivial or utopian.

It is a response that, in appealing to a false view of realism, also betrays a misunderstanding of programmatic argument. A programmatic proposal, cleansed of necessitarian superstition, should mark a direction and suggest next steps. If we view the direction in a particular context, with attention to its initial moves, we can and must be concrete: we need to provide a wealth of alternative, partly equivalent ways of achieving, in that context, the same movement. If we explore the direction further, away from the immediate time and place, we provide detail at our peril, and we succeed only in revealing ambiguities in our understanding of the interests and ideals that inform the proposals we make. Programmatic thought is sequence, not blueprint, music, not architecture.

To imagine society and history as they really are we need a way of thinking that, like classical European social theory and unlike the contemporary positive social sciences, recognizes the central role of structural discontinuity in history and the decisive effect of the assumed institutional and ideological setting. It must do so, however, without allowing its insights to be contaminated by the deterministic assumptions classical social theory embraced, all of which it must reject to the hilt.

Having combined the idea that the established framework of social life is fateful in its effects with the idea that it is as ramshackle in its composition as it is accidental in its origins, the way of thinking must go on to develop a conception that was never part of classical social theory. This conception is the view that orders of society and culture differ in the extent to which they present themselves as natural objects, relatively immune to challenge and change, or, on the contrary, as susceptible to reshaping in the midst of our ordinary affairs. They are artifacts, not destinies, and they can be formed to make their artifact-like character more patent and more usable.

Today, all around the world, the educated and politicized sections of society believe that the established order lacks any deep necessity or authority, but that it is nevertheless almost impossible to change, except under pressure of crisis. They are almost right. It should be the work of an informed imagination of history and society both to vindicate and to correct this experience. The structure of society and of culture is the temporary product of interrupted fighting over the terms of our access to one another. With the cessation or the containment of the struggle, the established arrangements and assumptions gain a second-order necessity: they become a template for understandings of group interests and identities, definitions of collective strategies, and even the design of technologies. The constraints thus imposed are no less real for not going all the way down.

It nevertheless matters that they do not go all the way down. We soon discover that we can pursue any given definition of a group interest in contrasting ways. Some of these ways are socially exclusive and institutionally conservative. In taking for granted the present niche a group occupies in the social division of labor and in therefore seeing neighboring groups in this social division of labor as rivals rather than allies, such approaches also presuppose and reinforce the present arrangements. Other ways, however, are socially solidaristic and institutionally transformative: they propose alliances that imply changes in the understanding of interests, and they require reforms in the practical organization of society. Once begun, such reforms reshape the terrain on which people understand their interests. The feeling that an order lacking in necessity and authority cannot be changed, not at least by us, is less mistaken than it is exaggerated. It soon gives way to discoveries and opportunities produced by intellectual and practical initiative.

Suppose we could design institutions and invent practices that enable us more readily to change our collective situation, in small but repeated steps, inciting the imagination to do some of the work of crisis. Then our discoveries of opportunities for reconstruction would be brought closer to the surface of social life. We would see more clearly, and we would be more free. An understanding of society and history cleansed of all taint of rationalization is the form this movement takes in the realm of ideas.

If rationalization prevails in the positive social sciences, *humanization* rules in normative political and legal thought. According to the perspective of humanization we cannot change society fundamentally. If we could, the attempt would be too dangerous, as the adventures of the twentieth century demonstrate. Let us then make the best of a world we cannot reconstruct.

One way of making the best of it is through compensatory transfers, attenuating the inequalities and insecurities of the market economy by retrospective redistribution. The philosophical justification of such transfers becomes a major concern of a humanizing political philosophy. Another way of making the best of it is to idealize the law as a repository of principles that embody impersonal right and of policies that advance the public interest. We hope to improve the effect of the laws—especially on the most vulnerable and least influential groups—by reading them in the best light. The jurisprudential justification of such idealization becomes the focus of a humanizing legal theory.

In both instances the renunciation of reconstructive ambition serves as the starting point for an effort to soften the harshness of the unreconstructed social order. In both, the poverty of the imagination of structural change and of structural alternatives and the false view that we must choose between humanization and revolution—the substitution of one system for another—lend authority to the humanizing operation. In both, we empower a supposedly beneficent elite of administrative and judicial officials who conduct the humanizing enterprise. In both, we risk turning the intended beneficiaries into passive wards of that elite.

Consider more closely the humanizing political philosophy, which is most clearly exemplified by theories of justice that place a metaphysical gloss on the homely practices of tax-and-transfer under contemporary social democracy. Whether these theories are formulated in the language of Utilitarianism and Welfare Economics or in the vocabulary of the doctrine of the Social Contract, they have the same basic outlook and repeat the same characteristic moves.

There are two main strategies. One strategy is to generate a guiding clarity about justice out of our desires or intuitions. By summing up the desires of many individuals, according to some set metric, or by bringing out the principles implicit in our intuitions, we turn experience into vision. However, even when we succeed in overcoming all other familiar obstacles to this work of aggregation or clarification, we face a difficulty that although the least discussed is the most important: the ambivalent relation of our wants and intuitions to the present order of social life.

We have wants and intuitions that take this order for granted. However, we also have wants and intuitions that transcend its limits: for example, fantasies of adventure and empowerment, promising escape from the humdrum humiliations of everyday life. This dual structure of our consciousness is no casual feature of the mind; it arises directly from our inexhaustibility by the finite contexts we inhabit.

The methods of Utility or of the Social Contract generate principles of justice out of our desires and intuitions only by first disregarding our structure-denying longings and speculations, and by treating them as if they were only an insubstantial and insignificant penumbra around the real thing. By this flattening of the duality of consciousness, however, the humanizing philosophers deliver themselves into the hands of the social world over which they claimed to pass judgment. The humanization enterprise, with all its limits, follows as a consequence.

There is a second, parallel procedure by which the votaries of the method of Utility or of the Social Contract try to bootstrap themselves above their circumstance. It is to identify the method for the aggregation of desires or for the clarification of intuitions with an institutional machinery already available, albeit in imperfect form: representative democracy or the market economy. Embodied in these two great choice machines, the method overcomes its infirmity—its inability to generate out of its assumptions more by way of guidance and authority than it has first put into them. Having claimed to solve this difficulty, the method yields practical conclusions about the way to distribute social resources.

But what entitled us to identify an idealized way of aggregating desires or of clarifying intuitions with these real-world political and economic institutions, forged amid the struggles of unequal classes and interests, against the background of a repertory of institutional ideas that is, at any given time and place, both inelastic and accidental? The problem is not the existence of localized defects that, once corrected, would entitle the existing forms of democracy and of the market to represent the impartial method of collective choice and to enjoy the authority of such a method. The problem is that the reorganization of democracies and of markets is itself a major focus of conflict in history. It can move in radically different directions, with consequences for the whole of society and culture.

The two parallel procedures suffer from the same fundamental defect. They try to achieve authority by distance from the historical context and neutrality among the interests and the visions that clash within it. However, we cannot escape the gravitational field of the present situation by a methodological maneuver or a conceptual stipulation at the outset of our intellectual and political work, as the methods of Utility and Social Contract assume. We can escape it only by a relentless campaign within the context, uncovering its fault lines and discovering its hidden opportunities of transformation. If we pretend to hand ourselves through the cleverness of the intellect what we can in fact achieve only through a long struggle against our time, the result will be a more thoroughgoing enslavement to the circumstance we had plotted to overcome. We shall be left to sugarcoat what we no longer dare to reimagine or know how to remake.

The exercise of normative argument must acknowledge that our ideals as well as our interests are nailed to the cross of the institutions and practices that represent them in society. We cannot realize our ideals and interests more fully without rethinking and reforming their practical expressions. Only the prejudice that the entrenched system of institutions and practices must be either replaced in its entirety or merely humanized prevents us from recognizing that we can change it through piecemeal but potentially cumulative and directed transformation. Some combination of discontinuity and gradualism is not ours to accept or reject; it is a feature of the way history happens. However, we can take over this characteristic of our historical experience, altering its quality and bending it to our purposes.

The threshold attribute of a practice of political and legal argument serving a free people under democracy is that it acknowledge the internal relation between thinking about ideals and interests and thinking about our practices and institutions. The contest over the organization of society is not a technical afterthought to the definition of our ideals and interests; it is an intrinsic part of the way we define them. We shape and reshape them by settling on their practical forms of realization.

No sooner do we bring pressure to bear against the received ways in which our ideals and interests are realized in practice than we discover in them ambiguities of meaning and of direction that were hidden from us so long as their practical expressions remained unchallenged. A debate about the alternative organization of the market economy, for example, forces us to ask what matters more about the market. Is it the broadening of the number of economic agents who have effective access to productive resources and opportunities together with the diversification of the legal regimes under which they can use those resources? Or is it the extent to which each of those users enjoys unconditional power over the resources at his command? As we begin to disengage ideals and interests from the institutions and practices that supply their hidden ground of meaning, we become freer and more confused.

There would be no way to overcome this confusion other than through the fiat of a groundless political faith if the practice of normative argument failed to include a second, prophetic and visionary element. This second side relies on a conception of our humanity and of unrealized human opportunity. Such a conception is informed by a reading of the lessons of historical experience: prophecy tutored by memory. It acquires its relatively greater distance from the immediate context in exchange for the relatively greater fragility of its claims. To gain authority and direction, it must constantly seek to touch again the ground of immediate experience. The most common way in which it does so, in the teaching of all political and religious prophets, is by appealing to aspects of present experience, especially of our experience of direct relations among individuals, that can prefigure a route to the development of society and culture.

The relation of the visionary and the prosaic species of normative judgment varies. The more entrenched the arrangements of society and the dogmas of culture and the greater the distance between our ordinary context-preserving activities and our extraordinary context-transforming initiatives, the starker will be the contrast between the two sides of prescriptive discourse. As the arrangements and dogmas are disentrenched and the distance between our context-preserving and our context-transforming actions narrows, the contrast between the two aspects of normative controversy wanes. Our ordinary arguments become little prophecies, and our prophecies little experiments.

Rationalization in the positive social sciences and humanization in normative political and legal discourse is accompanied by *escapism* in the humanities. The humanities avoid confronting the practical structure of society. Instead they describe and explore adventures in consciousness. These adventures bear no manifest relation to the remaking of the social order. More generally, spirit—the human spirit as portrayed in the humanities—escapes from the stifling structure of everyday life. Having escaped, it then floats above, disembodied, unwilling and unable to infuse and reanimate the spiritless world of routine and repetition.

Two themes are paramount in this practice of the humanities, each entangled in the other. One theme is spiritual adventurism: the quest for extreme forms of consciousness and experience that deny in the mind the social shackles we fail to break or even to loosen in practice. Every move—from the idea that a text can mean anything to the view that every argument is as good as its opposite—serves as an invitation to an adventure beckoning beyond the walls. This invitation repeats in the language of a cultural elite—faintly singing in its chains—the bias of a popular culture that offers as fantasy what society fails to provide as experience.

Another theme is relentless negativity: giving up on the institutions and practices of society, viewed, tacitly if not explicitly, as the irreconcilable enemies of resistant and transcendent spirit. Social reality exists in the element of repetition. And repetition, as in the relation of marriage to romantic love, seems to be the annihilation of spirit.

The theme of adventurism rests on a misunderstanding of the nature of human desire, and it embraces an ideal of personality that is too one-sided and too self-defeating to deserve authority. Desire is relational: our deepest longings seek expression in connections to other people and in forms of social life. We cannot possess and develop ourselves except to the extent we succeed, in the daily experience of social life, in reconciling self-affirmation with connection to others. The organization of society and culture sets the terms on which we can hope to do so, raising or lowering the threshold of difficulty.

We cannot form and enhance personality without encouraging strong impulse and strong vision in the individual. Such impulse and such vision must seek a collective voice and a social expression. If they fail to do so, one of two things must happen. The impulse and the vision may wither. Or they may turn inward, into narcissism and self-cultivation: self-defeating because they are unable to deal with the implications of the link between self-affirmation and connection.

The theme of negativity is based on a mistake about structure and a mistake about spirit. The mistake about structure is the belief that the relation of our institutions and practices to our structure-defying action remains constant. On the contrary, one ordering of society and culture may differ decisively from another in the extent to which it nourishes our powers of reconstruction and creates occasions for their exercise. The mistake about spirit is the view that the transgressing and transcendent powers that help define our humanity can survive and flourish in long-lasting exile from routine and repetition.

To explore the countercurrents of consciousness in a given circumstance—uncertain promises of other futures; to trace the struggle between spirit and structure in every domain of social and cultural life; to show how vision becomes embodied in institutions and practices and, in being embodied, is both undermined and corrected, but in any event transformed; to reveal how we forfeit our freedom to imagine and reconstruct, and then regain it, even against our will; to commandeer alien wisdom the better to criticize the established order and present experience; to give voice to what has lost a voice or not yet gained one; to display in every department of our experience, from the micro to the macro and from passion to calculation, the revolt of the infinite within us against the finite around us—all this is the work of the humanities when they recognize us for what we are and might become.

Self-Consciousness Redirected

The criticism of misguided directions in the social sciences and humanities suggests an alternative approach to explanation and criticism. Such an approach represents us as the products of circumstance, of context, of structure—both of institutions and of beliefs—but not completely the products. We can turn the tables both episodically and systemically. We can turn the tables episodically by doing and dreaming up more than the established institutional or ideological order can allow—and then revising the order retrospectively so that it will accommodate those resisting deeds and dreams. We can turn the tables systemically by forging institutional and conceptual arrangements that diminish the distance between what we do within the framework and what we do about the framework.

Our interest in turning the tables systemically—whatever system is established—is more indirect, but it is no less strong, than our interest in turning the tables episodically. One of the many sides of this interest is intellectual. We cannot hope to jump out of ourselves and to see with the eyes of God, from a place immune to the influence of place and time. However, we can so arrange our societies and our ideas that we become less tempted to mistake the local for the universal and more capable of registering and confronting constraint without mistaking it for fate.

The resulting approach to the whole field of social and historical study must come to terms with the need for an intellectual division of labor and for the specialized disciplines this division of labor supports. However, it is incompatible with a form of specialization—such as now reigns over the university culture—that is based on the association of each subject matter with a canonical method of study. Our understanding of what exists or has existed is parasitic on our insight into what can come, or could have come, next. The opportunities for change always exceed the moves admitted as feasible and legitimate within the given structure; we can understand what is established only by reference to what is not. The imagination is the scout of the will, anticipating how we might get to the there—or to different theres—from here. If transformative action is opportunistic, confounding what habit separates, imaginative insight must be opportunistic in spades, discounting the habitual divisions that the specialized disciplines would force upon us.

A philosophy that takes sides with the resisting agent, wandering in an accidental world, extends, deepens, and radicalizes all these intellectual practices. Its theorems teach us how to look back, from the future, on the present.

An Initial View of the Mind

Implicit in this alternative approach to the problems of social and historical understanding is a conception of the mind and of human nature. This conception takes as its points of departure two apparent paradoxes that are of very different orders: one about the brain and the mind; the other about history and its protagonists.

The paradox about the brain and the mind is that no matter how much we affirm that we are natural beings all the way through and deny that any part of our experience lies outside our natural constitution we cannot adequately describe the experience of consciousness in physical terms. We can relate the different features of our conscious experience to the physical facts that may help explain how they became possible. However, we do not thereby account for what is most important to us about consciousness. In particular, we fail to reckon with the most important attribute of thought: its power to subvert itself.

We can render this point, for the sake of clarity, in the categories of our present-day science, although its significance outreaches those categories. Suppose that, relying on them, we distinguish three aspects of our mental constitution: a sensory-motor apparatus, a conceptual-intentional apparatus, and a capability for what has been called recursion. Recursion is the capacity, most directly expressed in language, for infinite variation on the basis of finite elements.

Even in the most rudimentary part of this constitution—the sensory-motor apparatus—we are active interventionists, constructing what we see, not just passively registering impressions aroused in us by the outside world. It was the central thesis of the criticism leveled against the old associationist psychology of the nineteenth century to insist that the responding agent helped shape and define the stimulus to which he responded. However, this dialectical relation between the agent and the setting of his actions and impressions cannot suffice to distinguish a feature of consciousness that modifies every aspect of mental life.

The third element—the capacity to produce the infinite out of the finite—changes everything, shaping our conscious experience in its entirety. It gives us our power of using limited means to generate unlimited variations in language and thought, to express different contents or meanings though similar formal relations among symbols, and to convey the same contents or meanings through different series of symbols. It results in the most signal trait of our conceptual-intentional experience: our ability endlessly to revise our thoughts by bringing pressure to bear against their presuppositions: an ability we acquire only through our more basic power to generate endless variation and complication. This power in turn informs our sensational-motor experience by allowing us constantly to change the tacit stories with which we infuse our perceptions and guide our movements.

From these facts there results an ambiguity in the use of the concept of consciousness. We can attribute consciousness to other animals, sharing with some of them, as we do, the gross features of sensory-motor and even of conceptual-intentional experience. We can even hope to identify more clearly the physical mechanisms through which different parts of each of these apparatuses operate. At the end of the day, however, we would not have provided a map of what we human beings can recognize as conscious life.

The missing element—the recursive power to complicate—is both integral and pervasive to consciousness. It, too, has physical preconditions. Of these the most important is the plasticity of the brain: the way in which pieces of the brain can expand, combine, or otherwise change what these brain parts do. Plasticity may in turn depend on homely natural facts, such as modest increases in brain size and new interactions between a bigger brain and sensory-motor development.

Nevertheless, in explaining the physical preconditions of this recursive power, we do nothing to elucidate its content: its inner workings and its many-sided consequences for our experience. The recursive mind is embodied in an organism with a natural history that has shaped the natural powers and the natural limitations of the individual. How far the recursive mind can go, and in what directions, given these powers and limitations, is not anything we can infer from the physical conditions that made the novelty-producing traits of such a mind possible. We do not understand the mind better by exploring those conditions more fully.

This is not a metaphysical point about our difficulty in relating the physical to the mental; it is a remark about a limited structure with indefinite capabilities. Such a structure may be the human mind. It may also be a way of ordering society that mirrors, through the relations and the faculties it supports, what the mind is like. The possible parallelism between the organization of society and the organization of the mind foreshadows the central idea of a political program faithful to the aspirations and assumptions of democratic experimentalism.

No direct passage takes us from analysis of the physical basis of our recursive power to an understanding of its nature. The exercise of this power and therefore its meaning are decisively shaped by the way we order society and culture. The more we succeed in organizing society and culture as a series of structures that invite their own revision, and the shorter the distance we therefore allow to subsist between our framework-preserving and our framework-transforming activities, the more thoroughly does the recursive element in the life of the mind come to penetrate all aspects of our experience of consciousness. To that extent, we make ourselves less animal-like and more godlike. We spiritualize our natural condition, spirit being only another name for this power of transcendence: this ability to make if not the infinite out of the finite, then the less finite out of the more finite.

Consider now a second apparent paradox with which this argument about the expression of our humanity in the constitution of our minds begins: a paradox about human nature and history. Two propositions are true that may at first seem incompatible.

The first truth is that every feature of our experience, no matter how intimate and elusive, is up for grabs in history: for example, how we experience jealousy and what it means for us, or how we relate, in our most immediate and complete attachments to other people, power and love. We cannot separate our experience into two parts—the changing and the changeless parts. The appearance of changelessness can be upheld only by depriving of detailed content what we suppose to be immune to history. The changeless will then be the lifeless or the empty—the counterfeit image of an enduring and universal human nature.

This fact is a consequence of other facts. We can make a life only against the background of a habitual ordering of society and thought; we must therefore interrupt or contain our strife over the terms of such an ordering. There is no natural or definitive ordering, although there is a way of ordering that is truer to our humanity because it acknowledges and nourishes the qualities that make us human by making us godlike. Our natural history and our natural constitution do not suffice to describe or to explain what it is about ourselves that most interests us. In particular, they throw little light on how to answer, in each domain of social life, the question: What should we do next?

The second truth, which at first appears to be in tension with our susceptibility to the influence of context and history going all the way down or running all the way through, is that we can change what collectively we are only slowly and at the margin. The practical meaning of the idea of human nature is simply what we are like now. What we are like now is not malleable material, open to rapid or radical reshaping.

We do not need to attribute such constraints on malleability to our natural history and our natural constitution, nor could we, for although these natural influences are powerful and even intractable they are also remote and indeterminate. The more immediate and determinate constraint on malleability results from the ways in which our societies and cultures have made us who we are. Our being up for grabs in history does not set us up for easy reengineering; on the contrary, it entangles us in resistant material.

We cannot wipe the slate clean. Neither, however, are we powerless to loosen the stranglehold of constraint embodied in the established practices and institutions of society as well as in the practiced dogmas of culture. We can change the relation between repetition and novelty in our collective experience, using the repetitious, embodied in standard practices and in machines, to facilitate what does not yet lend itself to repetition. We can make the passage from our framework-preserving to our framework-transforming activities more continuous. By so doing, we can diminish the dependence of change on calamity.

The outcome of such reform is not to make us into plastic material, freely and deeply open to new projects of collective self-transformation. Nor is it to cancel the sense in which we are, all of us, at risk in history. However, it does diminish the force of path-dependency: the sense in which what can come next is determined by what happened before. It also strengthens the power of agency: the sense in which the history that shapes us becomes something we do rather than something we suffer. In both of these ways, it contributes to the divinization of humanity.

The meaning and value of this effort become clear when it is compared to the corresponding problem in an individual life. As society and culture must take a certain hardened form, so must the personality lean on habit. This habitual form of the person—of his dispositions toward others as well as toward the prospects of his own existence—is his character. We have been taught that his character becomes his fate, which is simply this hardened self, seen from outside or projected outward, and now recognized as an alien and irresistible force.

The vitality of the individual, however, depends on his success in fashioning a character resistant to the narrowing of experience, to the rigidity of response, and to the consequent constriction of possibility that surrender to a hardened version of what the self implies. "He was so extremely natural," said Santayana of William James, "that there was no way of telling what his nature was, or what came next." It is an observation that states an ideal, suitable to the ambitions of personality under democracy. The point is not to make war against habit or to make war against one self. It is to fashion a style of existence, a mode of the self, in which we lower our defenses enough to strengthen our readiness for the new, our attachment to life, and our love of the world.

The Initial View Developed by Contrast

This conception of mind and of human nature stands out by contrast to another view. Although it claims the credentials of science, this opposing view embodies the prejudices that have prevented us from developing a better alternative to the perennial philosophy.

This influential doctrine sees the mind as a computing machine, organized into discrete, modular elements. It emphasizes the extent to which this computable and modular structure is innate. And it claims that the composition and the workings of the mind can best be understood as products of natural selection according to the same enlarged and qualified Darwinism that we now apply to the explanation of other parts of our natural constitution. This view is not wholly mistaken, except insofar as it is too one-sided. It describes only one of two sides of the mind, and by failing to grasp its relation to the other side, it fails as well correctly to represent the part that it does recognize.

In the first place, the mind is not a computing machine, nor, in its most distinctive powers and movements, does it resemble one. For one thing, the mind is not formulaic. It can spin parts of itself off into formulas and encode such formulas in machines, like computers. Not only do its own workings resist reduction to closed systems of axioms and of the inferences that may be drawn from them, but all its most powerful productions—including mathematics and logic—bear the marks of this same openness and irreducibility.

For another thing, the mind does not simply move from similarity of syntax to attribution of meaning. It uses similar syntax to convey different meanings, and it conveys similar meanings through different syntax. Its use of syntax to transmit meaning is accessory to its more fundamental faculty of dissociating syntax from meaning. This faculty is in turn only a manifestation among many of its ability to produce more complication and variation than any definite structure, operating according to a fixed and complete set of rules, can incorporate.

In the second place, the mind is not, in the most important respects, modular. To be sure, it has discrete parts, and these parts, subject to the enrichments and transpositions resulting from the plasticity of the brain, perform certain functions. However, the way in which these discrete operations are put together and directed is not modular. The putting together is not just another discrete task. We cannot attribute it to any distinct part of our mental life. Nor can we bring it under a closed set of rules. The work of integration constantly confirms the power of the mind to produce results—of thought, emotion, and even perception—that no such closed set can encompass or allow.

The point is not just that the mind synthesizes. It is also that the mind subverts. It synthesizes and subverts at the same time. It achieves new connections by undermining old ones. No purely modular account of the mind can make sense of this association, central to our conscious experience, of synthesis with subversion.

In the third place, the most characteristic faculties of the mind are innate only in a sense that turns upside down our conventional idea of the significance of innateness. We associate innateness with constraint. However, our most significant innate faculty is a structure for outreaching and rebuilding all structures. This structure is the mind in its least computable and its least modular aspects: what we call imagination.

It may seem strange that there can be a structure for breaking all structures and that it can have a precise, limited form, and be built to particular specifications. Yet we have two major examples of such a structure in our experience. One is the mind as imagination. The other is society, progressively recast on the model of the imagination: organized to shorten the distance between our context-preserving and context-transforming activities and to diminish the dependence of transformation on crisis.

The significance of the first of these two instances of the idea depends in part on the prominence achieved by the second. If society is organized to insulate its own arrangements from challenge and change, and thus to give itself the semblance of a natural object or an alien fate, the noncomputable and the nonmodular aspects of the mind will remain no more than a penumbral light around the darkness of computability and modularity. However, as society acquires the features of democratic experimentalism, those aspects become central to the life of the mind.

The hold of the innate mental faculty on our experience gets turbinated by a political construction.

In the fourth place, natural selection applying to the evolution of the brain and of behavior is overtaken by the counterpart to natural selection in history: competition of forms of social and cultural life. The outcome of this contest shapes our experience of mind. It determines, for example, the relative importance of the computable-modular and noncomputable and nonmodular aspects of mental experience. It shapes this relation far more closely and powerfully than do the selective forces that continue to operate on the evolution of the brain and of the organism in which the brain is embodied.

These selective forces matter much less than those competitive struggles because they work much more slowly—too slowly to matter in the historical dimension in which we live our collective lives and above all in the biographical dimension in which we lead our individual lives. A mortal being is in a hurry; in his time clock, the forces of natural history, though decisive in having made him possible, are too slow to matter for the imagination of the next steps and therefore too remote to count for the analysis of the present situation.

Criticism of the functionalist and evolutionary determinism in the social thought of the last two centuries has taught us that similar levels of practical power to produce or to destroy can be supported by alternative sets of institutions. No one-to-one relation exists between institutional arrangements and functional advantages.

We have also discovered that there is no short, closed list of alternative forms of social, political, and economic organization on offer in world history, much less an evolutionary procession of indivisible institutional systems, succeeding one another by an inexorable logic of transformation.

Different orderings of society and culture compete. The results of the competition do throw light on what works and what does not. It is, however, a dim, shadowy light. Only a small number of living options are on offer and in contest at any given time. Options long established and associated with major world powers enjoy advantages that comparably effective rivals may lack. Moreover, the tests of superiority are too many-sided to allow for straightforward conclusions: they include success in seducing hearts and in converting minds as well as in delivering the goods and in defeating the enemy.

There is one type of functional advantage that enjoys in this dark struggle unique status and deserves special attention. As the force of path dependency in history wanes, and as different forms of life and consciousness get more jumbled together, this force gains in importance. It is negative capability: the power to act nonformulaically, in defiance of what rules and routines would predict, a power that may be inspired and strengthened, or discouraged and weakened, by our arrangements and practices as well as by our ways of thinking and feeling.

From negative capability, embodied in institutions, practices, and modes of consciousness, a wealth of practical competitive advantages result. However, negative capability is not merely a source of such advantages; it is a direct manifestation of our godlike power to outreach the established settings of action and thought and to split the difference between being inside a framework and being outside it. History, we may suppose, selects for this advantage more powerfully and above all more quickly than any form of natural competition for reproductive success, at the level of the species, the organism, or the genotype, can exert selective influence. Negative capability is power to the mind in its least modular and computable aspects: mind-making continued through politics.

The Two Sides of the Mind

Imagine a person and a machine. As soon as the person learns to do things repetitively, he sets the machine to do them. The better he learns to set the machine this way, the more of his time he can spend on the activities he does not yet know how to repeat. He and the machine are inseparable, more inseparable than Robinson Crusoe and Friday.

There are only two things in the world that answer to this description. One of them is the human mind; the other is society. They are not just homologous in this respect; they are internally related in a particular way. Each is involved in the constitution of the other.

The mind exhibits two different sets of powers. In one of its aspects, it is indeed modular and formulaic. It has specialized parts. Each of these parts operates according to what we would understand to be formulas. In this aspect of its workings, everything has a beginning, a middle, and an end. There are no surprises, except the surprise of finding that an apparatus capable of solving problems by breaking rules should nevertheless contain within itself something so rule-bound.

If the mind had only this first aspect, the experience of consciousness would be unnecessary. What contemporary neuroscientists call the "zombie" activities of the mind would wholly occupy our mental life. Our ability to solve problems in a temporal world, full of difference and change, would be far more limited than it in fact is. We would cease to be ourselves.

The mind, however, also has a second aspect. In this second life, it exhibits two characteristic powers: the power of recursive infinity and the power of nonformulaic initiative. By the power of recursive infinity, the mind makes infinite combinations out of finite elements. By the power of nonformulaic initiative, it does things that are not rule-bound.

The powers of recursive infinity and of nonformulaic initiative sustain a power that is yet more general in its scope and more far-reaching in its effect: the negative capability of the mind. The negative capability of the mind is its power to turn against itself, testing, denying, subverting, escaping, and transforming the presuppositions on which it has operated and the routines by which it operates. We can always think and discover more than we can justify, or even fully make sense of, and find the justification and the sense-giving procedures in retrospect.

In this second aspect—the aspect expressed in its negative capability—the mind is totalizing, transcending, and surprising; these qualities result from the characteristic powers of the second side of our mental life. They are the attributes that distinguish the experience of consciousness and that would remain forever denied to the zombies we are not. Without them, the automatisms of response that we initiate before we are even aware of having initiated them, produced according to formulas that a third-party observer could state, would exhaust the whole of our mental life.

Consciousness is totalizing: the experience of consciousness is one of movement within a wide, open scope of possible attention. Any particular object of attention is no more than flotsam floating in an ocean of awareness. There are parts to our mental activities. However, consciousness moves among the parts as if it were not just a collection of them. Indeed, it is not.

Consciousness is transcending. It cannot be confined within a closed framework of presuppositions. We understand a particular piece of the manifest world only by representing it as both absent and transformed and by relating the particular not just to other particulars but also to a structure of categories that is itself incomplete and revisable. We perceive more than we can understand, and we understand more than we can prospectively justify. We turn enigma and anomaly into prophecy: the intimation of another way of grasping some part of the reality around us.

Consciousness is surprising. It can operate in ways that no set of rules formulated definitively and in advance can capture. As a result, it can generate true novelty of experience and belief, not just the pseudonovelty of the spectral idea of possibility: the possible state of mind, waiting for its cue to be actualized in an individual mind at a given time.

The mind is then the combination of these two aspects—the one, piecemeal and repetitious; the other, possessed of the powers of recursive infinity, nonformulaic initiative, and negative capability and therefore totalizing, transcending, and surprising.

The mind is embodied. Built to the scale and to the situation of a finite and mortal organism, it is a problem-solving device. Its thoughts have action as their background. Its totalizing, transcending, and surprising qualities produce much of its capacity to solve problems. If it were a formulaic contraption, it could not cope with contingent danger and opportunity in the temporal world in which we must act nor with the open-ended and changing nature of the interests motivating our actions. However, the very features that enable it to solve particular problems also allow it to roam beyond them, imagining distant danger and remote opportunity in a world yet to be created and discovering hidden connections in a reality beyond the horizon of our individual actions.

As we move beyond the scale in which thought shadows action, fortified by our experimental tools and explanatory conjectures, our ideas do not become more reliable pictures of reality; they become less reliable. They are infected by metaphor. To make sense to us, they must ultimately be translated back into terms we can relate to our action-oriented experience. They are not the view of the world from the stars. They are just our view, the view of beings who enjoy the powers characteristic of the mind.

The embodiment of the mind reveals something of immense interest. The combination of the two aspects of the mind is not like the mysterious marriage of the human and the divine. It is the outcome of the natural evolution of a particular apparatus, made from a small number of finite elements, largely forged before we existed, and recombined over time.

In the course of that evolutionary history, variation and novelty were once produced chiefly by the adaptive radiation of different species. Then, in the Cambrian period, there began a dramatic reduction in the number of animal body types and species. The chief source of variation became the power of the regulatory genetic mechanisms that arose within the narrowing funnel of species difference to produce difference: at first, at the molecular level; then through a brain with a certain measure of plasticity; and finally through a social and cultural order able to multiply occasions and instruments for its own revision. The production of the new became internal. It became, in a sense, the main point.

The passage of humanity and of the mind through this natural history may have left us burdened by a dross of imaginative constraint: for example, the limitation of altruism by reciprocity and of love, greater than altruism, by narcissism. Thus, great religions have arisen in history that, like Christianity, have proposed an altruism beyond reciprocity and a love untainted by narcissism, and they have entered into a struggle with our habits and predispositions that has not yet ended.

We cannot fully describe the relation between the two sides of the mind looking to the mind alone. The relation between them depends on something else, the other thing answering to the two-sided description of the man and the machine: society and its culture. Our social and cultural life displays the same duality that is central to the mind: repetition within a framework of arrangements and assumptions that may be ordinarily unchallenged and even unseen; and then, occasionally, practical or imaginative action to change that framework.

Society and culture may be organized to insulate themselves against challenge and transformation, lengthening the distance between the ordinary context-preserving moves and the extraordinary context-changing ones and tightening the dependence of change on crisis. In such a circumstance, the second side of the mind will continue to exist; it will be implicit in the experience of consciousness, in the practice of thinking, and in the use of language. However, its powers of recursive infinity, of nonformulaic initiative, and of negative capability will not be at the forefront of our mental life; they will remain in the background.

Suppose, however, that society and culture are arranged to open themselves to challenge and change, shortening the distance between reproduction and revision of the institutional and ideological context, and diminishing the dependence of transformation on calamity. Then the powers of the second side will no longer be implicit or seem anomalous and marginal. They will come to the center of our conscious concerns and of our self-conception. The relation between the two sides of the mind will have changed thanks to change in the character of society and culture.

The mind is thus an unfinished project: unfinished not just as the ramshackle product of natural history that it is; unfinished also because no metric exists by which to measure the relation between its parts that does not depend on what we do to ourselves in history.

From the Conception of the Mind to the Marking of a Direction

This conception of the mind, when seen against the background of the view of the human situation explored in the earlier parts of this book, helps us make sense of a contest between two families of views of human nature that have warred, and that still war, in history. In so doing, it brings us to the threshold of the questions: what should we do with our lives, and how should we organize our societies?

A single family of ideas about human nature has exercised unrivalled influence in the history of thought. It forms part of what I earlier described as the perennial philosophy; it is the decisive conclusion to that philosophy—its whole point. In one or another variation, it was the ruling doctrine of the agrarian-bureaucratic empires that, together with the world religions, were the main protagonists of history before the last few hundred years of world revolution.

According to these ideas, the vividness of sense experience obscures the true nature of reality rather than revealing it. The manifest world of change and distinction is illusory. Our surrender to its illusions enslaves us and makes us suffer, inciting the rebellion of desire against illusion and imprisoning us in an unhappy world of distraction and self-regard.

What is desirable is to achieve freedom from illusion, indifference to suffering, and benevolence, from on high, to all who suffer around us. To this end, we must establish right order within the self and within society. These two orderings—of self and of society—will sustain each other.

Within the self, the sensuous appetites must be subordinated to the action-oriented emotions, and these in turn to the understanding of deep and universal reality, beyond change and difference. Within society, those who work must be subordinated to those who fight and those who fight to those who rule, think, and pray.

The social sign of success in this endeavor of ordering the world will be a hierarchical order in society, wedding right to power. The moral sign of success will be the discipline of indifference and serenity by which we shall put an end to the anxiety and frustration accompanying our engagement in the delusive realm of change and difference. Those who have achieved this freedom of serenity will be benevolent to those who remain in the toils of the phenomenal world. Itself free from danger, because given, from a distance, by the free to the unfree, such benevolence will express and sustain the happiness of the invulnerable—invulnerable to the suffering of dependence and frustration because invulnerable to the illusion of time and distinction. Its basis will be the marriage of empathy with insight: empathy for the suffering of others not yet free and serene; insight into the universal condition of entanglement in the evanescent world of change and difference. Its message to all will be: Stay out of trouble.

Such a project has had its philosophical grounding in a metaphysic of hidden prototypes of reality, more real than the phenomenal world of transformation and time. According to this metaphysic, there are timeless natural kinds—or even a single reality of undifferentiated being—underlying the phenomena. The ascent of inquiry is the revelation of these prototypes. By counteracting the immediacy and the appeal of sense experience, we prepare to cast on ourselves the spell that will allow for serenity and benevolence. At the limit, we participate in the experience of an impersonal God in a timeless world.

For the last two hundred years, an opposing family of beliefs about humanity and society has acquired unrivalled influence throughout the world. It accepts the reality of the phenomenal world of time and difference. It treats history as real, unrepeatable, and decisive—the theater in which our human hopes must be realized or undone. It struggles with the implications of the divergence of scale between the historical time in which these hopes come to fruition or frustration and the biographical time in which we must live our lives.

It repudiates the effort to find happiness in serenity and serenity in invulnerability. It recommends looking for trouble: the individual forms himself, he becomes bigger and freer, by struggling against the constraints of his epoch and his society. To this end, however, he must cast down his shield, accepting a heightened vulnerability as the price of transformation and self-transformation.

There is no reliable hierarchical order in either self or society. Progress consists in the subversion of such order and in the enhancement and refinement of the capabilities of ordinary people. This subversion is dangerous and painful, but there is no alternative to it that is compatible with our rise to greater power, insight, and self-possession.

The most important incidents in this ascent are those that allow us to moderate the conflict between the conditions of our selfhood: engaging in a particular world without surrendering to it our powers of resistance and transcendence; and connecting with other people, especially through innovation-friendly cooperation and through personal love, in such a way that in connecting with them we do not cease to be and to become ourselves.

The supreme form of engagement without surrender is to live for the future and to struggle over its direction as a certain way of living right now as a being not fully and definitively shaped by established arrangements and beliefs. The supreme form of connection without self-suppression is love among equals, given not as benevolence from a distance and from on high but as imagination and acceptance between equals who can rebuff, betray, and therefore hurt each other.

Humanity, individually as well as collectively, in the person as well as in the species, has infinities within. We demand the unlimited from the limited: an assurance that all is well from another person, even the world from a cigarette. Our experiences of addiction and obsession, for example, are adventures in false transcendence: the incongruous and seemingly arbitrary association of unlimited longing with all too limited objects. Our experiences of boredom and anxiety attest to our restlessness in our chains, to the weight of our unused capacities and of our hidden powers. Our insatiability is the stigma of our infinity.

Freedom, even divinization, would be to enlarge in our experience the chance to engage without surrendering and to connect without ceasing to be or to become ourselves. The advancement of that project requires that we reshape society and culture. It is not enough to replace some institutions and practices by others. We must change the relation of these social and cultural structures to our structure-defying freedom, creating structures that multiply opportunities and means for their revision, and in this way denying them their mendacious semblance of naturalness. Today we must reinvent the institutional forms and the ideological assumptions of political, economic, and social pluralism—of democracies, market economies, and free civil society. We must make repetition in society and in culture as well as in the internal life of the mind subservient to the creation of the new.

If we succeed, we shall be better able to be in a particular social and cultural world and to be outside it at the same time. We shall develop more quickly the powers, the instruments, and even the insights by which to hasten economic growth and technological innovation, lightening the burdens of poverty, drudgery, and infirmity that continue to weigh on human life. We shall melt down, under the heat of repeated pressure and challenge, all fixed orders of social division and hierarchy, and prevent them from working as the inescapable grid within which our practical and passionate relations to one another must develop.

There is good and deep reason for these hopes. It is not true that a fixed relation exists between institutional arrangements or cultural assumptions and our power to resist and transform them. Such arrangements and assumptions vary in quality—in the quality of their relation to us, to our power to oppose and reshape them—as well as in their discrete content. It is not true, as the liberals and socialists of the nineteenth and twentieth centuries believed, that a preexisting harmony holds between our practical stake in economic progress and our moral stake in the emancipation, empowerment, and enlightenment of the individual.

Neither, however, is there is an insuperable, tragic conflict between these interests as the fatalistic postliberals and postsocialists are inclined to think. A zone of potential intersection exists between the institutional requirements of practical progress and the institutional requirements to make people freer and greater. Although these two sets of requirements do not intersect automatically, we can make them intersect. It is in that zone of potential intersection that we must advance.

The reason for believing that such a region of potential overlap exists is the affinity of both sets of interests to the social expressions of the second side of the mind: its powers of nonformulaic initiative, recursive infinity, and negative capability. The freer we are to redefine practical tasks in the course of executing them, to develop a regime of cooperation that is to the greatest possible extent hospitable to permanent innovation, and to soften the contrast between order and chaos or design and improvisation, the better our chance of quickening economic growth and technical innovation. We disentangle our relations to one another from the established scripts of society and culture, and we turn them into in a collective representation of experimental inquiry.

Similarly, we undermine entrenched and naturalized hierarchy and division in society through a twofold movement. On the one hand, we deny immunity from pressure to the arrangements and dogmas on which all such hierarchies and divisions within humanity depend. On the other hand, we develop the powers of the individual—mental, political, and economic; that is to say, we give practical expression to the goal of making the person more godlike.

The deep basis for the hope that we can advance in an area of intersection between the conditions of material progress and the requirements of individual emancipation is therefore the role that must be played in the advancement of both these families of interests by the social expressions of the second aspect of the mind. When society and culture are organized to put the totalizing, transcending, and surprising qualities of the mind at the center of social experience, we produce the convergence of moral and material interests that the classic liberals and socialists mistakenly believed to be preordained.

The institutional forms and the ideological conceptions of democracy, of the market economy, and of free civil society now ascendant in the world and established in the richer countries represent a subset of a much larger set of feasible next steps that we would need to take in order to serve these interests and realize these ideals. Globalization itself is not there on a take-it-or-leave-it basis. We need not have to choose between having more of it in its present form and having less of it in that same form. We can have more of it on different terms.

We do not have to choose between the wholesale revolutionary substitution of the established order and its humanization, through compensatory redistribution by tax-and-transfer or through the idealization of law as a repository of principles of right and policies responsive to the public interest. In fact, the idea of total, revolutionary change is no more than a fantasy, providing an alibi for its opposite, the project of resigned humanization. We can, we must, jumble up the categories of reform and revolution, preferring change that, though perforce piecemeal, may, in its cumulative effect, become revolutionary.

Yes, but we still depend on crisis as the midwife of change, and we must still learn to arrange things so that we may depend on it less. Yes, but the particular forms of the advance always remain obscure and controversial. We cannot even agree whether they should occur chiefly at the subnational, national, or supranational levels; whether the ideas that animate them should appear as local heresies—proposals, for example, of a national path—or as a universalizing heresies—doctrines, as liberalism and socialism were in their day that convey a message to all humanity; and how we should understand and practice the relation between change of institutions and change of consciousness. Because the forms of change are obscure and controversial, they will continue to give rise to conflict and even to war. They will be dangerous. Yes, but all of this will take place, or fail to take place, in the long time of history, not in the short time of biography. We cannot wait; we must find a solution for ourselves now: a way of foreshadowing in life as we can now live it that which the species has yet collectively failed to achieve.

I ask myself in this book: on what assumptions about the world and the mind, the self and society, do these beliefs—mere translations and developments of a creed that has already taken over the world and set it on fire—continue to make sense? Within what larger combination of ideas can we ground, develop, and correct them?

The ideas on which this creed once relied, such as the great evolutionary narratives of social progress bequeathed to us by the nineteenth and twentieth centuries, have misled us, sometimes catastrophically, their vindication of hope and change tainted by appeals to false necessity. They were unable to do for the modern projects of social and moral transformation what the perennial philosophy did for the old attempt to achieve serenity through invulnerability and to establish right through hierarchical order in the self and in society. It is the ambition of this book to show that we can make sense of these transformative projects, a larger sense illuminating our situation in the time of an individual life as well as in the history of the human race. Making this larger sense of them will help us rescue, reinterpret, and redirect them.

8

What Then Should We Do?

Conception and Orientation

The preceding parts of this book have developed a conception of humanity and of its place in the world. This conception amounts to an alternative to the perennial philosophy, and this alternative represents an interpretation of the hidden or unfulfilled program of philosophy.

The subsequent parts of this book outline a series of transformative projects—in politics, religion, and speculative thought—animated by that conception. They offer not a blueprint but a direction and a series of next steps. Their programmatic proposals appeal for authority and energy to the conception inspiring them. Thus, they make a central, contentious claim: that the alternative to the perennial philosophy, rightly understood, does not leave us directionless. It does not abandon us to whatever direction we might glean from our local circumstances and interests such as they existed before we undertook the work of thought. The alternative calls to us to reconstruct society, consciousness, and philosophy itself in a certain way. The ideas describing this orientation may at first seem indeterminate and even perplexing. They nevertheless exclude much and compel action. They argue for a particular revolution, a world revolution that is spiritual as well as political.

This chapter explores the hinge between conception and orientation. A willingness to admit that such a hinge exists implies no mysterious passage from the "is" to the "ought." Rather than entering into the metaphysical dispute about "is" and "ought," and claiming that we can move from one to the other, it sidesteps this pseudophilosophical dispute.

The hinge from conception to orientation turns on the normal and natural problem-solving activity of the mind, when that activity is made both general and self-reflective. Instead of being directed to the solution of particular problems in particular domains, this power may take as its subject the whole of our situation in the world. It cannot do so without shaking loose the inhibitions imposed by the methods of particular disciplines and the assumptions of particular traditions.

This push beyond limited contexts and guideposts, however, is not a philosophical extravagance in defiance of the limitations of thought. It is an irresistible expression of the second—surprising and transcending—side of the mind, and therefore, as much as anything else we do, of our natural constitution. Its connection with the constitutive facts of our humanity does not expunge it of danger. On the contrary, it is full of the dangers of illusion and misdirection. Better, however, to struggle with such perils than to be enslaved by the fears, the pieties, and the dogmas that, in the absence of such struggle, will rule our lives.

The Indifference of Nature

The first feature of our situation that must strike us when we try to decide how to orient ourselves in the world in which we find ourselves is the indifference of nature to our concerns. This insurmountable alienness is inseparable from the unthinkable disparity of scale between our human life and its natural setting. We occupy a tiny corner of the universe, in which we emerged only a moment ago. We are unable to look into the beginnings and the end of time. Our individual lives, when viewed retrospectively, even from within the reality of our own experience, are suddenly and surprisingly spent.

The alienness of the world—its rushing past us, its overpowering us, its crushing us by its parade of bigness before our littleness, its impenetrability at the horizons of time—forces itself on us in a way that is both direct and irrefutable. It does so through the finality of death. Our condition as dying organisms seems to be in irresolvable conflict with the infinite fecundity of personality, the power of the self always finally to defy constraint and to transcend context, a power affirmed in the philosophical enterprise in which we are now engaged.

We may be tempted to view the universe as neither favorable nor unfavorable to our endeavors. Such a view would serve the antimetaphysical metaphysics that suits the intellectually deflationary temper of our age. It would, however, be false and reveal the same cowardice from which only a few of the philosophers—like the great Schopenhauer—have been exempt.

In the most important respect, the universe is unfavorable to our pursuits. Its disproportion to us, and its submission to a power—time—that ultimately crushes the projects and the attachments by which we define our humanity, creates a distance, an estrangement, a horror that we can never overcome. Its answer to our experience of infinite fecundity is to decree our death.

Yet this conflict between the inflexible constraints on our lives and the inexhaustible depth of our experience, confirmed by all our powers of rebellion and transcendence and inscribed in the second side of the mind, is terrible only because it casts a shadow over something wonderful. This wonder is the joy of being alive in the moment, right now—of being rather than not being and of finding ourselves overwhelmed by wonders on every side. It is a joy so intense, and so likely to be strengthened rather than to be undermined by reflection, that we cannot think of it too long or too directly. To do so is to risk paralysis by a delight more dangerous than the melancholy acknowledgment of the contrast between our mortality and our transcendence.

He who wrote that we can no more look directly at death than look straight at the sun would better have put life in the place of death. The anticipation of death forces us to confront our limitations of insight as well as of power. The experience of life, focused and concentrated in the happiness of the moment, the happiness at the possession of life itself, is dangerous because it transports us to an exulting that is incomparable to any other joy. Engagement with the universal in the immediate can absorb all our attention and prevent us from resisting and transforming the world and ourselves. All our art, our philosophy, and our science is a war between this ecstatic wonder and the somber discriminations that our reckoning with time—the time of the world and our own time, wasting away—imposes upon us.

If we could fight to occupy in our minds an imaginary position equidistant between our rejoicing at being alive and our sadness at the conflict between our inexhaustibility and our finitude, we would come closer to solving an enigma that is central to our existence. This enigma is not the incomprehensible nature of our place in the world, resulting from our inability to see into the beginning and the end of time. It is rather a riddle internal to every facet of our experience. It is distinct from the issues raised by our powerlessness to grasp how we fit into the overall scheme of things. This mystery binds together every aspect of the view developed and defended in this book—from its picture of time, nature, and mind to its conception of politics, religion, and human striving. We can best begin to understand it as another contradiction, not in our ideas but in our experience.

We can be human only by resisting the constraints of all the established structures—of life, organization, thought, and character—within which we move. Surrender to such constraints, giving the final word to them rather than keeping it for ourselves, denies our defining attributes of agency, transcendence, futurity, and experimentalism. There is a sense in which we may be content for a while in such a surrender. However, it is a sense that presupposes a shrinking of experience, consciousness, and self-consciousness: a lowering of our energy, a dimming of our sights, and a waning of our hope. It is a stupefaction that we may try to redescribe as happiness and freedom but that deserves no such redescription.

To redescribe in such a way this shrinking of experience is what the perennial philosophy urges us to do when it admonishes us to give up the world of time and distinction and offers us reasons to cast a spell on the restless will and the transforming imagination. The chief outcome of such a surrender is the belief that we should try to stay out of trouble. Against this belief stand the revolutionary projects of social reconstruction and self-transformation that have taught us to look for trouble. What I propose is a view giving us reasons to look for trouble.

It is a central thesis of this book that we find and wage this rebellion against the limits of circumstance in every aspect of our experience: in the inability of any scheme of categories, or of any list of such schemes, to exhaust our perception of particulars; in the inadequacy of the methods and practices in all disciplines and sciences to our powers of discovery, proof, and justification; in our mental faculties of recursive infinity, nonformulaic initiative, and negative capability; in the tendency of our powers of production, innovation, and cooperation to outreach what any particular way of organizing them can allow; in the need endlessly to challenge and to change the practical forms in which we realize our recognized interests and our professed ideals and, having challenged and changed them, then to revise these interests and ideals themselves in the light of the insight gained in the course of those changes; in our commonplace experiences of boredom, diversion, and hope; and in our effort never definitively to hand ourselves over to the rigidified version of our self that is our character.

It would be a sad and heroic task if all we could do would be to rebel. It is, however, another thesis of this book that we can change our societies and cultures and our own selves so that they express and invite our further acts of resistance and invention—a greater vitality of initiative, imagination, and experience. Thus we are justified in hoping for a happiness that is based on our liberation and enlargement, not on our servitude and belittlement. Such a happiness will not be a stupefaction; it will be an awakening.

However, unless we can anticipate some of the effect of this work right here and now, in our opening to other people and to the unfamiliar and the unprecedented, and indeed to the whole world of time and change as it bears down upon us, we shall find ourselves caught on a treadmill of endless frustration. Our fight against confinement will seem to have no purpose other than its own continuance. The recognition of this threat to both our insight and our happiness, and the conviction that we can master this threat only by escaping isolation in our own individual consciousness through a determined movement outward to the world around us, are the twin psychological truths on which the enslaving mystifications of the perennial philosophy have always traded.

If we must struggle against the established context to become more godlike and therefore more human, how can we be more godlike and more human right now, before the struggle has come to its end, in the history of humanity as well as in the life of the individual? And if we could not become more godlike and more human right now, would we not be compelled to dismiss our exultation at being alive as the delirium by which the imagination steels the will against the fear of death?

The hope held out by the thesis that we can change our relation to our contexts will remain hollow unless we can change this relation in biographical as well as in historical time, independent of the fate of all collective projects of transformation. It will be hollow as well unless that change will give us other people and the world itself more fully. That the hope is not hollow in any such sense represents part of the thesis implicit in the idea of futurity: to live for the future is to live in the present as a being not fully determined by the present settings of organized life and thought and therefore more capable of openness to the other person, to the surprising experience, and to the entire phenomenal world of time and change. It is in this way that we can embrace the joy of life in the moment as both a revelation and a prophecy rather than discounting it as a trick that nature plays on spirit the better to reconcile us to our haplessness and our ignorance.

The chief teaching of this book is that we become more godlike to live, not that we live to become more godlike. The reward of our striving is not arousal to a greater life later; it is arousal to a greater life now, a raising up confirmed by our opening up to the other and to the new. A simple way to grasp the point of my whole argument, from the vantage point of this its middle and its center, is to say that it explores a world of ideas about nature, society, personality, and mind within which this teaching makes sense and has authority.

False Escape

The whole problem of human life consists in this: how are we to respond to this our situation in the world without allowing ourselves to be overwhelmed by despair and defiance and without delivering ourselves to diversions that kill time by belittling us and by making us die many small deaths while we continue to live? How can we, in the face of this enigma and this terror, purify ourselves through simplicity, enthusiasm, and attentiveness, and make ourselves more godlike through openness to the other and to the new?

Against the backdrop of the disproportion between nature and humanity, we must develop a human world capable of sustaining itself. We must decide whether to accept the alienness of nature as a precondition of this enterprise or to escape and deny it.

There are two main forms of escape and denial. One is a dead end, inimical to our interest in life and to our stake in the construction of the human world. The other, although beset by illusions that may become misdirections, can help in that construction.

One form of escape is the denial of the truth—at least of the ultimate reality—of distinction and change. We assert the all-consuming reality, the eternity, and the oneness of impersonal being. The distinctions and changes that occupy our experience of the world are unreal, or enjoy a derivative, superficial reality as projections of something beneath them.

In our understanding of the world, this path—the path of denial of the reality of difference and of time—requires a fast of the imagination, which is the faculty by which we represent the production of distinction through transformation. The monistic doctrine of the unity and permanence of being, though qualified by a view of how the phenomenal world of distinction and change may participate in the reality of ultimate, unified being, is immune to challenge. At least it is immune to all challenges except those that result from our continuing to live and to perceive as natural beings in a world of change and distinction. As it denies the requirement of life, it is itself lifeless; turning away from experience, it is unable to learn from experience.

In the organization of action, the effort to deny and escape the world of time and difference results in the suppression of the will. To live as a dying organism and a context-resisting self in a world not designed on our scale or in our interest is to be chained to a wheel of insatiable desire. We may seek to escape the painful dialectic of desire and insatiability by casting on ourselves a spell of satisfaction and resignation. We then renounce what we suppose to be the vain objects of desire.

The result, however, is a shrinking of experience. The violence this forced truncation does to our nature betrays itself in two complementary ways: the crankiness of compulsion and the pain of boredom. We undergo the feigned renunciation of desire as a mutilation and a straitjacket even in the midst of our apparent success at making the will passive; it is only by resistance and reconstruction that we live and develop our humanity. We remain restless under the yoke of our vaunted and enforced inaction, feeling as boredom the larger life we have given up. When the spell we have tried to cast on ourselves is broken, we deliver ourselves haplessly to diversion and distraction, seeking variety of our experience when we have ceased to hope for transformation of our world.

There is another familiar way of escaping and denying the indifference of the great world of nature to our human concerns. It is to rely on a secret partnership between us and the forces governing that world. If we imagine those forces as limited powers in our own image, to be pleased and won over, we may succeed in dulling our sense of the alienness of the world from our concerns. We shall do so, however, only by misrepresenting those deified natural powers as privy to our concerns and subject to our constraints. If we suppose the partner to be the ultimate being—impersonal, unitary, and remote—we cannot hope for partnership; only for acceptance, worship, and surrender. We then overcome the strangeness of the world from us only by renouncing our singularity and by suppressing our powers of criticism and resistance.

There is, however, an alternative that has played a decisive part in the moral and religious history of humanity. We may believe our human experience to be placed in a larger context, of creation and love, radically removed from our affairs and yet intelligible to us by analogy to our sense of personality and personal encounter. The analogy points back to the experience of human engagement in finite circumstance and of human transcendence over finite circumstance.

The central theme of this variant of the second way of escape and denial is the penetration and transformation of the world by spirit, as spirit is revealed in the infinitudes within us. What, as dead creed, might seem a refusal to acknowledge the alienness of the world may then become, as living faith, an active hope: hope that the world, at first our world and then the whole world, may change in time and that it will lose its alienness; that it will be lifted up and, as they say, redeemed.

The analogical tie between divine and human reality saves this variant of the second response to the indifference of nature from being mere escape and denial, and explains its historical connection with the great transformative projects—the cause of democracy, the practices of experimentalism, the cultivation of selfhood and subjectivity in the ordinary man and woman—that for two hundred years have brought hope and revolution to humanity. The result is to point us back to the social world and to its reconstruction, but not to show the way: the direction and the next steps.

A conception of mankind recognizing our contingency and finitude but also our transcendence over circumstance and our orientation to the future, can begin to inform our search for a direction. It can do so, however, only after we have refused to conceal the strangeness and indifference of nature to our concerns. The alienness of the world is the reverse side of our humanity. It sets the stage for our work. This work is to sustain a world, our world, capable of generating its own meanings against the background of a vast and meaningless void.

How are we to set about this work? To what ends and in what spirit? If we fail to struggle for a sense of the direction, the established routines of society and culture will dictate the direction for us. We shall then be reduced to acting as if we were the automata that we in fact are not. Acquiescing in our own enslavement, we shall not begin the effort to make ourselves great and free. Consequently, we shall not be in a position to give ourselves to one another, or even to cooperate more openly, except insofar as the preordained scripts of our society and culture tell us how to work together.

Will and Imagination

We can begin to form an impression of the way forward by considering the role that the will and the imagination should play in opening it. The imagination does its work of double displacement: the displacement of distance and the displacement of transformation. It enables us to grasp the situation by having us let go of it: by representing it first as absent and then as changed. Through this double work, it informs and inspires the will. The will supplies the practical interest—the interest in resistance and reconstruction—on which the imagination can go to work.

The product of the joint work of the will and the imagination is to give us a world we can make our own: a world that is not irretrievably foreign to our concerns. Nevertheless, this happy union of the will and the imagination begins to dissolve as soon as the imagination ceases to shadow our actions and reaches beyond the phenomena that these actions can touch. Through experiment, made possible by the tools of science, we can augment, fitfully and for a while, the region of reality that the will and the imagination, working together, are able to reach.

However, the imagination is doomed to outreach the will, even the will magnified by the contraptions we devise. As it leaves the scene of action and will behind it, it loses its power to rob reality around us of its strangeness. It ceases to help in shaping a human world, sufficient unto itself, and within our power to treat as a projected part of our selves or as a friendly backdrop to our endeavors.

The marriage of the will and the imagination is an intrinsic and central feature of our first nature, our natural constitution, even before it is remade by the second nature we receive from society and culture. It takes on its full measure of effect in the light of the two-sidedness of the mind: at once modular and formulaic, and totalizing, transcending, and surprising. It gives us a first hint of the path to take in dealing with the indifference and the inhuman vastness of nature. The direction is to open a clearing, penetrated and reshaped by us, within which we can be and become ourselves, unshaken, unseduced, unterrified.

There are three great domains in which we can and must take this direction: our understanding of the world, our relation to other people, and our struggle with our own rigidified selves: our characters, routines, and habitual perceptions. In each of these domains, the effort to give ourselves a world we can accept, and in which we can accept ourselves and one another, comes up against intractable contradictions. In each instance, the combination of our intentions with our circumstances prompts us to act in two seemingly divergent and conflicting directions.

What we achieve by moving in one of these directions is radically insufficient unless combined with what we can obtain by acting in the other. We need the results of both directions to be and become ourselves, to make ourselves greater and freer. However, we do not know how or whether we can have them together, reconciling what seems irremediably opposed. As a result, an immense unhappiness, generated by the lasting disharmonies of experience, overshadows our lives. In what sense and by what means are we entitled to hope that we can overcome this unhappiness?

The Manifest World and Hidden Reality

To live and to act successfully, we must contend with the manifest world. It is more than an impulse successfully to assess opportunities for action and obstacles to action that drives us. It is also the desire to "save the appearances," to enhance and to deepen the visionary immediacy of the world of change and distinction in which we live.

If the phenomena of the manifest world were at best an allegory made useful by the guides to successful initiative that we were able to infer from it, our lives would pass among shadows, like a race of men and women unaided by any of the five senses and guided only by computers. These computers would instruct them on how to use things and how to move among them. They would not, however, tell these deaf and blind people what this furniture of the universe was actually like. We would remain imprisoned within a delusion, made tolerable only by our shared powerlessness to escape it and by its demonstrated utility in our efforts to inform behavior and to solve problems. We would make our sightless way through a manipulated but unimagined world. Only our ignorance of our situation, our vain diversions, and our half-awake efforts to postpone death could then dull our sense of the world's strangeness and reconcile us to our hopeless exile within it.

The effort to achieve or to regain visionary immediacy—to hold the manifest world, with all its wealth of difference and change, in the mind—is not, however, enough. It is not enough to enable us to act transformatively; it leaves shut the door to our causal investigation of reality and of its transformative variations. It is not even enough to support its own goal of saving the appearances; the quest for visionary immediacy degenerates into the union of habitual perceptions with familiar categories and replaces vision with a stare.

For the sake of both causal insight and transformative power—the former, the indispensable basis of the latter—we embark on the scientific investigation of the world. This investigation carries us to orders and magnitudes of reality far removed from the setting of human life, in which imagination can remain wedded to action. Now inquiry leaves action far behind, and with this overreaching begins to draw pictures of the world that can no longer remain in communion with our experience of manifest reality. Or it remains in such communion only by conjecturing a long series of links between those pictures and this experience, explaining, at the end of the chain of conjecture and experiment, how we can perceive the world one way when it is in fact another way.

For all these reasons, the effort to understand more and more of the world causally—including the world remote from the scene of our actions and our lives—is not an endeavor we can refuse. It threatens, however, to move us further and further away from the vindication of the manifest world, raising the specter that our phenomenal experience may, under its light, seem an allegory or a hallucination. The more we penetrate the causal background to this experience, and represent it in the time-resistant language of mathematics, the further away we move from the experienced reality of time, difference, and action.

Moreover, a striking feature of the world revealed to us by our causal inquiries besets all our attempts to fight our way back to the manifest world—the world of our living experience—and to harness the discoveries of science to this project of recovery. This feature is the puzzle about counterfactuals I first presented when arguing for the thesis of no closed configuration of possible states of affairs, in the course of the earlier discussion of the reality of time.

To understand a state of affairs, we must be able to imagine it transformed under a range of conditions. These anticipated or real transformations pose the problem of the constancy of the laws of nature. A change allowed by the laws of nature may change those laws. Indeed, if time is real, sooner or later the laws will change. The struggle for counterfactual insight—the attempt to see what things might become along a periphery of possible next steps around how things are now—presents us with what at first seems to be a conundrum of the understanding. When we imagine a different state of affairs, it is always unclear whether the counterfactual situation merely illustrates an alternative consequence of the laws to whose explanatory force we appeal or whether it implies or foreshadows a change in those laws. As the world changes, the rules by which it changes also change. Thus, what at first appears to be only a riddle for the intellect turns out, according to the doctrine of the reality of time, to be a source of upheaval and transfiguration in the world itself.

Either the laws do not govern everything (the way particular pieces of reality are configured or sequenced, or the seemingly arbitrary constants of nature), and some of what they fail to govern can change them, or they do govern everything, but some of what happens under their rule can change them anyway. The practical consequence of this fork is to diminish the force of the distinction between saying that the laws do and do not govern everything: even if they do, they are not immune to the temporal world. They are less like a Semitic God transcendent over nature than they are like the gods of the Greeks and Romans entangled in the contests and vicissitudes of this world.

If we cannot close the configuration space of the possible states of affairs and bring them all under the regime of a closed and timeless set of laws, we cannot be sure that we shall be able to fight our way back from our flight of causal inquiry to the recovery of the phenomenal world in its visionary immediacy. We shall be unhappy because our consciousness of the world will remain divided between the poetry of experience and the science of nature. Our ability to act successfully in the world will require us to hold on to both that experience and this science, but the truth about the world and about all the situations in it will forever seem sundered between the two. Instead of the whole of our understanding seeming more than the sum of the parts, each of the parts may seem less than the half, its meaning rendered uncertain by its uncertain relation to the other half.

There is an aspect of our mental life in which we enjoy such a reconciliation. However, its presence there instead of reassuring us ought rather to arouse and disturb us all the more. It should do so both by suggesting what we lack in the remainder of our conscious experience and by implying that the reconciliation is a mirage, never to be grasped. This part of our experience is dreaming. Dreams regularly join two features, the combination of which eludes us in our waking lives: counterfactual insight and visionary immediacy.

In a dream, some things are different from how we met them in the waking world. However, we dream as if we understood effortlessly the changed rules according to which the changed things happen in the changed world. If some of the phenomena of the dream world differ from the phenomena of the waking world, the laws by which they were produced and by which they persist must also differ. A premise of the dream work is that we already know how they differ; this knowledge is implicit in that work.

In a dream, the manifest world can appear to us in its full glory, with a degree of presence and particularity carrying conviction. The counterfactual sleight of hand of the dream work gives us the particulars; we have in our grasp, with irresistible immediacy, a reality whose workings we also seem to understand. Having, or appearing to have, this combination when we dream, we lose it when we awake. Our understanding remains divided against itself, and unhappy. We cannot dream without overcoming this division by renouncing our wakened powers.

The Conflict between the Enabling Requirements of Self-Possession

The second space in which we must undertake the work of making a world for ourselves that can sustain meaning and value in the midst of tremendous and impassive nature is our relation to other people. Here too we find that the task seems to require us to move in divergent and contradictory directions.

We need one another. Our need is pervasive: it goes all the way from the material sustenance of individual life by means of the division of labor and the reproduction of the species through sex and child-rearing to the exchange of recognition and acceptance. The personality exists, develops, and thrives only through the multiplication of connections to other people.

Every entanglement in such a set of formative bonds, however, also poses a threat. It is a threat of subjugation: that the price of connection may be dependence and submission. It is also a threat of loss of self-direction: that the cost of connection will be living out our lives under the guidance of collective scripts telling us how, in our assumed roles, to think, feel, speak, and act.

We need others, and we need to be apart from them, to achieve self-possession while imagining and accepting other people and being imagined and accepted by them. We move uneasily back and forth, between distance and closeness, and wonder whether we can hope for something better than the middle distance.

We face a conflict between the enabling conditions of self-construction. This conflict makes us less free and less great. It diminishes and enslaves us. It jeopardizes the effort to annul in our experience of society the terrors of indifferent nature. To contain this conflict, if not to rid ourselves of it, would be to become greater and freer.

There are two incidents of our experience that answer, more clearly than any others, to the idea of overcoming this conflict between the enabling conditions of self-assertion. They are personal love and innovation-friendly cooperation.

The personal love that achieves this result is neither *eros* nor *agape*. It cannot be given, as benevolence, from the protection of superiority, by the higher or the more powerful to the weaker and more dependent. It cannot even be a romantic projection of the self or an idealization of the other person, to suit the self's own needs. It does not float above routine and repetition, as an anti-institutional interlude of pure feeling; it seeks to survive repetition and routine in encounter, and to transform them.

The innovation-friendly cooperation that moves toward this goal moderates the tension between the imperatives of cooperation and innovation. This moderation is a gateway to the practical progress of humanity. Recognizing that both cooperation and innovation are necessary and that each jeopardizes the other, we seek to design the form of cooperation that is most hospitable to permanent innovation. To this end, we must not allow any established scheme of social division and hierarchy to predetermine the ways in which people can work together. The individual must achieve mastery of generic capabilities, and must command instruments and opportunities that do not depend for their possession on holding any particular job. The experimentalist impulse—at once piecemeal in its method and revolutionary in its ambitions—must be diffused through all society and culture.

Understood in this manner, both personal love and innovation-friendly cooperation require that we learn to deal with one another and to see ourselves as context-transcending originals rather than as specialized functionaries of a collective plan we obediently, even unwittingly, carry out. In our real experience, as it has developed in history, they are at best exceptions, limiting cases, regulative ideals. They may show us what is most to be valued, but they are not—at least not yet—the stuff of ordinary experience. They are windows into a world we have only begun to make, and mirrors of a humanity we have barely expressed.

To understand the direction in which they would point us, we must see how the conflict between the enabling requirements of self-assertion relates to another fundamental complication in our experience, and one that has played a major part in the account of our situation developed in the earlier parts of this book. This other complication is our relation to the social and cultural orders we develop and inhabit. These orders make us who we are; we cannot completely separate ourselves from them. However, there is always more in us than there is in them: they never exhaust us. No matter how entrenched they are against challenge and revision, and how successful in reducing us to their agents, we do in the end always retain the power to defy and upset them. They are finite with respect to us. We are infinite with respect to them.

To be free, and to come more fully into possession of ourselves, we must be able to engage in them, even single-mindedly and wholeheartedly. We must also, however, retain—if possible through them but if necessary against them—our active powers of criticism and transcendence.

In historical experience, things are not arranged to facilitate this achievement. Engagement may be surrender. Defiance may be isolation. To have to choose between such surrender and such isolation is to be diminished and unfree. This choice is another conflict between the enabling requirements of self-possession.

The solution would be to form practices and routines diminishing the distance between the ordinary activities by which we reproduce a social world and the exceptional activities by which, little by little and step by step, we change it. Then we could be inside and outside our worlds at the same time. We would learn how to engage without surrendering.

The two great problems of our experience in society—the relation of the self to the other and the relation of self and of humanity to context—come together. Our spilling over all limiting social and cultural orders—a spilling over that reveals the residue of infinity within us—touches and transforms our relations to one another. It is because of this residue that we may be able, in personal love or in innovation-friendly cooperation, to recognize one another and to give ourselves to one another as role- and context-transcending originals. It is because of this residue that our forms of self-bestowal and of evasion are incapable of being circumscribed by any formula.

A sign of the way in which the problem of transcendence—of our relation to our contexts—transforms the problem of connection—of our relation to other people—is our insatiability, including our insatiable desire for recognition and acceptance. We demand from other people—from those we love as well as from those we do not—what no human being can give to another: an unconditional assurance that there is a place for each of us in the world, not just as a dying organism but also as a context-transcending spirit. Nothing and no one are enough.

Our insatiability is an expression of our immensity. It is therefore also related to our elusiveness—to ourselves as well as to others. When Heraclitus said that the soul of another person is a dark continent that can never be visited or explored, he failed to recognize that the imagination, including the imagination of the experience of other people, might have a history, but he recognized the consequences of our immensity for our hiddenness.

This insatiability is not something that we can ever overcome without doing violence to our humanity. If we cast a spell on ourselves to quiet insatiable desire and offer to one another serene and distant benevolence rather than dangerous love, as the ancient and universal teaching of hierarchical order in self and society recommended, we dull insatiability only by dimming life. We poison our relations to one another by denying to one another the acknowledgment of the infinity within. We cannot stop being insatiable—demanding the unconditional from the conditioned—without ceasing to be human.

Nevertheless, the relation between the problems of connection and transcendence is a historical discovery and a political achievement, not just a timeless fact about human nature. Every religious invention affirming the transcendence of spirit, every social conflict shaking up the entrenched divisions and hierarchies of society, every political prophecy of cooperation without coercion and subjugation; and every strengthening of our power to imagine the hidden experience of other people contributes to its advance. Just as the second side of the mind—its powers of nonformulaic initiative, recursive infinity, and negative capability—may come, in greater or lesser measure, to the forefront of our mental experience according to the way society and culture are organized, so the world of society and belief may be arranged to exhibit and arouse, or to conceal and suppress, our insatiability.

So everything about us may be reinvented, not through a sudden and general regeneration but through a continual stretching at the limits: the way we are bored and addicted, or vain and proud. We may form the idea of being bored by forming the idea of being insatiable. We may find the character of our vanity—our dependence on other people's opinions of us—or of our pride—our pretense of indifference to such opinions—transformed by the demand increasingly to be recognized not for something in particular—the performance of an honorable calling or a customary role—but for something general—the pathos of a self that awakens to its own infinity by struggle against its context. Like everything else, the relation between the problems of connection and transcendence is played out in time. Like everything human, it is played out in history.

Now, however, we come to the threshold of another aspect of the self-division that causes our unhappiness. We are not yet, at least not yet fully, these beings who are able to engage without surrendering and to give ourselves to one another in personal love, or to work with one another in innovation-friendly cooperation, as the radical originals we may all wish to be. We are not yet these people. We must remake society and culture so that we can become such people more completely: so that we may realize, in a larger portion of our experience, the forms of experience exceptionally embodied in the limiting cases of personal love and innovation-friendly cooperation. In this way, we can make a world safe for humanity and lift ourselves up. We can make ourselves more godlike.

The commitment to this direction, and the conception of a human being animating this commitment, live in the great projects of democracy and empowerment that for some time now have enjoyed unrivalled authority throughout the world. Nevertheless, the determination to re-shape society in their name remains far from being uncontroversial. On the contrary, it is resisted at every turn. Even among its adherents, its implications for the reorganization of social life are contentious. The resulting disagreements form the stuff of the ideological conflicts of the last few centuries. Those conflicts will not come to an end; they will simply change in content and express themselves in unfamiliar forms.

To progress in resolving the problems of the self and the other as well as of the self and the context, we must reconstruct our world— the social world. This reconstruction, however, will become a fight; the path of advance will always be contestable and contested. The fight may be peaceful or it may be violent. Even its peaceful forms will be full of hurt and danger. Consequently, it will arouse fear. We may hope to diminish its perils by organizing, through democracy and experimentalism, a form of social life open to organized self-revision. However, we shall still be opposed to one another, even in our quarrels over the way collective self-transformation should be arranged as well as over the ends to which it should be addressed and the values for the sake of which it should be suspended or contained. The more we succeed in diminishing the dependence of change on crisis, the more deep-cutting our antagonisms may become.

It is a path we cannot rightly forswear. If we hold back from this contest, not only about ideas but also with other people, we shall fail to soften the twin tensions between the enabling conditions of self-affirmation—the tensions about our relation to other individuals and about our relation to the collective context of arrangements and beliefs. A sign of this failure is that our loyalties and attachments will be tainted by submission, concealing and weakening the powers of defiance and self-reinvention that are intrinsic to our first nature and that should become central to our second nature. At the extreme limit, society and culture will be organized to mix subjugation, exchange, and allegiance in the same relation; the sentimentalizing of unequal exchange will become the characteristic formula of social life.

The ultimate source of division and unhappiness in this realm of our experience is not that the enabling conditions of our self-possession conflict in the ways I have described. We can address this conflict and diminish it over time. Success in diminishing it even supplies a criterion of progress. The source of division and unhappiness lies in the price we must pay for this solution. The price is the need to fight with other people over the way forward. To struggle with these problems is to struggle with one another, when part of what we wanted, and needed, from the outset was reconciliation. How can we reshape without fighting or fight without hurting?

Self and Character

The third domain in which we face the task of building a human world adequate to dying organisms that are also embodied spirit is our relation to the rigidified form of the self in a settled character and in its routines of behavior and perception. We must accept repetition, and we must also make endless war against it.

We must accept repetition, and its codification in a character, because repetition and its codification represent the principles of economy and of integration that are indispensable to the development of a self. To refuse repetition and its expression in a settled version of the self is not to accept oneself. It is to set the stage for an insoluble contradiction between spiritual ambition and everyday life. In the manner of romanticism and of the *via negativa,* the spirit will forever float above the prosaic world, in which repetition must abound for novelty to be possible.

We would then live our lives under the shadow of a mistake: we would wrongly suppose that we can be fully alive only in interludes when we briefly manage to lift the dead hand of institutions and practices, of routines and compulsions, knowing that the hand will soon fall again. We would fail to recognize that we are not limited to replacing some institutions and practices by others; we can devise institutions and practices that, by diminishing the distance between the ordinary moves by which we reproduce them and the extraordinary moves by which we change them, make us greater, freer, and more fully human. More generally, we can change the place of repetition in individual and social life, and turn it, at great cost and by slow, painful steps, into a condition of invention and transcendence.

In reducing ourselves to a routine version of our selves, we cease to be fully human. We make ourselves little, and we begin to die. We deny the attribute of transcendence over every finite determination that is the condition of embodied spirit. As a result, we lose our grip on the means with which properly to grasp, much less to solve, the problems presented by our relation to others and to our contexts. To find something better than the middle distance in our relation to others, we must be able to experiment with ourselves. To seek change in our relation to the collective settings of arrangement and belief, we must be able to seek change in our relation to our own characters and habits. We cannot move our world if we remain ourselves unmoved.

Here then is yet a third source of division and unhappiness in our experience, and another obstacle to our self-possession. To say that we must both embrace our characters and habits and be able, from outside or beyond them, to destabilize and transform them, is not a solution. It is only the name of a solution. It would be vital to form a certain idea of the self as contextual and yet transcendent over context. However, it would also be necessary to live in a certain way, deliberately placing oneself in circumstances that would weaken the protections of habit and destabilize the stratagems of character, with a hopeful and patient availability to what might come and a consciousness that what could come might be disappointment and heartbreak.

This work of self-reinvention could be supported by an organization of society that gave everyone equipment and protection, loosening the constraints of dependence and incapacity and attenuating the distractions of fear. It could be inspired by a culture that established at its center an ideal of heightened vulnerability accepted for the sake of self-transformation and self-transcendence. However, we cannot wait for this work to be accomplished in the long time of history because we live only once, right now.

Historical and Biographical Time

These three causes of division and unhappiness in our experience allow and require a response. The response is to reorganize society and culture in a particular direction. The result, however, is not a solution, at least not a satisfactory solution, for the individual who must live his life within the brief span of the years allotted to him; it is at best a solution for the species in the long run of history.

That the existential problem allows of a political solution—to the extent that it can be solved at all—is clearest with respect to the second of the three domains discussed in this chapter. How could we begin to overcome the conflict between the enabling requirements of self-affirmation: to be connected to others, and yet not to pay, for this connection, the price of subjugation and depersonalization; to be able to engage in a particular society and culture and yet not to surrender to it our powers of resistance and transcendence? And how could we struggle with other people, as we must, over the forms that such change should take without forfeiting our chances for reconciliation with them? Only by changing the background conditions of social life.

There seem at first to be no answers that an individual could give, within the span of his own life, to these questions, only political answers, to the extent that there are answers at all. These political answers demand the cumulative revision of the terms of our life together. In the next part of this book I discuss the attributes and requirements of such a generalized, ongoing practice of social revision.

As society comes to be reformed and re-imagined in the direction marked by this practice of self-discovery and self-revision, we gain a better chance of engaging without surrendering and of connecting with other people without renouncing the affirmation of the self. As a result, we also have less need to fight—to fight with others—to become ourselves.

That we can address the other causes of division and unhappiness in our experience by reshaping society and culture may seem less clear. Yet we can.

For the individual to have a better chance of forming a set of routines of behavior and of perception that he can nevertheless shake up, he must live in a society that makes him both secure and capable, that expands his opportunities to experiment with the possibilities of life and that prevents him from playing the part of the mouthpiece to a script he never wrote and barely understands. He must live in a culture whose practices and discourses turn against themselves, and shorten the distance between the reproduction of the existent and its reorganization.

For the mind to maintain its grasp on the manifest world while freeing itself from the union of habitual perceptions with familiar categories, the individual must live in a culture that progressively dissolves rigid contrasts between science and art as part of a more general effort to make relative the distinctions among methods of inquiry, and that uses its science and its art to deepen and refine, rather than to suppress and subvert, our experience of the reality of time and difference. He must live in a society committed to arouse and to equip in the whole of the people, rather than only in an elite of visionaries, the powers of imagination.

Solutions to the problems of our division and unhappiness that require the long-term reshaping of society and culture are, however, in a sense not solutions at all. They take place in historical time. We live in biographical time and are dead before they become more real.

The contrast between historical and biographical time—between what the species and what the individual can achieve—threatens to reestablish within the human world the disproportion between indifferent nature and fragile humanity. What good does it does it do us to develop a world, our own world, capable of sustaining its own meanings over the void, if we can do so only on a time scale that is not the scale of a human life? If we try to make ourselves into the sacrificial instruments of a collective project of transformation, we risk becoming not only enemies to ourselves but also dangers to humanity. The real, embodied self, with its recalcitrant interests and its limitations of vision, will fight back, manipulating to its own advantage the pretense of sacrificial magnanimity.

The answer, to the extent that there is an answer, lies in a translation that is also a prophecy. The individual must translate the collective hope into a way of living right now. For example, he must learn to imagine and to treat others as the context-transcending beings and the radical originals they can become. In the midst of his fighting, he must allow himself to be entranced by some of these others. He must rebel against the strictures of science and art, demanding and foreshadowing in the imagination what they are not yet able to deliver: the reconciliation of visionary immediacy with causal probing. He must treat repetition as an incitement to do what is not yet repeatable. In all these ways he must live for the future—both the long future of humanity and his own short future—as a certain way of living in the present as a being not fully determined by the present circumstances of his existence.

The Prophecies of Art

We have a sign that this direction for the change of individual and collective existence is no mere speculative fantasy; that it has a basis in the same realities of existence that are also the sources of our self-division and unhappiness. This sign is the place of art in our lives.

Art is a promise of happiness. According to its content and to the level of its hope, it is a promise of two different types of happiness: the happiness of wholeness and the happiness of resolution. A tragic work of art does not show us a way to overcome our self-division, but it does show us how, by largeness of vision and of action, we can hold on to both sides of each of the divisions besetting our experience. We can resist becoming half of a human being; we can remain whole. A comic work of art promises us more than wholeness: the overcoming of the divisions, their reconciliation in a transformed life. If the alternative to the perennial philosophy for which I argue in this book is justified, comedy is indeed deeper or truer than tragedy.

Forget, however, about the content of particular works of art and look only to their form, and to the practice of making art and engaging with it, in any form. You will see then that art by its very nature, and regardless of the tragic character of its content, embodies the larger hope—the hope of resolution—and turns this hope into a form of vision. It is hopeful even when it seems to be despairing. Each type of art, according to its medium, is hopeful in a different way.

Music is a prophecy of our power to accept ourselves by accepting repetition while making ourselves free and great by defying repetition; it is an incantation, an exulting, an arousal produced entirely out of a dialectic between the repeated and the divergent in sound. Repetition ceases in music to be a prison-house; it becomes, as it should be in our experience, the condition of the new. What seems a remote exploration of consonance and dissonance expresses a hope that is central to our humanity.

The visual arts are a prophecy of our power to reconcile the imagination of the manifest world of distinction and change with the discovery of hidden structure; their universal theme is the depth of the surface. To cling to the surface of things or of their perceived qualities and yet to see into this surface, representing what is absent and imagining it transformed, is what we hope for in the visual arts.

The spoken and written arts are a prophecy of the power of each of us to connect with other people without renouncing his distinct experience and unique voice. Even when they are tragic in content, seeming to despair of resolution, they supply a kind of resolution in their making. The connection of the author or the speaker to the readers or the listeners affirms the hope that their communication can become more than an exchange of self-projections and reciprocal misunderstandings; he and they can escape imprisonment in their own consciousness.

No conception of human life can ring true that fails to make sense of these prophecies. No project for the transformation of human life should command authority that fails to suggest how we can begin to act on them.

9

Society

The Perpetual Invention of the Future

We are not yet fully the beings who not only transcend their contexts but also make contexts that recognize and nourish this context-surpassing capability. We must make ourselves into such beings. To do so is the work of democracy. More generally, it is the task of a direction of reform, in society and in thought, by which we shorten the gap between our context-preserving and our context-transforming activities. Once we have gone far enough in this direction we produce the permanent invention of the future—of alternative futures. To serve as the operational ideology of such an enterprise is the chief practical responsibility of an unshackled pragmatism.

To be fertile and realistic, this reform activity must connect with an actual development: one that embodies the project that most resembles and foreshadows the idea of such a direction of change—change in the very character of our relation to the organized settings of our life and thinking. There is such a project. Its institutional and conceptual expressions remain steeped in the accidents of history—the history of institutions and the history of ideas. It is rich in ambiguity and indeterminacy. We can steer it in directions that are either more inclusive and experimental or more restrictive and dogmatic. Its outcome is the outcome we shall manage to give it, but our future is no longer separable from its.

Call this project experimentalist cooperation. It is rooted today primarily in businesses and in schools—the best businesses and the best schools. However, its reach extends outward to the organization of politics and of culture.

Experimentalist cooperation is an innovation-friendly way of carrying out practical tasks characterized by the following features among others.

A first trait is softening of the contrast between supervisory and implementing roles. Tasks are redefined as they are executed, in the light of newly discovered opportunities and constraints.

A second attribute, closely linked to the first, is relative fluidity in the definition of the implementing roles themselves. There is no rigid technical definition of labor.

A third mark is ability to move the focus of new effort, as far as practical constraints may allow, to the frontier of operations that are not readily repeatable because we have not yet learned how to bring them under a formula. Whatever conceptual or practical moves we can formulaically repeat we can also in principle embody in a machine. We quicken movement between the repeatable and the not yet repeatable, using the mechanical embodiment of the former to save time and energy for the latter.

These first three characteristics make it possible for the practical dealings among the parties to experimentalist cooperation to embody the relations among the component parts of practical reason itself. The experimental decomposition and recombination of tasks translates into the organization of work all the variations of analysis and synthesis. Experimentalist cooperation amounts to a species of the effort to turn society into a mirror of the imagination.

The next two aspects of this practice suggest the character of the social dispositions most important to its workings.

A fourth property is willingness to combine and to superimpose, in the same domains, cooperation and competition. Under a regime of cooperative competition, for example, people compete in some respects while pooling resources, ideas, or efforts in others. As a result they moderate, even if they cannot overcome, the tension between economies of scale and flexibility of initiative.

A fifth sign is a predisposition for groups engaged in experimentalist cooperation to reinterpret their group interests and identities as they go along—and to expect to reinterpret them—rather than to take them as given.

Here is an approach to working together that the Smithian pin factory or Fordist mass production cannot adequately represent. From the vantage point of the vision of productive opportunity informing this approach, Smith's pin factory and Ford's assembly line represent limited and limiting variations, justified only under certain conditions and increasingly unsuited to the conditions of innovation-oriented economies and of the societies and cultures in which they exist.

The most familiar home grounds of this set of practices today are the advanced, knowledge-intensive firms and schools. It is from them that we increasingly expect novelty and wealth. The worldwide network they have begun to form promises to become the commanding force in the global economy. Yet such vanguards remain weakly linked to the rest of the economy and society: even in the richest countries, the vast majority of people remain excluded from them and have no prospect of joining them. The vanguards depend for their vigor on special conditions—for example, traditions of independent craft labor or of high educational endowment, community organization, and good government—that are missing in most of the world.

The two great devices available to redress the unequal and exclusionary consequences of the divisions between these vanguards and the economic and social rearguards surrounding them—compensatory redistribution through tax and transfer and political support for small, family-based property and business—are not enough. They attenuate a division they are unable to remake or to replace. Their work is to humanize the supposedly inevitable. They leave society divided. The vast masses of ordinary men and women are denied the arrangements and the endowments that would develop and tap their energies.

What is required to overcome this division rather than just to counteract, weakly and selectively, some of its consequences? We need to recognize that this advanced experimentalism is simply the most recent and the most extreme version of a broader range of cooperative and experimental capabilities. It is on their possession and propagation that the practical success of nations has increasingly come to depend.

Some countries seem to succeed at both market-oriented and *dirigiste* arrangements. They demonstrate an ability to move among such arrangements as circumstance requires or suggests, as if the institutional models they adopt, discard, and combine were so many masks to be worn according to occasion. Other countries have made a mess of both *dirigiste* and market-oriented approaches. They have not managed to remedy their failures in one of these directions by moving in the other one.

The familiar institutional and ideological disputes of the last two hundred years, with their single-minded focus on state and market as opposing mainstays of economic organization and economic growth, fail to capture something important about the requirements for making a practical success out of social life. What they fail to capture goes to the argument about the conditions and the advantages of the permanent invention of the future.

Some regimes of cooperation are more hospitable to innovation—technological, organizational, social, and cultural—than are others. They moderate the tension that inevitably exists between the imperatives of cooperation and innovation that are central and pervasive to all practical activities, including the production and exchange of goods and services. The experimentalist cooperation described earlier is only a step in a direction and a subset of a larger, open set of practices diminishing the interference between the mutually dependent imperatives of cooperation and innovation.

Certain ways of organizing society and education favor movement in this direction while other ways discourage it. Helping to reconcile the imperatives of cooperation and innovation, they also enable societies to shift according to circumstance among different institutional and policy orientations, with similar success. No society is condemned to remain at its present level of comparative disadvantage in the possession and diffusion of the capabilities that such practices make possible. Every society can go about reorganizing itself to master them more fully and to reap their benefits.

Consider the following three conditions, each of them rich in institutional content and consequence, that help societies achieve such a mastery, propagating throughout our social experience a power of revision and transcendence. They are at once demands and attributes of a generalized democratic experimentalism. They are not simply the social basis for the strengthening and spread of innovation-friendly cooperation; they are also the favored instruments of a political response to the problem, discussed in the previous chapter of this book, of the conflict between the enabling requirements of self-affirmation. It is thanks to them that we can hope to develop forms of social life that better allow us to connect with others without renouncing ourselves and to participate in a society and in a culture without surrendering to them.

A first condition is the avoidance of extreme inequalities of opportunity, respect, and recognition, as well as of relentless insistence on equality of resources or results. It is less important that the individual be able to improve his lot (or to see his children improve theirs) than it is that the structure of social division and hierarchy not tightly predetermine how people can work together. What matters is that the social and cultural script guiding the approach to cooperation be openended. Room for maneuver in the business of working together is what counts most.

This goal will require limiting the hereditary transmission of economic and educational advantage through the family. Moreover, it will be incompatible with an entrenched and extreme meritocracy, one that privileges a single hierarchy of talents and concentrates advantages on those who rise in this hierarchy.

Equality of opportunity will be too little: it may be compatible, for example, with a meritocracy that prevents broad-based decisions in the decisions of social and economic life and that places society under the rule of a meritocratic elite. Equality of circumstance, even when reduced to a principle of tolerance for the inequalities that benefit the worst off, will be too much; it will give undeserved priority to an aim that is in fact accessory. The point is to make ourselves, individually and collectively, bigger and freer, banishing extreme and entrenched inequalities because they get in the way of the initiatives by which we raise ourselves up.

No accumulation of entrenched inequalities—whether of opportunities and resources or of respect and recognition—must be allowed to subsist that has as its consequence to deny any group or class the occasions and the means for action and engagement (the principle of agency). Moreover, no diminished individual capacity for action and agency must be left without a compensating effort by society to minister to weakness and to the weak, not just by transfers of money but also by personal care. People must be made responsible for caring for one another (the principle of solidarity). We must lift the grid of social division and hierarchy weighing on our relations to one another.

A second condition is to enhance the capabilities of ordinary men and women, both by safeguarding them against governmental or social oppression and by giving them educational and economic equipment. The grant of such equipment must not depend on holding particular jobs or performing particular roles. It may include, for example, a claim on lifelong education, in both generic practical and conceptual capabilities and specialized skills, as well as on a minimum stock of basic resources or a social inheritance.

An education that prepares the individual both to act and to resist and that supports the progress of innovation-friendly cooperation has distinctive features. It is analytical and problematic rather than merely informative, selective rather than encyclopedic, cooperative rather than individualist or authoritarian, and dialectical (that is, proceeding by contrast of views) rather than canonical. The school must speak for the future rather than for the community or the government. It must recognize in the child the tongue-tied prophet, rescuing him from his family, his class, and his time.

Any set of arrangements for capability-protecting guarantees and for capability-enhancing resources will need to be exempted from the agenda of short-term politics: for example, by being constitutionally entrenched. However, some forms of exemption will be much more rigidifying of society than others; we must prefer those that rigidify it the least, leaving the most openness to experiment and invention.

A third condition is to extend in social life the susceptibility of all arrangements and practices to experimental transformation (the principle of revision). One social and cultural order may differ from another in the degree to which it bars itself against challenge and change, lengthening the distance between the ordinary moves we make within an institutional and ideological framework we take for granted and the extraordinary moves by which we challenge and change pieces of the framework. The more such an order becomes entrenched, the more it disguises itself as a natural object rather than our own artifact; the more it becomes a false fate. The practical consequence is to maximize the degree to which change depends on crisis, enslaving us to our own collective creation.

It is in our interest to move in the opposite direction, adopting practices and institutions that shorten the distance between our context-preserving and our context-transforming moves, diminishing the dependence of transformation upon trauma and denaturalizing the structures of society and culture. This interest applies with special force and precedence to our political arrangements: they set the terms on which we revise all other arrangements and revise their terms of revision.

The revisionist practice should also include innovations in the legal-institutional organization of both the market economy and free civil society. Different regimes of private and social property should coexist experimentally within the same regional, national, or global economy. Economic agents should be as free as possible to move among the regimes according to the nature of their enterprise.

A sign of success in the fulfillment of these three conditions, and most directly of the third, is that we shall have diminished the dependence of change on crisis and brought society and life itself to a higher level of awareness and intensity without the provocation of catastrophe.

These are not simply the conditions favorable to the distinctive capabilities I have labeled experimentalist or innovation-friendly cooperation. Nor should we value them merely because they promote material progress, helping lift the burdens of poverty, infirmity, and drudgery that continue to weigh on mankind. At one level, they form part of the basis for our advance in giving a political and collective response to the fundamental conflict between the enabling requirements of self-affirmation. At another level, they support the public culture of an inquisitive democracy, within which the concerns and ambitions of an unchained pragmatism have the best chance of flourishing. They lift plain humanity up, increasing our power to find light in the shadowy world of the commonplace and to discover constructive genius in the abilities of ordinary men and women.

However, they will not do so automatically and necessarily. They will do so only if these arrangements and conditions are combined with the development of the institutions, the practices, and the spirit of a high-energy democratic politics. Such a politics will be organized to favor the rapid resolution of impasse, the sustained engagement of the citizenry, the expanded testing, in particular places and sectors, of alternatives to the dominant solutions in national life, the generalization of a form of social inheritance guaranteeing access to capacity-enhancing endowments and immunities, and the targeted breakup of whatever instances of entrenched disadvantage and exclusion people are unable to escape by the forms of economic and political initiative that are available to them.

The deepening of democracy must now take place on a global scale. In a world of democracies, the value of difference among nations and of national sovereignty is to develop the powers and potential of humanity in different directions. Not only is there no natural form for human life; there is also no definitive institutional and cultural formula for a democracy, a market economy, or a free civil society. The nation-states and regional communities of the world must thus become instruments of moral specialization within humanity.

We are faced with a double paradox in the construction of such a global order. On the one hand, we need difference for the sake of sameness. The development of a common humanity requires the strengthening, not the weakening, of divergent national, subnational, and supranational experiments. Not real difference, open to experiment and compromise, but an impotent and enraged will to difference in the face of the waning of actual difference among nations is the danger most to be feared. As nations come to be more alike in organization and experience, they may hate one another all the more for the difference they want and for the difference they have lost. To endow them with the tools of collective originality is one of the greatest interests of humanity.

On the other hand, we need sameness for the sake of difference. The ability to create difference on the ground of individual rights and democratic empowerment rather than on the basis of fossilized tradition— to make the differences we create matter more than the ones we inherit—may require contemporary societies to pass through a common gateway of democratizing and experimentalist innovations in the organization of politics, economies, and civil societies. In every domain of social life, we now find in the world a narrow range of available institutional options—different ways of organizing the state or the firm, the family, or the school. This institutional repertory is the fate of the contemporary societies; to enlarge the repertory is to rebel against the fate.

Beginning from where we are, however, our first task is to develop the institutions and the practices of a high-energy democracy, a democratized market economy, an organized and independent civil society, and an educational and economic endowment of the individual for resistance as well as for action. The reforms capable of producing this effect may seem similar over a broad range of countries in which they may be enacted. Yet one of their justifications is to facilitate subsequent more radical divergence, on the basis of individual rights and endowments, democratic politics, and generalized experimentation.

This is not a program for an unqualified pluralism of forms of life. It embraces the value of openness but repudiates the illusion of neutrality. It therefore denies the unconditional distinction between the right and the good. It wants a global order that will make the world safe for democracy and experimentalism, containing, counterbalancing, and ultimately undermining all hegemonic power. It proposes a global trading regime that elects as its organizing aim the reconciliation of alternative trajectories of national development within an opening world economy rather than the maximization of free trade. It rejects a principle for the construction of a global economy that would leave goods and capital free to roam the world, yet imprison labor within the nations or within communities of relatively homogeneous nation-states. It insists that capital and labor should win together, in small, incremental steps, the right to cross national frontiers. And it sees in this freedom of labor mobility the most powerful of all equalizing forces and a mainstay of individual freedom: a guarantee that the individual be able to escape the nation into which he happens to have been born and to join another one.

For all its commitment to development through difference, this proposal adheres to a particular vision. It identifies its vision with the strongest material and moral interests of humanity, and it seeks to advance it through an open but qualified set of collective experiments in national life. It sides with the classical liberals and progressives against the liberals and social-democrats of today in two decisive and connected respects.

First, above equality it values greatness—the enhancement of the powers and the experience of ordinary humanity and the proliferation within mankind of strong and contrasting personalities and forms of life. Heroic and aristocratic variants of self-possession—self-deceiving and self-defeating as well as oppressive—must be reinvented in the process of being democratized. Extreme and entrenched inequalities raise an insuperable barrier to this diffusion of power, opportunity, and intensity. However, the quest for a rigid leveling of circumstance is a sorry substitute for such a tapping of energy and such an expansion of personality.

Second, it refuses to restrict its ambitions to attenuating, through social entitlements and compensatory redistribution, the effects of established social arrangements on inequality and exclusion. It insists on reentering, with reconstructive intention, the terrains of the reorganization of politics and of production that twentieth-century social democracy soon abandoned. In this sense, it shares the determination of the classical liberals to advance their project through reform of practices and institutions. However, it insists on the inadequacy not only of the classical liberal institutional program but also of the account of institutions and institutional change that liberals and socialists have shared. It sees as its task the demarcation of a direction, defined by cumulative and piecemeal change, rather than the provision of a blueprint—a direction that becomes far-reaching by the continuance of its experiments rather than by the suddenness and breadth of its impact. Moreover, it presses on both sides of the dialectical connection between reform of our institutions and revision of our conceptions. It brings us to another view of democracy, forming part of another view of ourselves.

We cannot achieve a deepened democracy within a reoriented globalization if we continue to believe that the creation of difference is the problem rather than the solution or to accept the idea that small politics makes for big people. Neither, however, can we reach it through doctrinaire devotion to a wholesale program of institutional reform. We can attain it only through the persuasive reinterpretation of recognized interests.

The most powerful interest throughout the world, in poorer countries as well as in richer ones, is the interest of the vast multitudes of people who aspire to a modest prosperity and independence, dreaming of both a small business and a bigger self. Can this longing be redirected by the transformation of its accustomed vehicles in the institutions of society and the myths of culture? This is everywhere the overriding question before progressives.

They cannot answer this question in the affirmative if they insist on combining theoretical radicalism about redistribution with practical conservatism about institutions. They can answer it in the affirmative only by discovering how to reorganize the practical setting of our lives in ways that open the arrangements and presuppositions of society to challenge and change without help from crisis and calamity. The shared cause of democratic experimentalism and radicalized pragmatism is not to humanize society; it is to divinize humanity—in the life of the individual as well as in the history of the species.

10

Politics

Democracy as Anti-Fate

Democratic Experimentalism

The permanent invention of the new requires that we shorten the distance between the habitual moves we make within our social worlds and the occasional moves by which we remake pieces of these worlds. It demands that we diminish the dependence of transformation on crisis, making change internal to social life and weakening the influence of what came before over what comes next. It assumes that even without the provocation of trauma we can render our daily experience more intense even as we enhance our powers.

It is easier to bring a group of people to order than to bring them to life. The largest ambition of politics is not to help bring them to order; it is to help bring them to life.

In the prosecution of this program, one set of practices has priority over all others: our political practices. They set the terms of revision, and of revision of the terms of revision, for all our other practices. The form of a people's political life that is suited to the program, and to its animating goal of making us more godlike, must be one that frees itself from two familiar oppositions of thought.

The first contrast we need to overcome opposes routine and revolutionary politics. Revolutionary politics would change the institutional arrangements and ideological assumptions of society, at the behest of visionary leaders and energized majorities, in circumstances of national crisis. Routine politics redistributes material and symbolic resources within an institutional and ideological framework it leaves unchallenged, through compromises of interest and of vision, brokered by professional politicians, in circumstances undisturbed by great economic or military danger.

The idea of revolutionary politics, however, is only a myth or at least a limiting case. It is tainted by the prejudice of classical European social theory according to which the institutional and ideological orderings of social life are indivisible systems, whose individual parts stand or fall together. Were this prejudice justified, the political life of a people would be restricted to reformist tinkering when the absence of crisis denied it the opportunity for revolutionary change.

With its fantastical idea of changing the whole, the notion of revolutionary politics becomes in practice an alibi for its opposite: the humanization of an order we no longer know how to reimagine or to remake. In contemporary societies the two main forms of this humanization are compensatory redistribution by tax and transfer and the idealization of law as a repository of impersonal principles of right and of policies addressed to the public interest. Real change in the structure of arrangements and assumptions shaping our conflicts over the resources of political power, economic capital, and cultural authority by which we make the present within the future is always change of part. The real revolutionary politics is revolutionary reform.

It is true that in all modern polities we observe a succession of moments of refoundation and periods of normalization. In the history of the United States, for example, the moments of refoundation were the establishment of the independent Republic, the Civil War and its aftermath, and the time of economic depression and world war in the middle of the twentieth century. Nevertheless, the rhythm of heating up and cooling down is not a natural fact about society; it is a product of the way institutions, practices, and ideas organize the relation between repetition and innovation in the political life of a people.

All past and present polities, including democratic polities, have failed completely to rob the social and cultural order of its mendacious semblance of natural necessity and cracked it open to our powers of recombination and renovation. They have, for example, established an exaggerated and unnecessary association between the safeguarding of individuals against governmental or private oppression and the insulation of the established social life against experimental challenge and revision. To this extent, they have helped produce the alternation of heating up and cooling down that we then mistake for an ineradicable feature of history.

We need to jumble up the categories of reform and revolution. What we should want is a form of political life enabling us to change everything in social life, one thing at a time. It may be gradualist in its method and yet revolutionary in its outcome. It produces an endless stretching and bending that dispenses with ruin as the incitement to change. It allows us to bridge the gap between thinking practically about problems and thinking prophetically about alternatives and to change our contexts, piece by piece, as we do our jobs, day by day.

The second opposition from which we must free ourselves is the contrast between a mythical republic in which political concern absorbs private interest and a disenchanted view of modern democratic politics in which politics expresses and serves material and moral interests formed outside the political realm. There can be no real synthesis between the two sides of this opposition: the second side is real; the first one is merely an idea by which we express our shame at the consequences of the now influential belief that politics must be made smaller if we are to be made greater.

The task is to take the real side—the side of the embodied and situated individual, with his shrinking from the drumbeat of history, with his partiality of interest and of view—and, from that side, to expand the scope of his responsibilities, his sympathies, and his powers. A sign of success in this endeavor would be a simultaneous and connected heightening, in the absence of crisis, of the energy level and of the structural content of politics—its fecundity in the production of experiments and alternatives. A second sign would be the attenuation of the exceptional or ecstatic quality of political life: its distinction from the forms of decision and coordination in our ordinary, daily existence. A third sign would the generalization in society of the experience of effective political agency: of solving collective problems through collective solutions, shaped in the midst of organized controversy and conflict. A fourth sign would be the strengthening, in the minds of large numbers of individuals in many walks of life, of an idea of political life as an antidote to fate and as a guarantee of our ability to engage a social world without surrendering to it.

A politics capable of overcoming these two contrasts in the direction I have described must today be a democratic and experimentalist politics. It must see in democracy the practical, institutionalized expression of faith in the transformative potential of ordinary men and women, in their ability to govern their own affairs and to wrest power away from any class or group claiming privileged access to the means for making the collective future within the social present. But to what kind of democracy does this doctrine point?

The Radicalization of Democracy

Our ideals and interests are always hostage to the institutions and practices that represent them in fact. After the calamitous adventures and conflicts of the twentieth century and the downfall of many of its utopian hopes, humanity finds itself tied to a very restricted repertory of institutional options for organizing each part of social life. These options are the fate of contemporary societies. We can escape that fate only by renovating and enlarging this repertory.

To do so, we must free ourselves from the illusions of false necessity that corrupted the guidance given by social thought to transformative politics: the ideas of a closed list of systems of social organization, of the indivisibility of each of these systems, and of their historical succession under the pressure of law-like forces. We must recapture, from the bottom up and from the inside out, the imagination of alternatives. To this end, we must realize that small institutional variations can exert vast practical effects and that the direction taken matters more than the length of each step.

No part of this work is more important than the reconstruction of democracy, given the role of politics in setting the outer limits for the revision of every aspect of society. Consider five combined sets of innovations, made entirely from the materials of ideas and arrangements that are widely available in the life and thought of contemporary societies. Each reveals a distinct aspect of a general way of thinking about how to make the future within the present. The particulars of any such program are of circumstantial and ephemeral interest. The procedures of thought and the habits of mind informing it may live longer. The direction it takes reveals the way in which a conception of humanity like the one developed in this book can be realized in a practical form of life.

The first set of innovations favors a sustained raising of the level of political mobilization, of popular engagement in civic life. These will be initiatives that reform the financing of politics, that give greater free access to the means of mass communication to social movements as well as to political parties, and that encourage a contrast of clear alternatives in national life.

The principle is to heat politics up, but to do so in an organized fashion rather than by anti- or extra-institutional means; to deny that, we must choose between Madison and Mussolini. It is a principle in direct contradiction to the assumptions of a conservative political science that supposes there to be a fixed inverse relation between the mobilizing fervor and the institutional organization of politics. On the contrary, political institutions differ crucially in the extent to which they encourage and support popular political engagement.

The underlying idea is that of a connection between the level of energy in a form of political life and its fertility in the production of alternatives. The higher temperature renders the structures of social life more liquid. This first set of innovations is thus directly connected to our interest in shaping arrangements that better allow us to split the difference between being inside a social world and being outside it.

A second set of innovations deepens and broadens the accomplishments of the first by combining features of representative and of direct democracy. Direct, participatory democracy, unassisted by representative institutions, does indeed fail to work in large states. Nevertheless, the assumption that direct and representative democracy can or should never mix is a dogmatic prejudice, revealing an impoverished imagination of the potential for reciprocal influence between our democratic ideals and our institutional experiments.

The cumulative incorporation of features of direct democracy into the organization of representative democracy is the most powerful antidote to oligarchy in all its ever-changing forms. It is also the most effective instrument by which to strengthen in the political life of the people the sense of effective individual action, overcoming the sense of the futility of political action and shortening the distance between politics and the rest of social experience.

This embedding of direct democracy in representative democracy can take forms as varied as the engagement of local communities in the formulation and implementation of social policy and budgetary decisions and the use of comprehensive programmatic plebiscites to break impasses between the political branches of government under a system of divided government or to change the course of policy and of law under any system of government.

The animating idea is that action and responsibility produce capacity and hope. They do so not by subordinating or sacrificing private concerns to public devotions but rather by expanding, little by little, the range of our ordinary interests and sympathies, so that they become more penetrating and inclusive. In this way, we rob the structures we have created of their patina of naturalness and necessity. We advance in the effort to dispense with calamity as the midwife of change. We succeed in making change come more from within: from within society and from within us.

A third set of innovations has as its aim to hasten the pace of transformative politics and to facilitate the political remaking of social life by resolving impasse among centers and sources of political power quickly and decisively. A feature of liberal constitutionalism under the separation of powers (as in the American presidential system) is to associate the liberal goal of fragmenting power with the conservative aim of slowing politics down. The result is to establish a table of correspondences between the transformative reach of a political project and the severity of the constitutional obstacles its adoption must overcome. This association is both false and prejudicial to the ambitions of democratic experimentalism. We can uphold the liberal principle while repudiating the conservative one.

For example, under an American-style presidential regime, we might allow the Congress and the president to call for anticipated elections, which, however, would always be simultaneous for both branches, so that the power that exercised this option would have to pay the price of running the electoral risk. Or we might have them refer their impasse to national debate and decision through referendum. By such simple and familiar devices, we could invert the political logic of the regime, turning it into a machine for accelerating transformative politics rather than for slowing it down.

Where there is no separation of powers (for example, under a classic parliamentary system) such innovations may seem unnecessary. Nevertheless, the same effect of naturalizing the social order by weakening the opportunities for its political transformation may result from the practice of striking bargains among powerful organized interests, each of which is effectively able to cast a veto. The solution is then to insist on the first two sets of innovations in this program for the radicalization of democracy. They undermine the oligarchic stranglehold on power. At the same time, in the absence of trauma, they melt down the crystallized understandings of group interests that depend, for their semblance of naturalness, necessity, or authority, on the political demobilization of the people.

The guiding idea is that only the limitations of our arrangements and our insights prevent us from learning how to break power up without sterilizing its transformative potential. To uphold political liberty, we do not need to organize political life so that it is a rehearsal of each party's second-best solutions. The rapidity of a people's political life is an essential virtue: making each moment count as it would in the midst of the crisis on which we would no longer want to rely.

A fourth set of innovations increases in yet another way our power to experiment decisively in a particular direction while hedging our bets. These innovations allow particular places or sectors to opt out of some part of the established rules of law, and to try other rules out. Thus, as a country goes down a path, defined by decisions made in its national politics, such arrangements make it possible to experiment, within a part of its territory or of its life, with another model of its future.

It is a principle only imperfectly realized in conventional federalism: first, because under that regime it takes only territorial form; second and more fundamentally, because different federal units typically enjoy only the same measure of freedom for variation. The point is to increase the extent to which decisive action at the center can coexist with bold deviation in the place or the sector that opts out of the rules. The crucial constraint on this power to opt out is that it not be used to entrench a new form of exclusion and disadvantage from which its new victims are then unable readily to escape.

The informing idea is that politics is not just a registering of preferences; it is a process of collective learning and self-formation. Our ideas about the alternative futures we can make must be tangible if they are to be illuminating and authoritative; we must touch the wound if we are to believe.

A fifth set of innovations strengthens the guarantees and the capabilities of the individual as a condition of our ability to open society up to a more intense experimentalism. Just as no invariant inverse relation exists between room for decisive action at the center and at the periphery, or between fragmenting power and strengthening its transformative uses, so there is no such fixed inverse correspondence between the rights and powers of the individual and the experiments of society. The extent to which the ideals and interests in contest remain incompatible depends on the particular arrangements by which each of them is realized; the task of the practical programmatic imagination is to dissolve tragedy into comedy, distinguishing empirical tradeoffs or tensions from insuperable conflicts.

We can infer the principle at work in this fifth set of innovations from a criticism of the traditional language of fundamental rights. Deprived of its metaphysical superstructure, this language has two elements: a practical instrument and a motivating conception.

The practical instrument is to withdraw certain arrangements from the agenda of short-term politics and give them some immunity against attack. Constitutional entrenchment—the requirement of a superma-jority—to abrogate the rules defining these arrangements is one way to achieve this effect. The bestowal of a halo of ideological sanctity is another.

The motivating conception is best understood as the giving of se-curity and capacity for the sake of larger human possibility. Think of it by analogy to the relation between the unconditional love a parent gives a child, assuring the child a place in the world and the willingness of the child to brave the risks of self-construction; to become if not fearless at least less fearful.

To radicalize democracy, we must not abandon this practical instru-ment or repudiate this motivating conception. We must instead enlarge the motivating conception by reshaping the practical instrument.

The arrangements securing the individual in a haven of protected interests and capabilities represent by definition a constraint on the plasticity of social life. They are, however, a constraint that makes pos-sible a greater, faster breaking of constraints. Without them the indi-vidual would be both too afraid and too incapable. We would sacrifice the aim of bringing people to life to the goal of bringing them to order.

The practices and institutions by which we define and provide such security may rigidify more of social life or less of it. A caste system, entangling as it does the sense of security in the preservation of deter-minate and defined forms of group life, rigidifies more of society than does the classical system of private and public rights with which clas-sical liberalism equated, in the nineteenth century, a free society. Yet this system still equips too little and rigidifies too much. What we want is a set of arrangements standing in the same relation to the classical system of rights that this system has to an idealized regime of caste. The fulfillment of this task requires, in addition to core, traditional safeguards of the individual against governmental and private oppres-sion, both a gift and a rescue.

The gift is the gradual development of a universal principle of social inheritance: that everyone will be able to count on a basic, minimum set of material resources, as soon as the economic progress of society may allow it, in the form of either a social-endowment account on which they can draw or a claim to a minimum income. The minimum, whether as a fund or as an income stream, should vary upward according to the countervailing principles of special compensation for exceptional need and special encouragement, in the nature of added equipment and opportunity, to make use of extraordinary talent.

The rescue is the establishment of a distinct power in the state, designed, financed, and equipped to intervene in those localized citadels of social exclusion and disadvantage from which people are unable to escape by means of the economic, social, and political action that are available to them. To intervene in a particular organization or practice, to invade the causal background from which the entrenched disadvantage or exclusion arises, and to reconstruct this organization or this practice until its participants can stand on their own feet are tasks for which no branch or part of contemporary governments is well suited by reason of either practical capacity or political legitimacy. They must nevertheless become a major responsibility of government under deepened democracy.

The vision informing this fifth set of innovations is that of the transformation of the political life of a people as an incident in the larger project of making ourselves more godlike, as if we go about advancing and revising our recognized interests and our professed ideals. It is part of the process by which we lift the burden of entrenched social division and hierarchy and of compulsive social roles weighing on our relations to one another. It is a lifting up, both through the powers it bestows and through the experiments it helps make possible.

In all these ways it is anti-fate. However, in diminishing the place that social fortune and misfortune have in shaping our life chances, it does not liberate us from the misfortunes for which society is not responsible: the misfortune that results from the fate of our genetic inheritance; from the fate of the accidents and infirmities that beset us; from the fate, at once self-imposed and hard to escape, of our rigidified selves, our characters; and from the fate of the acts of rejection to which we are subject by virtue of our universal need to be rescued by the gratuitous kindness and love of other people. These other forms of fate do not become weaker as we radicalize democracy; on the contrary, they become stronger. We see them more clearly, and we suffer their effects more bitterly, when undistracted by the artificial injustices of the social order.

What we can ask of society is that it not aggravate the consequences of these other forms of fate; that it encourage the diversification of our standards of accomplishment; that having undermined class for the sake of opportunity it then limit meritocracy in the name of a vision of our sharing of that part of fate we cannot overthrow; that it supply means for the development of talent but limit its rewards, not only in the hope that talent will find reward enough in its own active expression but also in the recognition that such limits may impose some loss of foregone achievement; that it nourish our power to imagine the experience of other people; that it multiply chances for engagement and connection; and that it respond to extremes of misfortune with extremes of mercy, affirmed not just through compensatory transfers of resources but also through commitments of time to care directly for others in need, outside the family, as part of the normal responsibility of every able-bodied adult.

What we must ask of ourselves is that, understanding the limits of politics as well as its uses, we not seek in the transformation of society a surrogate for the transformation of the self.

Hope and Strife

These combined institutional ideas do not supply a blueprint; they exemplify the proper work of the programmatic imagination by suggesting a direction and next steps. Not only is the direction controversial; so is any interpretation of how best to take it in the circumstances of a particular country.

The contestable character of the direction results from an ineradicable feature of our political ideas: the impossibility of any complete separation between the vision of the good and the conception of the right, a separation that has been one of the chief tenets of classical liberal philosophy. No form of social life is neutral among the adjacent next steps in the development of human experience (the adjacent next steps being the practical residue of the meaning of the possible). Every institutionalized ordering of social life favors some forms of experience and discourages others. In choosing to take one direction rather than another, we choose to develop human nature in a certain direction: marginally, to be sure, but nevertheless cumulatively and forcefully.

It is a virtue of a form of social life to allow for a broad range of experience and to lay itself open to challenge and change. However, the mirage of neutrality gets in the way of attaining the realistic and connected goals of catholicity and revisability. It does so by immunizing, even by sanctifying, a particular set of institutional expressions of the idea of a free society.

The taking of any direction is a gamble but also an expression of hope. The hope animating this political program appeals to our basic stake in advancing within the zone of intersection among our practical interests in the development of our productive capabilities, our moral interest in emancipating the individual from entrenched social division and hierarchy, and our spiritual interest in building social and cultural worlds that we can inhabit and transcend at the same time. To move forward in the area of overlap among the institutional requirements of these three families of interests, we must renovate and enlarge the restricted repertory of institutional ideas and arrangements to which social life is now held fast.

There is reason to think that the pursuit of these large and fundamental commitments can converge, through institutional experimentation, with the defense of our recognized group interests and professed social ideals, within contemporary societies and cultures. The grounds for this hope lie in two other features of political life: the duality of ways of defining and defending group interests and the internal relation between thinking about interests and ideals and thinking about institutions and practices.

We can always define and defend our recognized group or class interests in two different sets of ways. One set of ways is institutionally conservative and socially exclusive. It presupposes the present niche the group occupies, under the established arrangements, as natural, and it represents the neighboring groups in social space as rivals. The other set of ways is institutionally transformative and socially solidaristic. It treats the niche, and therefore the arrangements underlying it, as revisable, and it sees the neighboring groups as potential allies. It goes from tactical alliances to recombinations of group interests and group identities, on the basis of changed institutions and practices. It is this second set of ways defining and defending group interests that we must ordinarily prefer, seeking to combine the calculus of interests with the vision of alternatives.

Our practices and institutions are not just pieces of social engineering by which we can implement ideals antecedently defined. They are internally related to our understanding of our ideals and interests. Every ideal—social, political, or economic—points in two different directions: to inchoate, ill-defined, transcending aspirations and to a particular, contingent background of arrangements we ordinarily take for granted as the expression of that ideal. When we experiment with this institutional expression, whether in fact or in imagination, we disclose its hidden ambiguities of meaning and its multiple prospects of development through different series of feasible next steps. To master this process, to turn it from being an accident that befalls us into a method we can deploy, is part of the ambition of democratic experimentalism.

We may hope that the advantages of the direction I have described as the radicalization of democracy will prove appealing and even irresistible and that its flaws will turn out to be self-correcting in the light of experience. A hope, however, is a hope, not a guarantee. To proclaim this hope is not to announce the end of history, only its continuation, under the savage and warlike empire of time.

The contestability of the direction has a practical consequence: the permanent potential for conflict and thus as well for a struggle to the death in the form of war. We can hope to contain this strife, to organize it, to spiritualize it, and to render it peaceful for a while. We can quiet the passion of fear that accompanies it as a shadow if we ensure the individual in a haven of protected vital interests and capabilities, while minimizing the extent to which this assurance rigidifies the surrounding social space. We may hope that our power to imagine the experience of other people will increase together with our success in inspiring and equipping ordinary men and women to deepen and develop their imaginative life: the distinctions of subjective experience.

However, we cannot suppress the strife that is intrinsic to political life or guarantee against its escalation into violence. The first reason we cannot do so is that we cannot separate the constitution of the right from the choice of the good: in choosing the direction, we choose what collectively we are to become, and we announce what we most value and what we most fear. The second reason is that no insight can render the choice of the good uncontroversial. The third reason is that the differences among selves are deep and that our interest lies in deepening them despite the dangers of such deepening. The fourth reason is that human desire is relational: our strongest visions and impulses seek expression in shared forms of life, which then come into conflict. The fifth reason is that humanity can develop its powers only by developing them in different directions, whether through the nations and civilizations that have thus far been the chief protagonists in world history or in other forms yet to be invented. These five reasons combine not only to make antagonism a radical feature of political experience but also to render insecure and transitory our providential efforts to contain it.

A democracy reorganized in the light of the five institutional ambitions I have explored splits the difference between citizens and prophets as well as between practical tinkerers and citizens. The conception of political life it proposes is not a crushing of private concern by public devotion; it is rather a pushing outward of the range of our ordinary interests. Viewed in the light of this program, democratic politics is not just one practice among many: it is the counterpart, in political life, to innovation-friendly cooperation. It becomes the activity that most fully reveals and most effectively enhances our power simultaneously to engage and to transcend, denying the last word to the established order and reserving it to ourselves.

11

A Moment of Reform

The Reinvention of Social Democracy

To see what social and political change in such a direction means and what it requires, it helps to explore a particular contemporary experience. The particulars of that experience are of only passing interest. Even now they are changing into other, yet undreamt-of problems. Nevertheless, a democratic experimentalism that draws on a radicalized pragmatism suggests an approach to this ephemeral predicament. This approach illustrates a direction of movement for the reconstruction of society and a way of thinking about its future.

The model of social organization that exercises the strongest attraction all over the globe today is Scandinavian social democracy. It seems that if the world could vote it would vote to become Sweden rather than the United States. The extreme inequalities, the historical exclusions, and the sheer harshness of American society are widely viewed as too high a price to pay, if indeed such a price must be paid, for the material exuberance and the cultural vitality of the Americans. Throughout much of the world, a sugary center-left discourse—promising social democracy to poorer, more backward countries—has become the shared language of would-be progressives.

Paradoxically, however, the prestige of European social democracy has been contemporaneous with the hollowing out of its traditional programmatic core. An unsentimental view of European social democracy, as consolidated in the thirty years following the Second World War, would recognize that it has been defined by six commitments, arranged in three pairs. Different social democracies have developed these commitments in different ways and under different circumstances. They have embraced them nevertheless.

The first two commitments relate to restraints placed on market-driven instability for the sake of enhancing the economic security of certain groups of individuals. Thus, a first principle is the need to protect workers from instability in product and labor markets by granting them something close to a vested right in their present job. More often than not, this principle has been effectively applied to privileged segments of the labor force rather than to all workers. The result has then been a division between insiders and outsiders, helping to account for historically high levels of unemployment.

A second principle has been the defense of the owners of productive assets against instability in capital markets, especially against threats posed by a market in corporate control. The characteristic protective devices have been cross holdings within a network of reciprocally related businesses as well as privileged relations of firms to institutional investors.

The second pair of commitments refers to limits imposed on the power of markets to undermine forms of business organization that are valued for their social as well as their economic consequences. Like the first set of commitments, this second pair implies a trumping of the market economy rather than its cumulative reorganization.

The third principle protects small business, including agrarian smallholdings, against domestic and foreign competition. In many countries, the national government succeeded in making an alliance with the petty-bourgeoisie, an alliance that the nineteenth-century European left had so disastrously spurned. The defense of small business represents the anticipation as well as the vestige of a task that remains unaccomplished to this day: an institutional redesign of the market economy that would respond to the desire for modest prosperity and independence, more "middle class" than proletarian, that is now a worldwide aspiration. Such a reconstruction is needed to wean that aspiration away from its single-minded attachment to isolated small-scale property and to provide it with a less confining vocabulary of practical arrangements.

The fourth principle is the protection of family business, big or small, against competitive pressure: a compromise struck between meritocracy and nepotism. The role assigned to the hereditary transmission of economic or educational advantage through the family reproduces, though in weakened form, the realities of a class society. It also allows the regulatory and redistributive state to reach a compromise with loyalties and energies, rooted in family life, that only political and religious convictions can rival in power.

The last two commitments concern the conduct of macroeconomic policy as it relates to the distribution of income and wealth. According to the fifth principle, a "social partnership" of national and local government, big business, and organized labor should strike deals about the distributive impact of economic policy. Such deals help prevent distributive conflict from interfering with "sound" economic management of the economy and thus with the creation of wealth. Much of the society remains outside the realm of these organized interests; in the negotiation of the Social Contract, the unorganized should be directly represented by government as well as virtually represented by the organized.

The sixth principle is that retrospective redistribution through tax and transfer should be used to maintain a high level of social entitlements available to everyone, in particular entitlements to benefits that diminish the vulnerability of the ordinary working man and woman to economic instability and insecurity. By an apparent paradox, this limited, retrospective leveling through the compensatory programs of a "social market economy" or "welfare state" has been largely funded by reliance on the admittedly regressive device of the transaction-oriented taxation of consumption. The aggregate tax take and the way it is spent have mattered more: a regressive tax may nevertheless support a progressive project if it raises more public revenue for social spending, but with less disruption of established incentives to save, invest, and employ. What is lost by way of the progressive incidence of taxation may be more than compensated by the redistributive social spending a higher tax take makes possible.

This six-point program has been increasingly eviscerated. Social democracy, on its European home ground, has retreated from the first four commitments the better to uphold the last two, or even from the first five the better to defend the sixth. A high level of social entitlements has proved to be the last line of defense. The vaunted synthesis of European-style social flexibility with American-style economic flexibility has been a surrender disguised as a synthesis—a "third way."

Two great interests have collided with this historical social-democratic settlement and worked toward its undoing. The first force has been the interest of the restless and the ambitious among the wealthy or the educated: their impulse to undo the costly strictures of the vested rights entrenched by the protective policies as well as by the "social partnership" of the old settlement. It is this interest that has taken the lead in the hollowing out of historical social democracy. The second force has been the been the interest of the unorganized and the insecure, including millions of unemployed, underemployed, or unstably employed workers with petty-bourgeois identities—the orphans of this regime of prerogative and protection—in disturbing the arrangements that disfavor them. It is this interest that has regularly been denied influence over policy.

The watchword has therefore been more flexibility without more inclusion. This orientation has justified a program that strips away restraints on flexibility without developing devices by which to overcome or attenuate the stark divisions between advanced and backward sectors of the economy. A progressive alternative would demand flexibility with inclusion. However, unlike the program that it would replace, such an alternative could not work within the historical repertory of social democracy. It would need to reinvent the institutional form of the market economy so as radically to democratize access to productive resources. It could not do so without also deepening and redesigning democracy.

Neither the social-democratic settlement as redefined in the long aftermath of the Second World War nor the subsequent winnowing out of this settlement by the pseudosynthesis of European-style social protection with American-style economic flexibility solves the problems of the contemporary European social democracies. These problems can be effectively addressed only by a new set of experimentalist practices and alternative institutions. To develop such practices and institutions would be to take a direction recommended by a democratic experimentalism informed by the radicalized pragmatism for which this book argues. It would also, however, be to upset and to reshape the terms of the practical and ideological compromises that have made social democracy what it is.

Consider three such connected problems. They arise, in one form or another, in every European society in which social democracy has mattered.

The first problem of the social democracies is the narrowness of the social points of entry into the advanced sectors of the economy. The world economy is increasingly commanded by a network of productive vanguards, established in the front tier of the developing countries as well as in the rich societies. These sectors are in communion with one another, trading ideas, practices, and people as well as capital, technology, and services. However, they are often only weakly connected with the rest of the economy and society.

The heart of the productive vanguards has been less the accumulation of capital, technology, or even knowledge than the deployment of a set of revolutionary practices. These are the practices that define experimentalist cooperation, with its weakening of stark contrasts both between supervisory and executing roles and among executing jobs, its fluid mixture of cooperation and competition, and its commitment to the ongoing redefinition of group interests and identities as well as of productive tasks and procedures. The existing productive vanguards, however, ordinarily deploy these practices only by also bending them under the yoke of the inherited regime of property and contract and by making them serve the interests of those who, as owners or managers, effectively control the firms. The development of these practices and their propagation throughout broader sectors of the society and the economy depend in large part on the redesign of their institutional setting.

Two devices have been traditionally available to redress the inequality-producing consequences of the divisions between advanced and backward sectors. One instrument has been compensatory redistribution through tax-and-transfer, ever the pride and now the fragile residue of historical social democracy. The other tool has been the governmentally supported diffusion and protection of small-scale family property and business. Neither approach overcomes the vast inequalities rooted in the hierarchical segmentation of the economy. Both present themselves as constraints on economic efficiency for the sake of equity and on economic growth—at least in the short turn—for the sake of social unity and justice. They fail to anchor their commitments to inclusion and cohesion in the institutional logic of innovation and growth.

Even in the relatively egalitarian social democracies of Europe only a relatively small part of the population is able to gain a foothold in such productive vanguards or in the professional services that assist them. It is nevertheless in these advantaged sectors that wealth and fun are increasingly concentrated.

Under this dispensation, society is divided into four large classes. This class structure coexists more or less peacefully with the merito-cratic principle rather than being undermined by it: the transmission of educational as well as of economic advantage through the family, when combined with the genetic element in the distribution of partic-ular intellectual powers, makes possible the synthesis of meritocracy and class that now characterizes all the advanced societies, It is a syn-thesis that helps circumscribe the reach of democracy and hold the masses of ordinary men and women down.

On top is a professional and business class, anxious to reconcile with the advance of the meritocratic principle the hereditary transmission of educational and economic advantage through the family and aware that its position increasingly depends on its privileged relation—whether direct or oblique—to the advanced sectors of the economy. Beneath this professional and business class is a small-business class, which has taken refuge in a form of economic life antedating the contemporary variants of big business. The white-collar and blue-collar working class continue for the most part to work in offices, shops, and factories char-acterized by the old methods of passive execution of productive tasks they are powerless to redefine. At the bottom is an underclass of tem-porary workers, sometimes racially stigmatized, often legally unprotected, and always economically insecure, who perform dead-end service jobs.

The majority of the people, comprised of the small-business class and the working class, are free from extreme deprivation and insecurity, especially when they live under social democracy. However, they are denied access to the advanced sectors, with all their room for gain, discretion, and invention. They find solace in their families and their diversions.

The most important social consequence of this situation is to redraw the class divisions of society rather than to destroy them. Its most significant moral implication is to deny the majority of working men and women an opportunity to have anything more than an instrumental attitude toward their own work. Its most onerous economic effect is to waste energies and talents on a vast scale, depriving common labor of wings, if not of arms. A byproduct of this denial of opportunity to those who might create wealth is to impose on public finance a burden it cannot long sustain, the burden of compensation by transfers for the consequences of inequalities rooted in the organization of the market economy and in the deficiencies of public education.

The solution both to the basic problem and to its corollary for public finance is twofold. One element of such a solution must be a broadening of opportunity for engagement in the advanced sectors of production: a radical expansion of the terms on which people can have access to the types of education, expertise, technology, and credit that such engagement requires. More access for more people in a wider array of social and economic circumstances is also likely to require more ways in which people and resources can be brought together for productive activity.

Another element of such a solution is the creation of conditions favorable to the expansion of advanced economic practices outside the narrow, favored sectors in which they have traditionally flourished: vanguardism outside the vanguard. Where preindustrial traditions of craft labor and training, so often hospitable to the advance of these post-Fordist practices are missing, they must be substituted by an education emphasizing the development of generic capacities of practical and conceptual capabilities. Where a dense network of associational life and participation in local affairs is weak, inhibiting the higher trust required by experimentalist cooperation, such a network must be created by a combination of public and private initiatives setting the responsibilities, providing the resources, and opening the opportunities around which new examples of association can begin to form. Where economies of scale and scope are important to the success of varieties of flexible, innovation-oriented production more readily suited to small teams than to big firms, institutional arrangements and private-law regimes must be established that make it easier to achieve cooperative competition among private producers—the pooling of resources among teams and firms that otherwise compete.

Such a two-sided solution to the problem of the narrowness of access to vanguards and vanguardism in the economy calls in turn for an enlarged repertory of forms of collaboration between government and private enterprise. The architects of such a reconstruction must not let themselves be forced to choose between the arm's-length regulation of business by government and the centralized formulation of unitary trade and industrial policy by a bureaucracy.

To supersede this choice, they must develop new varieties of asso-ciation or coordination between public and private initiative. Such a partnership must be decentralized to the point of mimicking and even radicalizing the market-related idea of an organized anarchy rather than being imposed from on high. It must be pluralistic, encouraging the experimental coexistence of alternative strategies for production and trade rather than imposing a single one. It must be open-ended, taking as its subject the step-by-step fulfillment of the conditions of productive vanguardism, rather than conforming to a blueprint. And it must be inclusive in the range of its agents and beneficiaries, touching the back-ward sectors of production rather than remaining confined to the ad-vanced sectors.

A renewal of the institutional means by which public and private initiative work together can in turn serve as the starting point for an institutional reshaping of the market economy. Different regimes of contract and property may arise from the varying terms on which government and business work together. These alternative private-law regimes may begin to coexist experimentally within the same democratized market economy. In this way, we may generalize and deepen the liberal-market commitment to the freedom to recombine factors of production within an institutional setting that we take as given, turning it into a greater freedom to recombine and replace pieces of the institutional setting of exchange and production.

A second problem of the contemporary social democracies has to do with the nature and strength of the social bond. Imagine a society and an economy composed of four sectors. The first sector consists in the advanced forms of production and learning, responsible for an increasing share of social wealth and innovation. The second sector is made up of the declining mass-production industries. The third sector is a caring economy in which people take care of one another, and especially of the young, the old, and the infirm, in jobs largely created and paid by the state. The fourth sector is the realm of disenfranchised and unstable labor, peopled by temporary or illegal workers who are foreigners or belong to racial minorities.

A major responsibility of the chastened social state under the present, eviscerated form of social democracy is to collect money from whoever has it—especially from participants in the first sector—and to distribute it to the beneficiaries of social entitlements—particularly members of the third sector. Social solidarity comes down to the movement of checks through the mail. The different sectors are different worlds: people in one have almost no acquaintance with people in the others. The social bond is thinned to the point of breaking. Nothing in common remains other than an idea of a shared past, the sentimentalized afterglow of a national memory.

For social solidarity to become real, the principle must be established that it is not enough for the individual to give up some of his money; he must give up some of his life. Every able-bodied adult should in principle hold a position in both the caring economy and the production system. To his responsibility to care for others, outside his own family, he must sacrifice part if not of a working week or year, then of a working life. Moreover, government must help civil society to reorganize itself so that civil society becomes capable of arranging and monitoring the provision of social service. Then people will become responsible for one another. They will achieve the unmediated, embodied knowledge on which the social bond depends.

A third problem of the contemporary social democracies is the denial to the individual of opportunities to escape the confines of a small life. For large numbers of ordinary men and women in the European home ground of social democracy over the last hundred years, the life-giving escape from belittlement has come only through the deadly ordeal of war. Martyrdom for the nation, its glory and its freedoms, has for many been a way of living for something larger than oneself. Even when dreaded and hated, it has been an escape from routines that dulled and humiliated.

However, this experience of greatness, soaked in blood, poisoned by illusion and deception, and ending in suffering, exhaustion, and disillusionment, has been less an ascent of common humanity to a higher plane of consciousness and nobility than a repulsive proxy for that inaccessible ideal.

Peace brought narcolepsy. The European nations devoted the first half of the twentieth century to slaughtering one another and the second half to drowning their sorrows in consumption. Toward the end of the twentieth century, exhausted by their sufferings and their pleasures, they placed themselves in the care of politicians, entertainers, and philosophers who taught the poisonous doctrine that politics must be little for individuals to become big. Then the peoples of Europe fell asleep. If they later failed to awaken, they might well remain rich. However, they would also be less equal, less free, and less great.

How can society and culture be so organized that large numbers of ordinary men and women have a better chance to awake from the narcoleptic daze, outside the circle of intimacy and love, without having to do so as pawns and belligerents? This same question presents itself in another form, unburdened by the struggle between friend and enemy or by the terrible ambiguities of war. How can an individual born into a small country live a large life? How can the state help him widen the stage on which he can live such a life?

The general answer to all these questions is the development of political, economic, and social institutions and practices that both equip the individual and multiply his chances of changing pieces of the established setting of his work and life as he goes about his ordinary activities. Diminishing the dependence of change on calamity they raise him up; they make him godlike. The specific answer to all these questions is that the state should help the individual not to be little.

Education, beginning in childhood and continuing throughout the working life, must nourish a core of generic conceptual and practical capacities to make the new out of the old. It must also equip the mind with the means with which to resist the present. For this very reason, the school should not remain under the control of the community of local families, who tell the child: become like us. Nor can it be the passive instrument of a central educational bureaucracy, which delivers the child from these influences only to subjugate him to a universal formula. Relying on multiple supports and responsive to multiple responsibilities, it must also play them off against one another the better to open up the space in which collective memory serves individual imagination.

What the school begins the state should continue. It must help provide the individual with the economic as well as the educational means with which to take the initiative anywhere in the world. A small, rich country, for example, can set out deliberately to transform the nation into an international service elite. And when the whole world becomes the theater of individual initiative, from business to charity and social activism, the tenor of national life changes as well; global experience and large ambition are refracted back into the homeland.

These three characteristic problems of contemporary social democracy have in common that they do not yield to the regulatory and redistributive policies that have shaped the social-democratic program. Social democracy defined itself by its renunciation of the attempt to reorganize production and politics. Retreating from these two terrains, it developed what seemed to be an impregnable position within the sphere of distribution or redistribution. The present hollowing out of social democracy in the name of the reconciliation of social protection with economic flexibility has only confirmed the logic of this retreat. Now, however, it turns out that social democracy cannot solve its problems and preserve its life unless it returns to the two terrains from which it withdrew at its formative moment.

It cannot solve any of these problems without innovating in the institutional form of the market economy. It cannot democratize the market, without deepening democracy: that is to say, without creating the institutions of a high-energy democracy facilitating institutional experimentation and mitigating the dependence of change on crisis.

The real social force that can propel such a transformation, even in the absence of great economic or political catastrophes, is the desire of the masses of ordinary working people, locked out of the islands of advanced production and learning, to be admitted. They cannot, however, be let in, nor can more technical and economic plasticity be reconciled with more social inclusion, unless we begin to change the whole structure. We can change the whole structure piece by piece and step by step. We do not need, and should not want, a blueprint. All we require is a clear conception of the direction and a rich set of provisional conjectures about what next to do.

Experimentalist cooperation, with its loosely defined but exacting conditions, is both a means and an end, a method and an outcome. However, it remains blind until it is informed by a contest of programs, each of them suggesting a direction and a series of next steps. Radicalized pragmatism becomes transformative politics.

12

Religion

The Self Awakened

The Problems of Connection and Transcendence Restated

Only a fool would consult an abstract doctrine for clear, comprehensive, and reliable instruction about what to do with his life. The question—How should I live?—is nevertheless one to which a philosophy giving primacy to the personal must speak. The argument of this book draws on a conception of the self—the same conception motivating these ideas about the permanent creation of the new in society. This conception of the self suggests an attitude to some of the central problems of life, although it is unable by itself to generate or to support a developed moral vision. It provides neither a detailed description nor an authoritative defense of a course of life. It nevertheless points in a particular direction.

In thinking about the enigmas and longings that are central to our lives, we face two recurrent, pervasive, and overlapping problems: the problems of connection and transcendence. They are already implied in the conception of the self with which this argument began, and they came to the surface when the argument turned on its hinge, from conception to orientation.

The problem of connection is a conflict between the enabling conditions of selfhood. We need other people—practically, emotionally, and cognitively. Our need for them is unlimited and insatiable; we experience everything they do for us as a down payment on a transaction that cannot be completed. We build a self through connection.

However, the jeopardy in which other people place us is also unlimited: their existence, beyond every particular conflict of interest and of wills, puts constant pressure on ours. So we move toward them and then back away from them, oscillating between closeness and distance. Often we settle into an anxious middle distance.

Freedom as self-possession would be to resolve or to moderate this clash between the enabling requirements of self-assertion. Our most convincing experience of such a reconciliation is personal love. In its fullest expressions, personal love offers an experience of imaginative recognition and acceptance of another as a radical individual. Only with difficulty, however, does this experience gain broader purchase on social life beyond the reaches of our most intimate and all-encompassing encounters.

The problem of transcendence is a contradiction between two sets of demands we place on the organized social and cultural worlds in which we move. We cannot find a definitive setting for our humanity—a natural space of society and culture accommodating all that is worth doing, feeling, and thinking. There is no such natural space. There are only the particular worlds we build and inhabit.

These worlds make us who we are. They shape us. However, they never shape us fully. A residue of unused capability for action, association, passion, and insight worth having is always left over. There is always more in us than in any such context or in any retrospective or prospective list of contexts. In comparison to them, we are infinite; pushing up against their limits, we discover there to be more within us.

The realization of our recognized interests and professed ideals therefore forces us in the end to go beyond what the established framework allows. As we begin to do so, the specious clarity of our interests and ideals begins to fade. We discover that their apparent clarity depended on their association in our minds with conventional practices and familiar arrangements. Thus, the churning of the contexts is accompanied by fighting within each of us and among all of us, and when among us, by every means from conversation to war.

Our humanity as well as our particular interests and ideals require us to resist and to fight. Through all this experience, we face a conflict between two conditions of our humanity that are just as important as the conflicting demands we place on connection. We need to engage in a particular social and cultural world. Freedom comes from engagement as well as from connection. However, every such engagement threatens to become a surrender: to reduce us from authors to puppets. Thus, we seem forced to choose, at every turn, between an engagement that both frees and enslaves us and a holding back, by mental reservation if not by outward rebellion. This holding back preserves our independence only by wasting its substance. Engagement, wholehearted if not single-minded, without surrender, is what we need.

So it is that we come to conceive the ambition of changing the basic character as well as the particular content of the contexts of institutions and beliefs against which we must always finally rebel. We seek to build a world so organized that there is less of a discontinuity between being inside it and being outside it, between following the rules and changing them. To the extent we succeed, we are able not only to realize more effectively our particular interests and ideals but also to develop more fully our humanity. Our world becomes less of a place of exile and imprisonment. It bears more clearly the mark of infinity.

The problem of transcendence is implicated in the problem of connection. Our power to reconcile our infinite need and longing for other people with containment of the jeopardy in which they place us remains limited in scope outside the privileged domain of personal love. The best we can ordinarily achieve is to organize the middle distance. Even in the freest and most prosperous of contemporary democracies, we continue to do time as indentured servants to a compulsive scheme of social division and hierarchy and to a stereotyped allocation of social roles.

We cannot give ourselves to one another as full individuals beyond the frontiers of personal love because we have not yet made ourselves into such individuals. To allow us to do so is part of the work of experimentalist cooperation and of high-energy democracy. They equip the individual with greater and more varied capabilities. They strengthen his freedom from the inherited tropisms of culture and the automatisms of society. They make possible for more people, over a wider terrain, the magnanimity of the strong.

The problem of connection is implicated in the problem of transcendence. It is implicated both as a condition and as a goal. Just as a child is better able to run the risks of self-construction if it knows itself safe in the love of its parents, so are men and women better able to challenge and change pieces of their context if they are secure and strengthened in their connections to others as well as in their basic rights and abilities. And the freedom we acquire through the permanent reinvention of the future and the qualitative transformation of our contexts would be too harsh and dehumanizing a goal, too narrowly and dangerously heroic an ideal, if it did not promise a basis on which to connect more fully and productively with other people.

How We Encounter These Problems in the Course of a Life

The problems of connection and transcendence present themselves under disguise in a characteristic sequence over the course of a life—of the most ambitious lives, lived by those who have taken to heart the message of self-construction through resistance to the world and to the hardened version of one's self.

First, we must abandon our fantasies about multiple selves and multiple lives. We must embrace a particular trajectory and accept its consequences for the person we shall become.

Then we must follow this violent act of self-mutilation with a struggle to learn how to feel the ghostly movements of the missing limbs: by an act of imaginative love, we must imagine the experience of the people we did not become. This enlargement of the sense of self joins with our early experience of identification and compassion to establish a basis for accepting and imagining other people.

Later, as we struggle, from a particular position in the world, with the limits of our circumstance and of our insight, and face the temptation to mistake disillusionment for wisdom, a carapace, made of character and compromise, begins to form around us. Part of this carapace comes from inside: the habitual dispositions of the self form a character. Such routines are indispensable: they provide a coherent and secure place from which we can embark on adventure and experiment. However, our freedom and vitality also require resistance against our own character as yet another reduction of the unlimited to the limited and of the surprising to the formulaic. Part of the carapace also comes from outside: resignation to the limits of an individual circumstance. We begin to think that the lives we lead are the only ones we shall ever lead, and we fall down into the acceptance of what we take to be our fate.

This combination of hardened character and unchallenged compromise results in a mummification of the self. We begin to die many small deaths. We can then live only by ripping apart this mummy that begins to encase us. We do not rip it apart to be virtuous or righteous; rather, we rip it apart so that we can live in such a manner that we die only once.

We cannot rip it apart by a direct act of will. However, the will can operate indirectly and powerfully, if guided by a view of moral opportunity. We progress by a dynamic of engagement and self-transformation. If we stand back in a posture of ironic detachment, we turn from flesh to stone. By identifying with particular beliefs and forms of life, by subjecting ourselves, through such identification, to defeat and disappointment, by risking the subversion of faith at the hands of thought and experience, we continue to live. We learn, through action, to hope.

What is the idea of our situation that, recognizing its terrors of suffering and obscurity but building on the idea of the self from which I began, could justify such an ambition in the living of a life?

Consider first the larger circumstance within which we confront the dilemmas of connection and transcendence and undergo their characteristic expressions over the course of a human life. On one side, we find ourselves pushed back and forth between agitation and boredom. When we temporarily manage to quiet our ambitions, frustrations, and diversions—the ceaseless wandering among particulars, the desperate effort to make them bear a weight they cannot carry—we fall into a state of staring and boredom. Our happy moments of engagement with the task at hand and the other person are soon devoured by this alternation between lostness and emptiness. In this susceptibility we experience as suffering the overriding consequence of our humanity, which demands infinity from the finite and accessibility from the infinite.

On the other side, darkness surrounds our dreamlike and tormented existence, punctuated by joys we are powerless to make last and entangled in the drives, toils, and pains of the body. No advance of natural science could ever lift this darkness. In the end science can deliver to us only a history of the universe and of the ephemeral and bounded regularities that may arise at certain moments in this history. It can do nothing to split the difference between being and nothingness, or to explain how and why being could come out of nothing, or why we are not God rather than the doomed beings we in fact are. It can answer none of these questions—now or ever after—because it thinks with our embodied minds rather than with the mind of God.

Our mortality focuses our experience on a brief, irreversible, and dramatic procession from one mystery to another. As we turn to one another and to our chores and commitments, we place on these frail encounters, homely routines, and fallible devotions the burden of unlimited longing for the unlimited. They are not up to it.

Consider three solutions to the problems of connection and transcendence, seen against this background of trouble and ignorance: the narrative of salvation, the extinction of the self, and the awakening of the self.

The narrative of salvation places our struggles with the problems of connection and transcendence in a broader context of meaning and hope. The relations among people foreshadow our relation to God, who mysteriously needs us even as we need Him and who intervenes, dramatically, decisively, and irreversibly, in historical time. This intervention, beginning in history and continuing in eternity, prepares both us and the world for overcoming the conflicts between finite circumstance and infinite longing, between the need and the fear of connection. Even our great secular projects—like the cause of democracy and the alleviation of poverty and oppression—gain meaning from the part they play in this redemptive work.

Can we make ourselves believe in such a narrative by wanting to believe in it? If we try to save our faith by reducing it to allegory—translating the record of personal encounter with God into a vision of impersonal piety and morality—we eviscerate it of precisely those features that allow it to speak most directly and powerfully to our anxieties and hopes. We recover it only by undoing it.

We cannot evade a judgment of its truth—the truth of the historical and transhistorical events it recounts. If it is a way of arousing the will and consoling the mind, it suffers from the defect of the historical narratives of political, social, and economic redemption, like Marxism, which for so long inspired and misdirected transformative politics. The spell we cast on ourselves will lead us to misrepresent both the constraints and the opportunities of our situation. As a result, we shall see less clearly and be less free.

It may seem strange to invoke such a complaint of truthfulness in an argument that pursues pragmatist themes and commitments. For no feature of the vulgar understanding of the pragmatist tradition is more widespread than the idea that this tradition proposes a merely instrumental view of truth. Here, however, I have argued that the primacy of the personal over the impersonal rather than the subordination of belief to expedience is the element of this tradition we have most reason to rescue and develop.

It is precisely in the domain of the personal and the historical that we have the strongest basis to oppose the reduction of discovery to strategizing. It is our knowledge of nature that is less reliable as representation of the world rather than as a guide to practical intervention because it is knowledge circumscribed by the disproportion of the mind to its object and beset by the antinomies of the impersonal. To be sure, every powerful view of society and personality is, among other things, a self-fulfilling prophecy. It invites us to act in a way that makes it true. However, this impulse of self-fulfillment, though ineradicable, is also self-limiting: we soon hit against the resistance imposed by people such as they now are and by society such as it is now. Thus, the element of self-fulfilling prophecy in our social and personal ideas forces us into a confrontation with reality rather than allowing us to mistake comfort for truth.

A second solution to the problems of existence is the annihilation of the self. We can find different versions of it expressed in the philosophies of Schopenhauer and Plotinus as well as in some aspects of the teachings of the Buddha and Lao Tzu. It proposes the suspension of individual striving through an identification of consciousness with universal and ultimate reality beyond the self. We achieve reconciliation both with other people and with our societies and cultures through a radical devaluation of the reality of phenomenal distinctions and of individual selfhood.

There is a reciprocal relation in this response between the metaphysical picture and the existential orientation. Denial of the ultimate reality of distinctions within the manifold justifies the abandonment of striving, with its terrible alternation between disquiet and boredom. Cessation of striving turns away from the confrontations that can alone keep vivid in our minds the distinctions of the manifest world.

The moral cost of the annihilation of the self is the very effect that its proponents invoke as its benefit. What we lose by adopting this metaphysic and practicing this therapy is the world and, with the world, life. Our experience shrinks on the pretext of expanding. When, because of the reality of our embodiment and our social location, we are unable to keep up the pretense of returning from the self to the ultimate, we find ourselves imprisoned in a place that we have worked to make smaller.

This moral cost is aggravated by an epistemological one. We set up in consciousness a situation in which the invalidating test can come only from outside—the knock on the door by a personal and social reality that refuses to be mastered by distancing and denial.

A third solution is an awakening of self to other people and to the manifest world. Such an awakening is an intensification of our engagement with experience, especially with our experience of distinction both of people and of phenomena. It is a movement from narcoleptic daze, interrupted by moments of pain and joy, to presence, attention, and involvement. Nowhere is this link between intensification of experience and recognition of difference more fully revealed than in our sense of the reality of the individual self. We now see this reality as one that goes all the way down rather than dismissing it as an epiphenomenon.

This awakening is therefore in every respect a reversal of both the existential attitude and the metaphysical vision underlying the attempt at annihilation of the self. It takes a certain conception of the self and of its struggles with the world—the conception I proposed to put at the center of a radicalized pragmatism—and develops it into a response to the problems of existence. It gives many signs of its intention and subjects itself to many tests of its claims.

In politics and in culture, it leads us toward the permanent invention of the future and the enhancement of the powers of ordinary humanity and the dignity of ordinary experience. The structure of society comes to resemble more closely the workings of the imagination.

In the shaping of moral vision and action, it inspires resistance to the mummification of the self and, more generally, the effort to embed our solutions to the problem of connection in a response to the problem of transcendence. As we develop our practical powers, our overriding moral purpose becomes that of reconciling greatness with love in our experience of selfhood and encounter. We seek such a reconciliation in a form untainted by the illusions of an heroic ethic, open to the promptings of ordinary experience, and respectful of the abilities of ordinary people.

In the imagination of the world as a whole, such as we can see and understand it from our narrow and accidental vantage point, it inspires an attempt to recapture, chastened and transformed, the visionary presence of the world to the child. Art and science work together to deepen our awareness of distinction within the actual world by placing the actual against a backdrop of transformative variation and opportunity—seen, discovered, envisaged, prophesied, and created. Rather than dimming our sense of reality and real distinction, this imagination of change makes it more acute. Although we did not make the world, the whole wide world becomes our dream, and everything in it appears to us in the visionary relief of the dreaming mind.

Existential Options

Imagine the problem of the path of the self from another perspective—the perspective of the existential options presented to us by the most ambitious and inclusive thinking of our own times. We shall reach the same outcome from a different starting point.

Facing the certainty and finality of death and unable to dispel the mystery of our existence, or of the existence of the world, we are normally engaged in the affairs of life, in our attachments to others, and in our conflicts with them. Such engagement occupies our consciousness. If it is intense, it fills us with joy, even when it is accompanied by the shadows of antagonism, ambivalence, remorse, and fear. The intensity may run in the direction of devotion to a task or of longing for other people.

This intensity, however, wavers. It threatens to go under, submerged by routine. The problem is not repetition and habit, unavoidable and indispensable features of our experience. The problem is the failure to sustain our godliness—the quality of context-transcending spirit—in the midst of repetition; the failure to embody spirit in the routine.

As a result, we live out much of our lives in a daze, as if we are acting out a script someone else had written. The someone else, however, is not an individual or even a group; it is the impersonal, crushing collective authority of the others who set our terms of reference and who exercise power, or suffer servitude, in the world we inhabit. We become them, but they do not become each of us.

The flickering of the life force is a little bit of dying, or dying by steps. It comes with its own solace: the narcoleptic state of diminished consciousness into which we descend prevents us from focusing on the enormity of the loss or from confronting our situation. And the pressures of material need and economic scarcity keep us chained to our practical responsibilities.

Consider three responses. Each has played a role in the thought, art, and experience of our times. Only the third sets us on a path of divinization consistent with the facts of our existence.

One response is relentlessly to parade before our eyes the spectacle of our sliding toward death and of our dangling in meaninglessness. The point of this parade is to arouse in us a dread so terrible and a disgust so violent that we are incited to rebel against the denial of active and conscious personality.

But to what end? To the end of prompting us to compose ourselves. We compose ourselves less by reasserting the claims of life than by denying the importance or even the reality of the distinctions that fill up our everyday experience. Seeing these distinctions of the manifest world as the outreach of an underlying reality, we affirm the radiance of being. We attend to the world; we celebrate it; we identify with its onward rush. We triumph over ignorance and death by taking leave of ourselves.

This belated and strained paganism is another version of the ancient doctrine of the extinction of the self. It used to be justified by the metaphysical conceptions of the perennial philosophy. In our day it appeals more often to an idea of the exhaustion and the failure of everything else, including the tradition of philosophy: of all attempts to make sense of the particulars of the manifest world and to steer in that world a course of transformative action.

The consequences of this response reveal its errors. We cannot in fact sustain the engagement that enables us to resist our descent into the narcoleptic daze by standing and waiting, or by celebrating and attending. We can do so only by struggling against both ourselves and the world, even if it is the struggle of the individual philosopher or artist to renew under new disguises, and without reliance on the perennial philosophy, the ancient doctrine of the extinction of the self and its program of ecstatic and mindful quiescence. This first response is a doctrine that no one, least of all its own inventors, can live out.

A second response focuses on the suppression of individuality that accompanies both the dimming of consciousness and the automatisms of the will. It proposes resistance to the institutional arrangements, the stereotyped roles, and the hardened forms of consciousness that crush authentic personality. We can reaffirm the quality that makes us more human by making us more divine only if we tread an endless *via negativa*: we must say no, no, no to all the structures, through rebellion, both collective and individual.

The permanent rebellion against structure reveals a failure of insight and a wavering of the heart. It is a failure of insight because it refuses to recognize that the structures against which it rebels may differ in quality as well as in content: in the character of their relation to the structure-transgressing powers of the agent. They may be relatively more entrenched against challenge and change, presenting themselves to the agent as natural necessity or alien fate. Or they may be relatively more available to revision in the course of the activities of everyday life.

When we reform the structures in this alternative direction, we do more than enhance our practical powers and undermine an indispensable basis of entrenched social division and hierarchy. We split the difference between being inside a structure and being beyond one. We fashion a setting more suitable to the infinities within us. Not to recognize this potential of variation is to remain in thrall to a superstition that is also a form of subjugation.

This rebellion is also a wavering of the heart because the teaching of the endless *via negativa* betrays despair about our ability to make spirit live in structure: that is to say within routine and repetition, law and practice. This hopelessness is a sin we commit against ourselves: against our powers of transgression, transcendence, and transformation. It has two exemplary forms: the one, the political; the other, personal. The political form is abandonment of any attempt so to organize society and culture that we shorten the distance between our context-preserving and our context-transforming activities and make change internal to social life. The personal form is renunciation of all efforts to make love live in institutions, particularly in the institutions of marriage and in the long conversations and reciprocal sacrifices of a life together. Romantic love—spirit disembodied and incapable of incarnation in routine—sees repetition as its death. The political and the personal forms of this loss of hope represent two instances of the same closing down.

A third response is the one I have called the awakening of the self. Like the other two responses just described, it depends for the force of its appeal on an effort to force confrontation with our mortality and ignorance: how what we value most swings over a void of meaninglessness, concealed by need, busyness, and diversion.

The greatest threat to this moral project is the entrapment of the self. We may suddenly realize that the life we are leading is the only one we may ever live. We find ourselves trapped in a situation that denies our infinity, which is to say our humanity. We then resist.

One form of this resistance is the redirection of thought and politics to an effort to create structures that recognize, nurture, and develop our structure-transcending nature. Our orientation to such a future is also a way of living in the present as beings not fully determined by the established organization of society and culture. However, this is a path that even in the circumstances of the most free, equal, and prosperous societies is directly open only to a few. Even for these few it offers an inadequate solution.

Our lives are usually over before we have seen the things we fought for come to pass and turn out not to be what we wanted. The person before us, the moment we are living, the task to which we are devoted, the experience remembered now—the turning of consciousness to the manifest world, heightened as in a dream, transfigured by the imagination of the next steps as in thought and politics, yet subject, as in our everyday waking lives, to the discipline of constraint and to the demands of repetition—that is the antidote to the death-in-life of a diminished existence.

The conversion of the mind to the manifest world is paradoxically connected with the orientation to the future. The workings of the imagination throw light on this connection. To grasp a state of affairs or a phenomenon is to see it as capable of being changed into something else as a result of certain interventions. Until we set it within such a range of transforming variation, we do not see; we merely stare. The core setting of this imaginative work is our experience of acting in the world, of encountering resistance, and of overcoming it.

We cannot give ourselves fully to the manifest world and to the others if we remain the puppets of a script we did not write and the prisoners of a situation that does not recognize in us the context-transcending beings we really are. We do not need to await the transformation of society and of culture to begin our emancipation. We can begin right now. In every area of action and thought, and so long as we do not suffer the extremities of deprivation and infirmity, the question on our lips will be: What should we do next? The most ambitious forms of programmatic thinking and of reconstructive action simply extend the scope of this questioning and broaden the range of our answers.

What allows us to ask at every turn the question—what should we do next?—is the marriage of the imagination with an existential attitude: a hopeful and patient availability to novelty and to experience. What enables us to sustain this attitude is in turn the combination of growing confidence in the exercise of our own powers—security and capability—with love—the love of the world and the love of people.

The commitment to a zone of fundamental protections and endowments, established by rights withdrawn from the agenda of short-term politics, is simply the most important political expression of a more general truth. As the love of the parent for the child, assuring it of an unconditional place in the world, encourages the child to run risks for the sake of self-construction, so these capability-enhancing rights help the individual to lower his defenses and to look for the new. Taking these rights partly out of politics by surrounding them with rules and doctrines that make them relatively harder to change in the short run may have a paradoxical result. Entrenching these rights against political challenge may broaden the scope of politics and increase its intensity.

However, the aim must be to define such immunities and endowments in a manner that imposes the least possible rigidity of the surrounding social space. A caste system equating the security of the individual with the inviolability of detailed and distinct forms of group life represents an extreme of confusion of individual safety and identity with social rigidity. What we should desire is the opposite extreme, of disassociation between entrenchment of the capability-enhancing rights or endowments and entrenchment of all other arrangements. Of such an opposite extreme we have no available example: the existing forms of economic, social, and political organization, including the traditional modern law of property and contract, stand at varying intermediate points along this imaginary spectrum. So here, as everywhere, individuals must make up, by the way in which they relate self-possession to connection, for what politics and law have not yet provided as the ordering of social life.

It is not the radiance of a supposedly unified being underlying the phenomenal world that inspires this response of awakening, as it inspires the contemporary version of the doctrine of the extinction of the self. It is real love, the love of actual people, given and received. The love of the world now appears as an effusion of this human love. Plotinus's fountain flowed upside down, from hidden being above, into the manifest world below. Now, however, the fountain flows right side up. The love of the world is the penumbral light of a brighter flame, human love.

The first of the three contemporary responses to our condition of ignorance and mortality is no more than a contemporary version of the ancient doctrine of the extinction of the self. It translates the tenets of the perennial philosophy, which traditionally supported that doctrine, into a vocabulary gratifying to modern ears. The second response, of permanent romantic rebellion against structure, continues under democracy and in the form of political and moral views, the *via negativa* that has always existed, as a heresy, within the great world religions of personal salvation. The third response, of the awakening of the self, might be similarly seen as a continuation, without the theological backdrop, of some of the moral and psychological beliefs most characteristic of the narrative of salvation.

In the form of its statement here, the awakening of the self may seem no more than Christianity without Christ or the Church. In this respect, it would resemble many of the ideas of the last five centuries in the West, as an afterglow of Christianity, obtaining from its ambivalent relation to a lost faith whatever power it may enjoy. Because many were pagans when they professed to be Christians, some became Christians when they turned into pagans; the moment of their apostasy was the hour of their conversion.

Nothing for sure follows, however, for insight or action now from the limited truth of this genealogical remark. Are the transactions between God and humanity, in which the converted apostates are no longer able to believe, the indispensable repository of the most important truth about ourselves? Or does this view represent an attempt to provide grounds outside us for what can have grounds only within us?

As an orientation to life, the doctrine of the awakening of the self must recommend itself by its own force. It is not an inference from the radicalized pragmatism for which I argue, any more than the redirection of social democracy can be a consequence of that philosophy. The philosophical position only connects and generalizes the insights and impulses emerging from these different fields of experience. It returns to them a light that is largely reflected from them.

What is it like to do this work now? We lost the faith that inspired this view of the self and of its divinization. We consoled ourselves that in losing it we were in fact bringing it back to life again, but we could not be sure. All around us we had seen the idea that everything could in principle be different, combined with the sense that we could not change anything that mattered anyway; the victory over necessitarianism seemed hollow. We witnessed the revolutionary ideas of the West stab to death the leading doctrines of other civilizations, which survived only as props or fossils. Moreover, the triumphant ideas about social and personal transformation, having set the world on fire through revolution or subjugated it through empire, had then appeared, at the moment of their triumph, to wither and die. The dialogue of the major philosophical traditions of mankind had therefore become a congress of dead people. We aroused the transforming will through epic narratives of inevitable progress based on assumptions in which we were no longer able to believe.

We were repelled, however, by the conclusion that all that was left to us was to sing in our chains, to cast a spell on ourselves, to experiment with private pleasures, and to reinvent the ancient ethic of serenity. Ironic distancing would mean surrender and death. Always we had before us the perennial moral formula of our civilization, which the nineteenth-and twentieth-century novel had brought as the last glimmer of a fading light: you change yourself, although you cannot change the world; and the way to change yourself is to try to change the world—your world—even though you cannot change it. We said that these beliefs were true, and we wanted to discover the way of acting that would confirm their truth and the way of thinking that would save them from the appearance of absurdity.

The Two Awakenings of the Self

The self awakens twice. The first awakening of the self is the affirmation of consciousness and, through consciousness, of distinct personality. We affirm consciousness by entering fully into the experience of conscious life. To enter fully into it is to broaden it, stretching its limits. This stretching gives rise, however, to a contrary experience, of loss of distinct consciousness and identity. Horrified, we then step back into the citadel of the conscious self, holding on with new force and clarity to what we had risked losing. The central paradox of the first awakening of the self is that we must risk losing the sense of self—our grip on consciousness, our hold on distinction of personality—the better to reaffirm it.

Few are the thinkers in our Western tradition who, like Plotinus, have explored this paradox. For centuries, however, it was a familiar topic of discussion among the philosophers of ancient India.

There are two directions in which we may stretch and risk our experience of self-consciousness. In one direction we enter more fully into the life of our own body. It ceases to appear strange to us; consciousness becomes a detailed map of our bodily states of pain, pleasure, or perception, the mind transformed into what Spinoza thought it always was—the idea of the body. The more fully we identify in consciousness with the body, closely tracking its humors and changes and lifting the categorical grid we normally impose on perception, the greater the loss of the sense of distinction. The whole manifest world, and our embodied self within it, now begins to dissolve into an indistinct glow, an afterglow of the sense of distinct selfhood that we had upheld so long as we remained, vigilant and armed, within the fortress of consciousness, anxiously eyeing from a distance the body and the world.

In another direction we leave this fortress for the sake of two varieties of absorption: absorption in an activity, experienced as all-consuming as well as self-justifying, and absorption in a vision of the manifest world around us, experienced as sufficient to hold our attention.

By the first of these varieties of absorption, we surrender to a work that quiets for a while all restlessness and anxiety. In surrendering to it, however, we feel no boredom because it seems large enough to occupy the whole of our conscious life so long as we are doing it. Our experience of time changes. We undergo movement and transformation, making real the sense of time. Yet time as an uncontrolled fall toward death is seemingly suspended.

By the second of these two varieties of absorption, we find our eyes open to the phenomenal world. It appears to us with all its distinctions and radiance highlighted as if in a dream. And it commands our attention so completely that nothing of this attention is left over, as a residue of doubt, discontent, and suspicion.

Both these varieties of absorption lead outward. Both represent enhancements of our core experience of self-consciousness and distinction. Yet both also threaten what they enhance, undermining the clarity of the boundary between the self and what lies outside it, weakening the vigilance of distance on which our experience of consciousness relies.

From the descent into the body and the ascent into the two types of absorption, we step back, frightened and strengthened, into the walls of the defended self. This going out and coming back, this broadening and narrowing, this endless movement among the different levels of consciousness is the first awakening of the self: an awakening to the experience of distinct personality and embodied spirit. It takes place under a double shadow: the shadow of the need to reckon with other people and the shadow of the need to come to terms with the organized structure of the society in which we find ourselves.

Needing others for everything from the material sustenance of life to the confirmation of our sense of self but fearing them as threats to our independent existence, we move uneasily between closeness and fending off. Ordinarily, we settle into an ill-marked middle distance.

Recognizing that the order of society is simply the temporary interruption or containment of a fight that can begin again at any moment—a struggle over the terms of people's claims upon one another—we seek to uphold the rules, proprieties, and decencies that expunge from social life some of its undercurrent of savagery and danger.

The second awakening of the self is the discovery within us of the demand for the infinite, for the absolute. Once discovered, it is irresistible; it must be lived out. Its living out changes the meaning of everything we had experienced before. The second awakening is therefore a revolution in the experience of consciousness and distinction.

It takes place at first in the form of certain interruptions and redirections of the experiences characteristic of the first awakening. Once we understand the nature of these interruptions and redirections, we can see how their occurrence may be favored by the spread of certain beliefs about personality and society and how their expression may require developments in thought and in politics. The second awakening is inseparable from the history of democracy as well as from the progress of our insight into social and personal change.

Two connected events are at the root of the second awakening of the self. One event is the discovery of our estrangement from the social and natural worlds; of their indifference or antagonism to our trait of infinity—that is to say, of excess over circumstance and structure.

We are natural beings. Our powers of transcendence are foreshadowed by our physical characteristics, beginning with the plasticity of the brain. However, nature, which we can know only by a fragile and tentative overreaching of our powers of insight into the sphere of our own actions, is indifferent to our effort to make ourselves more godlike, and condemns us to frustration and dissolution.

We are social beings. We must express our capacity for transcendence in the exercise of a power to challenge and to change the established settings of life and of thought if we are to express it at all. We can express it in greater or lesser measure. However, no society and no culture that have yet existed have ever recognized and nourished this capacity enough for us to be justified in laying down our arms. Separation from nature and transformation of society are therefore the indispensable answers to the discovery of our estrangement.

The other event that is at the source of the second awakening of the self is our acknowledgment, alongside our estrangement from the natural and social worlds, of the unlimited character of our longing for other people. We demand from them, from some of them, more than any human being can give to another: not just material and moral support, but radical acceptance and assurance that there is a place for us in the world as the embodied spirits and context-transcendent beings we really are. Thus, everything we can give one another implies a promise no one can keep.

The only solution, we know, is only barely possible: love, understood as the imagination and acceptance of the other person, as who that person both is and might become, not as the projection of our need, love freely given and therefore also freely refused, complete only when not tainted by the benevolence of the protector for the protected, precariously penetrating the routines of a life together and fading as it moves away from the core terrain of personal encounter to the larger life of society.

The two events at the root of the second awakening of the self shape each other. We are estranged from a natural and social world that burdens our efforts to develop ourselves, and to recognize one another, as beings capable of imagining and accepting one another. We demand from one another that which nature and society seem to refuse us.

The first awakening of the self can happen anywhere and any time, in any society and culture. The second awakening of the self is a discovery that is also a disturbance—the discovery of the secret of our infinity and the disturbance of the arrangements and beliefs that conceal or repress it. Although it may be prefigured anywhere and any time as prophecy, its regular occurrence in human life is a collective as well as an individual achievement. It thrives only in a terrain prepared by the reconstruction of thought and of society. It is not a miracle; it is an accomplishment. Its advancement amounts to a large part of what justifies the project of democratic experimentalism and the teaching of a radicalized pragmatism.

Demands of the Second Awakening

How should people live for whom this second awakening of the self represents a guiding ideal? In social and economic life we must use repetition, embodied in standardized practice and in machines, to save time for what is not yet repeatable. So in the moral life we must use habitual dispositions—the virtues—to be ourselves by going beyond ourselves.

There are three sets of virtues: those of connection, purification, and divinization. The virtues of connection and purification have to do with two different aspects of our moral experience. They are at the same level; they complete and complement one another. The virtues of divinization are at another level. They presuppose the second awakening of the self, and they change the experience and the meaning of the other virtues.

The virtues of connection—respect, forbearance, and fairness—regard the way we reckon with one another. In their initial, unreconstructed form, they make this reckoning without benefit of the discoveries of the second awakening. These virtues draw on an ability to restrain our self-centeredness, which enslaves us as it oppresses others: our partiality of view and of interest. Respect is the individualized recognition of our common humanity. Forbearance is the restraint we impose on the expression of our views and the vindication of our interests, so that others may have the space in which to express and to vindicate theirs. Fairness is the treatment of other people by standards that lower the price of subjugation and depersonalization that each of us must pay to connect with other people. To act fairly is to contribute the most one can to this end, given what we can and cannot do and change right here and now.

The virtues of purification—simplicity, enthusiasm, and attentiveness—concern the ascent of the self in the course of its first awakening. They prepare or realize the twin forms of absorption, characteristic of this ascent, in all-consuming activity or in reception of the manifest world. Simplicity is the removal of clutter, especially of attachment to things, and the lowering of defenses. It prepares our rise both by disarming us and by focusing us. Enthusiasm is the readiness to give oneself to an activity that, once found not to violate the virtues and obligations of connection, absorbs us for a while without residue or reservation and seems to be eternal while it lasts. Attentiveness is the turning to the manifest world, received in perception and represented in the mind, as a fully articulated manifold, full of distinction and radiance. Although attentiveness may seem to be as passive as enthusiasm is active, the phenomenology of each of these two experiences belies this apparent contrast. In enthusiasm, we have the sense of being seized, and in attentiveness of an enhancement and expansion of consciousness. Their product is the experience of a mind on which nothing is lost.

The virtues of divinization—openness to new experience and openness to the other person—are the resources we deploy and the ends toward which we move in the course of the second awakening of the self. Through them, we become not God but more godlike, and we make good on the infinity within us. They are related; each equips us better for the other. One of the major aims of an experimentalist culture and of a democratic politics is to give us a better chance of experiencing and connecting them.

Openness to the new manifests the true relation between individual or collective humanity and the organized settings of society and culture: that they are finite relative to us and that we are infinite relative to them. As more than the flawed, corrigible, contingent, and ephemeral constructions they really are, they become idols. When they become idols, we must smash them to prevent them from sucking out the life that properly belongs to us.

Openness to the other person is most fully realized in personal love. In its more diffuse and weaker form, it becomes the higher trust on which the practices of experimentalist cooperation depend. The generalization of such trust among strangers cannot, however, be produced by a change of attitude alone. It requires as well a change of arrangements and endowments along the lines explored earlier: thus, once again, the connection between the progress of democracy and the success of the second awakening of the self.

The practice of the virtues of divinization modifies the meaning and content of the virtues of connection. It turns respect into compassion or fellow feeling (untainted by the self-defensive equivocations of a high-handed benevolence), forbearance into self-sacrifice, and fairness into mercy. It also transforms the experience—central to the virtues of purification—of losing the self the better to regain it. The ascent of the self, through simplicity, enthusiasm, and attentiveness, now undergoes a decisive reorientation. Instead of keeping out of trouble to find composure, the self looks for trouble to find, affirm, and express its own infinity.

13

Philosophy
Beyond Superscience and Self-Help

Philosophy has usually been either superscience or self-help. Most often it has been self-help disguised as superscience.

By superscience I mean the claim to general and foundational knowledge, more universal than the intimate but enclosed knowledge we can gain over our own constructs and more basic than the fallible and shadowy knowledge we can achieve through science. The idea of the primacy of the personal over the impersonal, in knowledge as well as in value, is fatal to the pretense of superscience.

By self-help I mean just what the word ordinarily describes in the book market: instruction about how to be happy and successful in a world that allows us little control over the defining circumstances of our lives.

To disguise self-help as superscience is to present a formula for our struggle with fate and luck, as well as with social constraint and internal division of the self, in the form of discourse about ultimate reality or higher knowledge. This bond between an imperative of life and a vision of the world is the hallmark of religious experience. The embedding of self-help in superscience is the claim of philosophy to do the work of religion. It is a claim that philosophy can only very imperfectly honor and even then only by jeopardizing the greatest contributions that it was always able to make to humanity and that it is now able to make to democracy.

The partnership between superscience and self-help is ancient. One of its most fully realized models is the philosophy of the Hellenistic period. However, it has now achieved a new and special significance through the combination of loss of faith in God with struggle for faith in ordinary people. The desire for a successor to religion could not but be intensified by the difficulty of overt religious belief. And the democratic creed of individual and collective self-invention raised the premium placed on ideas that would tell us authoritatively how and in what direction to reinvent ourselves.

The execution of the plan to ground self-help on superscience suffers, however, from a fatal flaw. There is no superscience, or at least none that philosophy can hope to establish. When we look beyond common experience for guidance in self-help, we must look for inspiration wherever we can find it: therefore, in art and literature, in religion and politics, in simple joys and great contests, in disappointment and disillusionment.

The waning of our hope to embed self-help in superscience threatens to leave philosophy without a sustaining view of its work. If this hope fails far enough, nothing is left for philosophy but a travesty of the old idea of a superscience. Philosophy becomes a thought police, attempting to clarify concepts now empty of reference and to discipline methods now robbed of purpose. This police operation offers a service that no one is interested in hiring. Its practitioners soon find themselves speaking only to one another.

Something can and should be saved from the wreck of the claim to a superscience and from the failure of the marriage of superscience to self-help. We should not feel forced to choose between the idea of a superscience and the belief that all knowledge is merely specialized knowledge in a particular domain. Once we have understood what the third option is—a way of thinking that is neither superscience nor self-help—we should be able to use it to help inform and even inspire our practices of individual and collective self-reinvention. We shall find in it a powerful instrument for the avoidance of personal mummification and institutional idolatry. It will serve us under democracy in our efforts to live for the future as a certain way of living in the present, as the context-surpassing beings that we are.

A philosophy that has ceased to entertain the hope of grounding self-help in superscience exists in the practical conditions of a professorial discipline at peace with the encyclopedia of specialized disciplines in the university system. However, to find something useful to do, to escape the justly derided make-work of the intellectual police, to rescue the rational pearl in the mystical shell of the marriage of superscience to self-help, and to develop intellectual programs like the one outlined in these pages, philosophy cannot coexist peacefully with this system of specialized knowledge. It must break the peace.

In the university system, each of the specialized disciplines is held together by a double glue: a subject matter defined as a certain range of phenomena and an analytical and argumentative practice. The conceit of the professors is that substance and method go naturally together. They believe that their way of thinking and arguing is best suited to the domain that helps define their discipline, although it may also apply to phenomena in other domains. For example, an economist may think that his specialty is both to study the economy and to think as an economist, which means to think according to the conventional analytical practice in which he has been trained. Once confident of the excellences of this practice, he is likely to begin applying it to neighboring domains, such as politics or psychology. Only then does the forced marriage of method and substance begin to dissolve.

The willingness to treat the methods dominant in each discipline as if they were intrinsic to the subject matter and expressive of a unique and enduring facet of human understanding is nowhere more damaging than in the study of society and culture. For there it is most likely to deny us the intimate and transformative knowledge that we can hope to secure of humanity and its constructions. Only by the painful triumph of vision over method, the periodic subversion of method for the sake of deepening vision, can we hope to advance insight. In the absence of this pressure, thought remains in constant peril of being seduced by the impulse to confuse its conventions with reality, and actuality with necessity. Only some unexpected upheaval then brings us up short and awakens us to the limits of our understanding. Such an approach to the development of knowledge corrupts our understanding and fails to do justice to our humanity-defining powers of resistance, transgression, and transcendence.

That these faults disorient our thinking even in natural science can be shown by the typical trajectory of an academic specialist. He masters in his early training an analytic and argumentative apparatus, and then he spends much of his subsequent professional life applying the slowly enriched but unchallenged machine to changing material. It is a species of the surrender of spirit to structure, the slow and repeated dying, to which we are all subject.

Philosophy is then the loose canon, strong because it is speaking not from the stars but from within, vindicating vision against exclusive method and spirit against established structure. It is the leftover in the organized collective work of the mind, the remnant that is saving because it is unassimilated and resistant to assimilation. Its general ideas work in the service of its incitement to particular rebellions. This residual but uncontainable power of subversion is what remains of the discredited project of a philosophical superscience.

The imagination, remember, is not a separate faculty of the mind. It is the mind itself seen in its least computable and least modular aspects. Philosophy is neither a discipline among others nor the master discipline. It is the imagination at war, exploring what the established methods and discourses do not allow to be thought and said. Whether these discourses and methods do not think and say such ideas because they cannot in fact be thought and said, or only because they cannot be thought or said yet, must always be one of the chief concerns of philosophical thinking.

Philosophy remains most faithful to this mission and most useful to us when the mind in arms wages this struggle in the spirit of the total wars of the twentieth century, not the limited wars of the eighteenth. The characteristic goal of such total war in thought is the development of a way of thinking and acting that makes use of the most significant truth about ourselves: our excess of uninterpreted experience and squandered capability over the structures, of organization and of thought, that would contain us. A radicalized pragmatism imparts a distinctive twist to this goal: it wants to develop a way of thinking that, because it gives direct expression to our residual powers, our secret stores of infinity, proves useful in everything that humanizes the world and divinizes humanity. The primary method of the total war is the forced selective mobilization of available methods and discourses, jumbled up as suits us rather than them, to the end of saying a little piece of what they deem inexpressible and of doing a little bit of what they suppose impossible.

For what then can we use philosophy? In the first place, we can use it to shake up the disciplines as organized and distinguished by the professional organization of specialized knowledge. In this respect, it serves as an incomplete antidote to superstition.

In the second place, we can use it to inform our practices of individual and collective self-invention. How it can inform both our collective efforts to empower humanity through material progress and democracy and our individual experiments in moral adventure was the subject of the four preceding chapters of this book. Used in this way, philosophy does not offer comprehensive programs for the reform of society or the reorientation of existence. Neither, however, is it limited to undermining the intellectual prejudices that inhibit and misdirect our struggle for individual and collective self-construction. It has a message. The message, is that we should live for the future as a certain way of living more completely and more fully in the present, unbowed, with eyes wide awake. This message, conveyed in the language of the concerns of a particular time, is what legitimately remains of the notion of philosophy as an exercise in self-help.

This idea of the work of philosophy stands in opposition to another contrast that is connected with the divergence between self-help and superscience but that differs from it: Hume's contrast between the subversion of social custom and mental convention under the pressure of a mind confident in its power to unlock the secrets of the world and the willingness to accept the reign of convention and custom the better to go on living and connecting. The hope for knowledge from the viewpoint of the stars, unlimited by the circumstance of any human agent, arises from the false notion that such a circumstance is merely a veil we must pierce to see the world as it truly is.

The claim to absolute insight results in a clash of arbitrary dogmas and withering skepticisms, undermining the conventions and customs that form, for all of us, the social and mental "cement of the universe." When speculative insight ceases to be disciplined by the practices of natural science and tied to its tools, it becomes delirious. We escape from this delirium by reengaging with other people in the customary and conventional world from which our metaphysical speculation had seemed to deliver us. The valuable outcome of philosophizing would then be merely negative: in the course of its excesses, it may help overturn superstitions that stand as intangible obstacles to the social and moral improvement of humanity.

This supposed contrast, with its foreseeable conservative outcome masquerading as sobriety and realism, rests on the denial of the idea of mind, self, and society that has been central to this book. Because our contexts make us who we are and because we can never hope to move in a context-less space above them, seeing from nowhere with the eyes of God, we must indeed abandon the voyage that ends in the delirium.

Surrender to custom and convention, however, is no less an insult to the claims of connection and engagement than is the willingness to pass judgment on our social and mental practices from the midst of our speculative delirium. Such a surrender prevents us from recognizing one another as the context-transcending originals we in fact are or can become; it is impossible to be respectful without being iconoclastic. No sharing in social life will allow us to live as who we really are that disregards the way in which our powers of transcendence become embedded in our experiences of connection. No participation in a social world will be compatible with our individual and collective ascent that stops looking for a way to make the second side of the mind—its powers of nonformulaic initiative, recursive infinity, and negative capability—preeminent in our ordinary social experience.

The conclusion of our disappointment with the results of our speculative delirium should not then be to surrender to the established context of order and belief as if our exorbitant dreams had no consequence for the remaking of our world. We can change the context. Indeed, we can change over time—biographical as well as historical time—the character of our relation to all contexts. We can do so by reforming all our institutions and practices so that we can be more wholeheartedly in the world, our world, and outside it at the same time, or, to use a hallowed phrase, so that we can be in the world without being of it.

This third position—the position beyond both the delirium and the surrender—is the position of philosophy and of humanity. From this standpoint, to be philosophical and to be human are one and the same thing. The most important premises of this position are the reality of time, understood as the transformation of transformation; the open-endedness of the possible made tangible and definite only by its translation into next steps; and the inexhaustibility of our powers by the finite determinations of our existence.

The attitudes accompanying this third place define a series of ambitions for the transformation of humanity. They prompt us to reconsider and to reshape the virtues of connection and of purification in the light of the virtues of divinization. They require an emptying out that is also an opening up. They describe a direction for the development of the moral experience of mankind under the reign of democracy and experimentalism. They promise a happiness that depends on no illusion and requires no indifference.

Some may object that even if the doctrine of this book offered us what we need, it would not offer us what we want. We want consolation for the sufferings of existence and for the void of meaning and purpose that surrounds our vanishing lives on every side. What does it profit us to become more godlike in power and self-possession if we are not in fact God but finite and mortal beings doomed to decline and death and deprived of insight into the mystery of existence? If we are falling toward an end that mystifies us before it destroys us, what good will it do us to quicken the felt pace of our absurd parade?

This objection, however, mistakes the message. We do not live that we may become more godlike. We become more godlike that we may live. We turn to the future to live in the present. The practices by which we invent different futures bring down upon us a storm of impalpable meteors. The risks to which these practices subject us, the commotions, the hurts, the joys, strike and break the coats of armor within which we are all slowly dying. They enable each of us to live in action and in the mind until he dies all at once.

They open us to the phenomena and to the people around us. They bring us back to the visionary immediacy we long since lost. They enable us to see the other not as a placeholder in some confining collective script we did not write and can barely understand but as the radical original each of us knows himself to be. They make it possible for us to come more completely into possession of ourselves as beings that our circumstances never exhaust. In all these ways they bring us face to face with the presence of reality as it is manifest, right here and now.

It is the vital paradox of our being and our thinking that we thrive and see in context, yet slowly cease to live and to understand if we fail to struggle against the limitations context imposes. As we die these small deaths, the phenomena and the other people move away from us; their recession foretells our annihilation.

We must therefore so accelerate and direct the permanent invention of the new that we are able to overthrow the dictatorship of the dead over the living and to turn our minds more freely and fully toward the people and the phenomena around us. The future of the imagination, like the future of democracy, is to create in society and in thought a better chance for us to recover these people and these phenomena.

Imagination over dogma, vulnerability over serenity, aspiration over obligation, comedy over tragedy, hope over experience, prophecy over memory, surprise over repetition, the personal over the impersonal, time over eternity, life over everything.

First Digression

Nature in Its Place

At first, we needed nature so much that we worshipped it. Now we need it less and less. We cannot undo the consequences of this liberation; we can go only forward, further and further away from the need that once obsessed us toward the freedom that now disorients us.

Civilization is the antidote to our dependence on nature. However, for much of human history we remained so vulnerable to the natural forces outside and within us that we continued to picture the divine in the image of the natural forces that held us in their grip. This sense of weakness, fear, and reverence was terrifying, but it was not tragic. We found respite in our powers of invention. Inventing institutions and machines, we began to overcome our helplessness. Recognizing that our minds could outreach our frail bodies and our demeaning circumstance, we came to imagine a God who, like us, rises above nature.

As a result of this growth in power, our experience of nature has fallen apart into four pieces, each marked by a distinctive attitude toward the natural world and a characteristic contest of aspirations. Only one of these four parts of our contemporary dealings with nature bears the marks of our early neediness and terror. Only another one of the four is tragic.

First, there is the delight of the gardener. We treat nature as a setting for escape from strife and striving into aesthetic freedom. That the object of this freedom should be something we found rather than something we made only increases its charm. Why not convert whole sections of the earth into global parks for the solace of people exasperated by the disappointments of society? We worry how much we can afford to subtract from production for the sake of recreation, anxiously calculating the terms of trade of tundra for oil wells or of jungle for paper. The truth, however, is that as we increase in wealth and dexterity and as population growth levels off, we can turn more places into gardens. Our mechanical and organizational devices can help insulate part of the earth from further artifice.

Second, there is the responsibility of the steward. We view ourselves as managers, in trust for future generations, of a sinking fund of non-renewable resources. We balance the call of consumption against the duty of thrift. It is an anxiety founded on an illusion. Necessity, mother of invention, has never yet in modern history failed to elicit a scientific and technological response to the scarcity of a resource, leaving us richer than we were before. If the earth itself were to waste away, we would find a way to flee from it into other reaches of the universe. We would later revisit our abandoned and unlovely planet to re-fertilize and re-inhabit it before its fiery end. Will the waters dry? Will the oil end? It is useful to be worried and therefore prudent. It is foolish to deny that no such event has yet proved a match for ingenuity.

Third, there is the infirmity of the mortal. Only a small fraction of the world's population is now likely ever to be threatened by the natural disasters that so bedeviled our ancestors—a smaller number by far than the number of victims of any major disease that continues to afflict us. Even floods and droughts have begun to yield their terrors to technological precaution, commercial substitution, and rural depopulation. There is, however, one area of experience in which we continue to suffer as humanity always suffered until it used mind to gain power over nature: our dealings with disease and death. Terrified and distracted, doubting both our own powers and higher providence, we work to cure the illnesses that waste us, and we dream of undying life.

Fourth, there is the ambivalence of the titan. Now that we need nature less, we face a conflict that our helpless forefathers were spared. We are able to question the effects of our actions on the animate and inanimate nature surrounding us. We wonder whether we should not sacrifice our self-centered desires for the sake of a more inclusive fellow feeling. Yet we are not gods, only demigods, too strong to be indifferent, too weak to forego exercising the prerogatives of our power over the forms of life, or even of lifeless being, with which we share our world. Here, at last, is a conflict we cannot hope to settle, only to endure, to understand, and to direct.

Our experience of nature is now torn into these four shreds. Where and how, in the resulting confusion, can we find guidance? What should we do with our halting triumph over need for nature? In what direction should we push our advance? And what constraints should we honor as we do so?

Not gray abstractions, deaf to the paradoxes of experience, but a simple conception, close to the ground of the history that has brought us to our present power, is what we require. The capacity to remain open to the future—to alternative futures—proves decisive. Consider two sides of the same view. One side speaks to our mastery of nature outside us; the other, to our experiments with nature within us.

We are unquiet in nature because the mind concentrates and focuses a quality diffuse in nature: the mind is inexhaustible and therefore irreducible and uncontainable. No limited setting, of nature, society, or culture can accommodate all we—we the species, we as individuals—can think, feel, and do. Our drivenness, including our drive to assert power over nature, follows from our inexhaustibility. We should not, and to a large extent we cannot, suppress, in the name of delight, stewardship, or reverence, the initiatives by which we reinforce our command over nature.

We nevertheless have reason to stay our hands from time to time and gradually to extend the areas of the planet and the parts of each human life that we set aside for activities free from the tyranny of the will and the dictates of society. By dividing our time between restless conquest of nature and artless reencounter with it, rather than trying to subordinate Prometheanism to piety, we can guard against brutalizing ourselves.

Consider another aspect of the same view. Our societies and cultures make us who we are. However, there is always more in us—in us, humanity, and in us, individuals—than there is or can be in them. They shape us. We transform them—more readily and constantly if they multiply the occasions, and strengthen the tools, of our experimentalism. We have no greater interest than in so arranging society and culture that they leave the future open and invite their own revision.

Under democracy, this interest becomes paramount, for democracy grants to ordinary men and women the power to reimagine and to remake the social order. That is why under democracy prophecy speaks louder than memory. That is why democrats discover that the roots of a human being lie in the future rather in the past. In a democracy, the school should speak for the future, not for the state or for the family, giving the child the instruments with which to rescue itself from the biases of its family, the interests of its class, and the illusions of its epoch.

These ideas can inform our efforts to fix, through genetic engineering, the nature within us. Nothing should prevent us from tinkering with our natural constitution, inscribed in genetic code, to avoid disease and deformity. The place to stop is the point at which the present seeks to form human beings who will deliver a future drawn in its own image. Let the dead bury the dead is what the future must say back, through our voices, to the present. To let the future go free would show more than power. It would show wisdom.

The Universal Grid of Philosophy

In the world history of philosophy, a small number of intellectual options keep recurring. However, the way in which they recur in the part of philosophy that proposes to deal with the whole of reality—metaphysics—has been completely different from the way in which they recur in the practical philosophy that deals with social life and human action: politics and ethics.

In metaphysics very little happens, and even less would happen were it not for the influence of two forces. The first force is that philosophers are different, by temperament and circumstance, even before they begin to think and that they are led by ambition as well as by enthusiasm to deepen the differences among themselves. The second force, of increasing significance over the last few centuries, is that natural science changes. Metaphysics must adapt to such change unless it can force science to temporize, which it almost never can. Because so little happens in metaphysics, metaphysicians can sometimes convince themselves that they have discovered, once and for all, as much of the world as the human mind can grasp, by which they generally mean the most important part of the world.

In the practical philosophy of politics and ethics, a few intellectual positions, developed in different vocabularies, have also accounted for the greater part of the most influential ideas. However, much does happen, or can happen, and sometimes very quickly. A contest of philosophical positions that may at first seem intractable is in fact resolved in a particular direction, setting thought on a course of cumulative change rather than eternal recurrence or oscillation.

The history of metaphysics has been organized around a single, overriding axis of intellectual alternatives. These alternatives have to do with the relation of being to appearance and therefore also with the relation of being to knowledge. We are more familiar with the expression of the main alternative positions in the categories of our Western philosophical tradition; we first learned from the ancient Greeks the words with which to name them. However, they have close counterparts in Indian and Chinese philosophy as well as in the Islamic philosophers who developed the thought of the ancient Greeks in forms different from those that became established in medieval and modern Europe.

At one extreme of this axis lies the idea that the manifest world of distinction and flux is not for real, at least not ultimately. It is an epiphenomenon: an artifact of our perception of the world. Being is one. Insofar as we are real, we form part of it. The theory of the manifest world, in its variety and transformation, is, on this account, an illusion. We can rescue ourselves from this illusion by clinging to what I earlier called, by Leibniz's label, the perennial philosophy. Spinoza's *Ethics* presents a version of this view that tries to make sense of the implications of early-modern science.

Further along this axis, in the direction of greater acceptance of the reality of the manifest world, is a doctrine of hidden prototypes. Plato's theory of forms (as explored in the *Parmenides*) remains the classic instance. There is a hierarchy of forms of being. The distinctions and transformations of the manifest world exhibit a repertory of natural kinds or basic types. All have their origin in the prototypes. The more real the being, the less manifest; the more manifest, the less real. True knowledge, to be won only at great cost, is knowledge of the hidden but plural prototypes rather than of their shadowy and ephemeral expressions in the phenomenal world.

If we move further in the direction of an attempt to save the appearances, toward what may seem the extreme opposite to the doctrine of being as one, we find that it is not as extreme as we may have expected. The metaphysician as realist, determined to hold firm to the

world of the manifest, needs somehow to ground appearance in structure if he is to gain purchase on the reality he seeks to uphold. By so
doing, he comes closest to the tenets of the common-sense realism that
has always been the trading partner of this metaphysical position: con-
tributing beliefs to it and receiving them from it.

In the absence of such a structure just beneath the surface of appearance, the mind will dissolve the world of appearance into in-
distinction; it will lack the means with which to bring the individual
phenomena and events under the light of a categorical structure. Consequently, it will begin to lose clarity about the boundaries among them.
As they sink into a mush, the effort to save the appearances will risk
turning into its supposed antithesis, the doctrine of the unity of being.
Such an extreme phenomenalism has appeared from time to time in
the history of metaphysics, but it has never succeeded in preventing the
effort to save the appearances from turning against itself.

The solution to this problem in the history of philosophy in many
different traditions and civilizations has been to stop one step short of
the last step. The metaphysician imagines that just under the surface of
appearances is a structure of kinds of being. Built into that structure is
a set of regularities governing the realization of the kinds in individual
phenomena and events. Aristotle's hylemorphism—his doctrine of form
and matter—as presented in his *Metaphysics* is the most famous example of such a structure, and the doctrine that each kind tends to the
development of the excellence intrinsic to it is the paradigmatic instance
of such regularities.

This solution creates another problem, however. If the structure of
kinds and the regime of their realization are not apparent, how are we
to prevent them from keeping the ultimate reality of individualized
being just beyond our grasp? The individual is the prize—not just the
individual person but also the individual phenomenon or event. However, the individual, Aristotle reminds us, is ineffable. Suppose we grasp
the particularities of the individual phenomenon or event by subsuming
it under a long list of kinds: each kind scoops out a little more of the
particularity of the event or the phenomenon. In the end, however, the
particularity of the particular remains an unreachable limit. We risk

dying of thirst for the real, our idea-laden perceptions outstretched to realities that remain just beyond their reach. From this derivative problem and from the familiar stock of attempted, inconclusive solutions to it there arises a familiar set of disputes in the world history of this metaphysical option.

The natural scientist, or the worshiper of natural science, may attempt to escape this fate—failure to reach the residue of particularity in the particular—by making two moves. First, he may insist on attributing to the concepts and categories of his science an uncontroversial reality. He may think of them less as conjectures and metaphors, warranted by the interventions and applications they inform, than as part of the furniture of the universe. Second, he may dismiss the individualized remnant of the manifest—the part that fails to be captured by the kinds into which he divides up the world and by the law-like relations of cause and effect he claims to reveal—as an unimportant residue, a byproduct of the marriage of necessity and chance.

It is, however, only by a hallucination that we can mistake the ideas of science for the structure of the world. What dispels this hallucination and returns us to our perplexity is not a metaphysical objection; it is the history of science. Scientific ideas change, sometimes radically. Their periodic subversion saps our ability to convince ourselves that they are nature itself rather than constructions of our minds. Bereft of the consoling hallucination, we find we have sold too cheaply, in exchange for counterfeit goods, the longing to grasp in the mind the particulars of the phenomenal world.

The recurrence of these intellectual alternatives in the history of metaphysics is too universal and too persistent to be marked down to the power of tradition and influence. What Kant said of the antinomies of reason holds true for these conundrums: they result from an overreaching of the mind. The overreaching, however, is not necessary. We can stop it, and so we should.

Metaphysics would better be called metahumanity. Its secret ambition is that we see ourselves from the outside, from far away and high above, as if we were not ourselves but God. We are, however, not God. We cannot begin to divinize ourselves, little by little, until we acknowledge this fact. The naturalistic prejudice—seeing from the stars—is the beginning of the insuperable problems and of the unsatisfactory alternatives that beset our metaphysical ideas about the relation of being to appearance.

The world history of practical philosophy presents a wholly different situation. Here too we find a small repertory of recurring problems and solutions. Something, however, can happen and has happened that changes everything. Political and ethical thought have no need for meta-humanity. This fact proves to be their salvation.

The central question in political theory is: What does and should hold society together, enabling men and women to enjoy the benefits of social life? There are two limiting solutions. By their extremity and partiality, each turns out to be insufficient. Nevertheless, each contains elements that must be used by any compromise struck in the large middle space that these extreme solutions define.

At one limit, the answer to the question is coercion, imposed from above. At the other limit, the answer is love, given by people to one another.

The ruler, having gained power, will put a stop to the relentless struggle of all against all. He will attempt, so far as possible, to achieve a monopoly of violence. He can then offer society its most fundamental good—security—without which people are unable to pursue all other goods.

He who brings the sword soon discovers, however, that he needs additional instruments to rule. For one thing, to consolidate his rule, he must destroy all intermediate organizations just because they are rivals to his power. For another thing, unless power becomes authority, acquiring legitimacy in the eyes of the ruled, rebellion will lurk always and everywhere. Sooner or later, fear will give way to ambition.

If coercion is not enough, neither is love. People may be bound together by both fellow feeling and erotic attachment. The difficulty lies in assuring both the constancy and the diffusion of this force. It wavers, and, as it moves through a larger social space, it weakens. Fellow feeling weakened becomes trust. Erotic attachment weakened becomes allegiance or loyalty.

Coercion and love are both insufficient. Both, however, are necessary props to the social bond. Both are warm. They must be cooled down. In the cooler, middle space of social life, we find law and contract. Coercive violence is turned into the ultimate, delayed guarantee of institutionalized practice and legal order. Love, diffused and rarified, shades into our faith in one another: especially into the ability to trust strangers rather than just other members of a group united by blood.

The rule of law and the experience of trust among strangers, backed ultimately by regulated coercion and diffuse love, are two of the three essential instruments for preserving of the social bond. Or so we have been taught in the world history of political theory. They are fragile. The different ways of understanding their fragility, and of compensating for it, account for many of the main options in the history of political ideas.

Law becomes more necessary the more people differ from one another and the greater the range of the differences they create. If, however, such differences of experience, interest, value, and vision become too great, the shared basis on which the law can be interpreted, elaborated, and applied falls apart. Where law is most needed—in the presence of radical divergence of experience and vision—it is least effective.

On the other hand, trust cannot easily dispense with bonds sanctioned—in fact or in imagination—by blood. When it does dispense with them, it is likely to be the low trust required, for example, by the traditional form of the market economy—a simplified form of cooperation among strangers; not the high trust, required as a background to the most advanced practices of cooperation and cooperative experimentalism.

Something must therefore be added to the rule of law and to minimal trust. This third element is the social division of labor, provided by a hierarchy of classes or castes. It is not enough to appeal to brute facts of class society; they must be enveloped in purifying and sanctifying ideas. A widespread conception is that society is naturally divided by classes or ranks, shaped by the distribution of social fates and individual capacities at birth. The belief, common among the ancient Indo-European peoples, of a natural division of society into three major groups—one charged with propitiation and guidance; the second, with fighting and ruling; and the third, with labor and production—is the most important historical example of such a conception.

An account must be provided of why the apparent accident of birth into a certain social rank, with its hereditary prerogatives or disabilities, should be accepted, and why it should be seen to imply a natural distribution of the talents required for the work of each of the social ranks. The position of each person in such a hierarchy of birth may, for example, be determined by what each accomplished or failed to accomplish in a previous life.

The outward hierarchy of classes and castes supports, and in turn draws sustenance from, an inward ordering of the emotions: the right disposition of the different faculties of the human spirit, with reason in command over striving, and striving fueled by bodily appetite and vigor. Social disharmony and moral derangement feed on each other.

The different ways in which law, trust, and the class-bound division of labor can and should be related, against the eternal backgrounds of coercion and love, generate the familiar repertory of problems and positions in the history of political ideas all over the world. It all seems similar, in character though not in content, to the history of metaphysics: a small set of concerns and ideas endlessly recombined in minor variations.

It only seems that way until everything changes. What changes everything in the global history of political thought are two connected developments: each of them, at the same time, a shift in our social ideas and a transformation in the practical arrangements of society.

The first development that changes everything is the halting, unfinished destabilization of the idea of class society: of a hierarchical social division of labor, sanctioned by natural necessity, if not by sacred authority. The differences among us, however, fail to go all the way down. The class organization of society—which, in its weakened, contemporary form, continues to be reproduced by the hereditary transmission of economic and educational advantage through the family—is not, according to the new idea, a natural or invariant fact. Its content at any given time and in any given place depends on the nature of the established institutions and the prevailing beliefs.

The vast differences in the measure as well as in the direction of talents among individuals should never override the recognition of our common humanity and the duty of equal respect to which this recognition gives rise. We should not deny or suppress, by failure of material support or moral encouragement, the essential doctrine of a democratic civilization: that ordinary men and women can lift themselves up and change the world. By improving their cooperative practices and by equipping themselves with more powerful ideas and machines as well as with better practices and institutions, ordinary people can make vast problems yield to the cumulative effects of little solutions. This ingenuity is a homely manifestation of our power to do more than the existing organization of society and culture can readily tolerate.

The second development that changes everything is a sudden, vast enlargement of the assumed repertory of institutional possibilities in the different domains of social life. The implications of the idea that society lacks any natural form assume their full dimension as we begin to rid ourselves of illusions of false necessity: the mistakes of classical European social theory—with its characteristic idea of a predetermined evolutionary sequence of indivisible institutional systems—and of contemporary social science—with its rationalizing trivialization of structural discontinuity in history.

Our interests, ideals, and identities are hostage to the practices and institutions we accept as their practical realization. By motivated and directed tinkering with these arrangements, we force ourselves to revise our understanding of those interests, ideals, and identities. We both illuminate and quicken the dialectic between the reform of society and the revision of our beliefs about ourselves.

The conviction that class division fails to go all the way down joins with the enlargement of the institutional imagination radically to expand our sense of alternatives. One consequence of this breakthrough is the ability to develop the four major conditions of the most developed forms of cooperative experimentalism. The result is therefore also to moderate the interference between the two great imperatives of practical progress in social and economic life—cooperation and innovation.

The first condition is the development of the capability-enhancing economic and education endowments. These endowments are shaped by arrangements that, although they withdraw something from the agenda of short-term politics—defined as fundamental rights, only minimally rigidify the surrounding social and economic space. The second condition is subversion of entrenched and extreme inequalities of opportunity as well as rejection of a commitment to rigid equality of resources and circumstances. The third condition is the propagation of an experimentalist impulse through all of society and culture, an impulse nourished by the school. The fourth condition is the preference for discourses and practices that make change internal to social life, lessening the dependence of transformation on crisis.

Each of these conditions in turn provides opportunities for experimentation with institutions, practices, and methods. None has a self-evident, uncontroversial institutional expression. Together, they strengthen the practices of experimentalism both directly and indirectly. They do so directly by loosening the hold of any closed script on the forms of association. They do so indirectly by making it more likely that, in dealing with one another, strangers will be able to move beyond the low trust required by the conventional form of the market economy to the high trust demanded by the most fertile cooperative practices.

The marriage of the idea that class division fails to touch the fundamentals of our humanity with the discovery of the institutional indeterminacy of our interests and ideals and indeed of the ideal of society itself puts an end to the endless refrains of political thought. Law and contract as the cooler, feasible middle point between the two impossible warm extremes of coercive order and erotic attachment now become simply the undefined, open space in which to accelerate the reinvention of social life.

A similar shift has taken place for similar reasons in the world history of moral theory. No one could guess from the histories of philosophy written by the professors what the chief line of division in the development of moral thought has in fact been. You might suppose from reading their accounts that it has been some high-order contrast of approach: whether, for example, the overriding concern of moral judgment should be the pursuit of pleasure, the quest for happiness, the achievement of virtue, or the obedience to universal rules. As soon as we begin to examine these supposed contrasts more closely, however, we discover that they begin to collapse into one another.

Then we hit on a more basic weakness of this view of what is at stake in the history of moral philosophy. We can translate any given vision of what to do with a human life into any or all of these seemingly incompatible ethical vocabularies. The message will not be quite the same in each of these translations. Neither, however, will it be clearly different.

The two overlapping questions that trump all others in the world history of moral thought are: what should I do with my life?, and, how should I live? To the extent that decrees of society and culture have predetermined the choice of life, the second question has been submerged within the first.

The answer to these questions has taken two main directions: stay out of trouble and get into trouble; serenity or vulnerability. In the history of moral philosophy, the reasons to take the first direction have until recently seemed overwhelming. Although certain religious teachers began to urge the second direction over two thousand years ago, their prophecy achieved its present astonishing authority only in the last few hundred years. It has done so by what must be considered the greatest moral revolution in world history.

Faced with the unchanging conditions of human existence, with its rapid march to dissolution in the midst of meaninglessness, the first response is: let us compose ourselves. Let us cast a spell on ourselves that can bring us serenity. Let us detach ourselves from vain striving in a world of shadowy appearances and insubstantial achievements.

It may seem that the doctrine of the epiphenomenal nature of change and distinction and the related idea of the unity of real being—the perennial philosophy—offer the most persuasive metaphysical backdrop for the ethic of serenity. Nevertheless, all the major recurrent positions about the relation of being to appearance—not just the one that denies the reality of change and distinction—have been bent into the service of this ethic of composure. We can see as much by considering the age in which the relation between these metaphysical options and ethical alternatives was most transparent: the Hellenistic period. Before then Aristotle had already combined his apology for contemplative passivity as the experience bringing man closest to the divine with his campaign to vindicate the world of appearances.

We must relate to other people in a way that affirms our overriding concern with putting a stop to vain and restless desire. The way to do so has often been to settle into some practice of reciprocal responsibility, recognizing one's duties to others, according to the nature of the relation, as defined by society. A posture of detached and distant benevolence is then most to be desired. This posture may be infused by love. However, it will not be love as the radical acceptance and imagination of the other person and as the demand for such acceptance and imagination, with all its consequent dangers of rejection, misunderstanding, and heartbreak. It will be love as kindness, whenever possible from afar or from on high.

All this changes when there takes place in the moral history of mankind an event that is at once intangible and unique: another vision of human life and its possibilities. The effort to reconcile our need for another with our fear of the jeopardy in which we place one another is now changed by a new insight into the relation between spirit and structure. We recognize ourselves as structure-transcending beings and require more than the middle distance from one another. Our relations are infected—or sublimated—by the unlimited demand for the unlimited.

The goal is no longer composure. It is to live a larger life, for ourselves and for others. To this end, we must change the world—or, at least, part of our immediate world—the better to change ourselves. We must look for trouble. We must be prudent in small things the better to be reckless in big ones. The good we gain from such sacrifices and adventures, and from choosing lead over gold, is priceless: life itself, the ability to continue living and to escape the many small deaths until we die all at once. It is to live more fully as the infinite imprisoned within the finite. It is to begin the work of our divinization without denying the inalterable circumstances of our existence.

On the way, as the moral thinking of humanity begins to move in this direction, and to abandon the ideal of a serenity at once deathless and lifeless, there comes the moment of universalizing obligation, of Kant's categorical imperative. It is a movement toward the other person, but under the distancing shield of moral law, with the hypochondriac's fear of others and the ascetic's fear of the body and its desires, as if incarnate spirit would read from a rulebook and wear an undershirt.

The acceptance of personal vulnerability and the struggle for world transformation (however small the part of the world thus changed) for the sake of self-transformation, and the striving for self-transformation for the sake of world transformation, become organizing ideals of life. This way of thinking has two roots. Over time these two roots become entangled in each other. One root lies in the history of our moral ideas, interrupted and redirected by prophetic inspiration and religious revolution. The other root lies in the progress of democracy and in the consequent loosening of the hold of any entrenched scheme of social division and hierarchy over what we expect and demand from one another.

A breakthrough bearing a message of universal value to humanity, such as the message conveyed by this world-historical reorientation in political and moral thought, cannot be the privileged possession of any civilization or any time. If indeed we can never be completely imprisoned by a society or a culture, such a message will have been anticipated in the countercurrents of even those times and situations that seem most alien or antagonistic to it. Long after the contests produced by the spread of the message, scholars will look back and say, for example: see, the thinkers of pre-imperial China shared similar concerns and made similar proposals. And indeed if the truth revealed by the turn is deep and strong, people must have recognized it—often only dimly but sometimes more clearly—always and everywhere.

Yet if time, change, and difference are for real and if history is as dangerous and decisive as it seems to be, the discovery and propagation of this universal message must have become enmeshed in the scandalous particularity of historical experience: carried by particular agents, in particular situations, through experiences of conflict and conversion that turned a precarious countercurrent into a triumphant creed. The particularity missing from the message belongs in spades to the plot. We have to take care only that the particulars of the plot—its passage through particular nations, cultures, classes, and individuals—not contaminate the universality of the message. The plot, full of surprise, accident, and paradoxical reversals, reminds us that embodied spirit must bear all the weight of a world of particulars—including the weight of imperial power and of resistance to it. Who would hear truth from the conqueror or accept wisdom from those who refuse to give recognition?

It is, however, a fact intimately related to the insights conveyed by this change in the direction of political and moral thought that our traditions and civilizations are not for keeps. Although they help make us who we are, we, in the end, are not they, if only because they ultimately limit us, and we ultimately transcend them. In the worldwide competition and emulation of the present time, the distinct national cultures are in the process of being jumbled up and emptied out. In the contest of cultures, the waning of actual difference arouses all the more the enraged will to difference. Emptied of content, national cultures cannot be objects of half-deliberate compromise, as they had been when they lived as detailed customary ways of life. There is less and less to compromise; only an assertion of willed difference, made the more poisonous by having been deprived of tangible content.

The solution, however, is not to preserve these traditions and civilizations as fossils under a glass. It is to replace the fictions of the collective will to difference by institutions and practices that strengthen the collective ability to produce real differences: distinct forms of life, realized through different institutional orders. It is to reinterpret the role of nations in a world of democracies as a form of moral specialization within humanity: the development of our powers in different directions and the realization of a democratic society in alternative sets of arrangements. It is to obey the law of the spirit, according to which we can possess only what we reinvent, and reinvent only what we give up.

The combination of the moral and the political turns breaks the world-historical mold of philosophy. The two turns, combined, abandon metaphysics to its routines, barely modified by the discoveries of science. But they change our ideas about ourselves forever.

What is the conclusion to draw from this inquiry into the universal grid of philosophy? It is that we cannot become God and that we can become more godlike.

Proper Name Index

Thematic Index

Totalizing (*continued*)
qualities of consciousness, 14, 102–103, 135–136; shared feature of philosophy and politics, 233–234

Transcendence: our inability to be fully contained by our contexts, 28, 55, 110; in our mental experience: negative capability, 14, 135–136, 160–161; in work of philosophy, 148–149, 162; in our social experience, 55; ideal of society as mirror of imagination, 163, 180; in our moral experience, 55; and enlargement of our sympathies and powers, 184–185; our's related to God's, 213, 222; society made hospitable to our context-transcending capacities, 185–192

Transformation: transformation of transformation as nature of time, 82, 84; shaped by context dependence and transcendence over context, 164; made internal to society: diminishing dependence of change on crisis, 43, 61, 112, 132, 138, 177, 181–182, 207, 251; triumph over repetition: in the mind, 137–138, 165–168; triumph over repetition: in society, 123, 141; transformation and mummification, 212, 216, 241; transformation and insight: the adjacent possible, 86, 94–97, 157–158

Truth: James's theory of truth and its equivocations, 33–36; pragmatism and instrumental conception of truth, 33–34, 214

Utilitarianism: as philosophical method harnessed recently to humanization of society, 119–120; as justifying compensatory redistribution, 143, 173; failure to reckon with conflict between context-preserving and context-challenging desires, 137–138, 219

Vanguards (economic) and rearguards: core of economic vanguardism today, 173–174; bases of vanguardism in second side of the mind, 135–136; network of vanguards of production as commanding force in world economy, 172–173; inadequacy of compensatory redistribution and small-scale property to redress effects of chasm

between vanguards and rearguards, 175–176, 180; means to expand access to vanguards, 173–175; vanguardism outside vanguard, 173–180, 203–204; vanguardism before its time, 173–180, 203–204; vanguardism without a blueprint, 180; requirement of subversion of entrenched inequalities, 175–176, 180; requirement of capability-enhancing endowments, 176–177, 221; requirement of propagation of experimentalist impulse, 159–160, 250–251

Via negativa: despairing of our ability to make spirit live in structure, 218–219; false alternative to perennial philosophy, 219; as mystical tendency within Christianity and other world religions, 222; in romanticism, 164–165, 218–219, 222; in contemporary thought, 223; as mistake about nature of our contexts, 163–165, 223; different way of relating to our contexts and character, 140–144, 148–150, 166–168, 184–185, 195, 223–229, 236–237, 249–256

Virtues: their nature and place in a view and path of the self, 217; virtues of connection: respect, forbearance, fairness, 218; virtues of purification: simplicity, enthusiasm, attentiveness, 227–229, 236; virtues of divinization: openness to new experience and to the other person, 228–229; relation of virtues to two awakenings of self, 227–229

Visionary immediacy: as ability to hold manifest world in the mind, 135; in relation to counterfactual insight and dreams, 157–158; struggle to reconcile visionary immediacy with discovery of underlying order, 156; promise of this reconciliation in art, 22, 168–170; its partial achievement through change in thinking, feeling, and acting, 167, 236–237

Vitality: our exhilaration at being alive, 147–149; our struggle with indifference of nature to our concerns, 26, 147, 153–154; and prospect of death, 26–27, 237; and orientation to future, 40–41, 150; preeminent teaching of this book: we become more godlike to live rather than